Acclaim for Arthur Levitt's

TAKE ON THE STREET

"Lively and illuminating. . . . Blends the backroom revelations of a first-rate political memoir with the no-nonsense advice of a basic investment primer. . . . Educational and entertaining in equal measure."
—*The New York Times*

"Knowledge is power, Mr. Levitt implicitly argues, offering investors valuable guidance about understanding corporate financial statements, the Byzantine workings of the securities markets and today's flawed system of corporate guidance."
—*The Wall Street Journal*

"Buy Levitt's book for its behind-the-curtains look at how Wall Street, Washington and corporate America work against giving investors a fair shake."
—*Kiplinger's Personal Finance*

"Tantalizing. . . . When the history of the recent corporate scandals is written, Arthur Levitt will surely wind up near the top of the list of good guys."
—*The Washington Post*

"Identifies hidden pitfalls and gives specific steps you can take to safeguard your financial future."
—*Bloomberg Personal Finance*

"Investor . . . take heart . . . Arthur Levitt is on your side. . . . Packed with insight and advice geared toward the wary and wearied individual investor."
—*New York Post*

"A startling behind-the-scenes book for anyone who has felt intimidated or baffled by Wall Street. . . . Levitt's eye-opening revelations are sure to make navigating the minefield of hidden potholes on Wall Street a little easier." —*BookPage*

"Candid, pointed, and eye-opening. . . . Of use to both the first time investor and the experienced policy wonk. . . . Provides a comprehensive indictment of the overwhelming influence of private-interest money. Devastating." —*The Washington Monthly*

"Engaging. . . . Succeeds admirably . . . educate[s] the average investor." —*The Economist*

"Timely and revealing. . . . Part personal finance guide, part 'I Told You So' to his former foes, and—mostly—a comprehensive 'caveat investor.'" —*San Jose Mercury News*

"Levitt comes across as engaged and focused on the key issues of the day. . . . An informed, opinionated and feisty raconteur. He names names . . . and shoots in the occasional partisan elbow." —*The New York Observer*

"Deserves much praise. . . . Could hardly come at a better time. . . . A good balance of introductory and advanced content. Beginners receive a crash course on how to become well-informed investors. . . . Veterans can immerse themselves in the almost gossipy Wall Street behind-the-scenes stories and Levitt's seasoned survival tips." —*Better Investing*

"Very effective. . . . Seeks to help the small investor fight back when Wall Street and corporate America try to hide ugly truths." —*Securities Industry News*

Arthur Levitt

TAKE ON THE STREET

First appointed in 1993, Arthur Levitt was the longest-serving SEC chairman. He was also chairman of the New York City Economic Development Corporation and the American Stock Exchange. He lives in Connecticut.

PAULA DWYER has worked for *Business Week* since 1985. She currently serves as deputy chief in the magazine's Washington, D.C., bureau.

TAKE ON THE STREET

To Ian
Help protect investors! 4/25/07

TAKE ON THE STREET

STREET

How to Fight
for Your Financial Future

ARTHUR LEVITT

With Paula Dwyer

4/25/07

VINTAGE BOOKS

A Division of Random House, Inc.

New York

The Library of Congress has cataloged the Pantheon edition as follows:
Levitt, Arthur
Take on the street: what Wall Street and corporate America don't want you to know; what you can do to fight back/Arthur Levitt with Paula Dwyer
p. cm.
1. Investments. 2. Investment analysis. 3. Investments—United States.
I. Dwyer, Paula, 1954– II. Title.
HG4521 .L339 2002 332.6—dc21 2002070422

Vintage ISBN: 0-375-71402-2

www.vintagebooks.com

CONTENTS

ACKNOWLEDGMENTS

No one writes a book alone. I owe thanks to many people for helping me with my first book, which proved to be more of a challenge than I thought. First and foremost, my friend and former colleague Russell Horwitz was an extraordinarily creative participant throughout the process. His patience, inspired editorial comments, institutional memory, and dedication to investor interests were invaluable. I can't thank him enough.

Harvey Goldschmid's assistance was also invaluable. Many times I relied on his knowledge of the securities laws. He also faithfully read and commented on much of the book. Joe Lombard gave countless hours of assistance with market structure issues, as did Lynn Turner on accounting matters. Gregg Corso and Jim Glassman are some of the most creative thinkers I know. I am grateful that they were always available to serve as a sounding board for ideas. Lenny Sacks has exquisite taste. His editorial and conceptual suggestions made this book better. Dan Tully, my friend of many years, was my beacon of balance in terms of investor relationships. Others whom I admire and respect read chapters and faithfully responded to my request for comment. They were Bob Denham, Holman Jenkins, Charlie Munger, Brent Baird, and Karl-Hermann Baumann.

I especially want to thank Warren Buffett for helping me get to the core of the matter on broker compensation, mutual funds, and corporate governance issues, and for making himself available when needed. He has been one of the strongest and most ethical advocates of the public interest, and America's markets have bene-fited from his wisdom.

Since I left the SEC, I have been blessed by the extreme loyalty of many aides who worked by my side and continue to provide valu-able counsel. Many of them gave unstintingly of their time. I want to thank Jane Adams, Tracey Aronson, Nick Balamaci, Barry Bar-bash, David Becker, Bob Colby, Carrie Dwyer, Rich Lindsey, Bill McLucas, Annette Nazareth, Susan Ochs, Lori Richards, Paul Roye, Jennifer Scardino, Michael Schlein, Nancy Smith, Mike Sut-ton, Mark Tellini, Chris Ullman, and Dick Walker.

I am very lucky to have Carol Morrow as my executive assistant and the person who helps organize my life. I owe her a huge debt of gratitude for keeping me on track every day. I would also like to acknowledge researchers Christopher Schmitt and Jennifer Reingold for their assistance on 401(k) and corporate governance issues.

My collaborator, Paula Dwyer, accepted the challenge of putting together with me our first book. Her knowledge of the Commis-sion, the securities industry, and the political environment yielded unique perspectives and insights. More than that, she has won my trust and inspired confidence through her sense of fair play, calm determination, and reasoned judgment.

Erroll McDonald, my editor, championed this project from the beginning. His encouragement and wisdom got me past many moments of doubt about how I could produce a book that would engage my mythical "Aunt Edna" and the millions of American investors who need to know more about the snares that can dimin-ish the likelihood of investing success. Erroll shares my obsession for protecting investors and helped me focus on producing some-thing that would help level the playing field for them. He is a patient, dedicated, and passionate advocate for the things he believes in and the people he trusts. I am better for our relationship.

PREFACE

Looking back over the past year, it seems a new reality has taken hold in America. Dozens of company officials have been indicted and await trial; dozens more have pleaded guilty. Arthur Andersen's conviction on an obstruction of justice charge has all but put the Big Five accounting firm out of business. Major brokerage firms, under duress, have agreed to construct a legal wall between their analysts and investment bankers to restore the integrity of research.

Washington also sent a strong message when Congress passed, and President George W. Bush signed, the Sarbanes-Oxley Act of 2002. The landmark legislation gives regulators an array of new tools to hunt down and punish wrongdoing when it occurs. It also aims to deter corporate and accounting fraud and clean up corporate governance practices. It creates an oversight board to rewrite the rules for corporate audits and requires the new board to review the work of certified public accountants, as well as discipline them when needed. With the board in the capable hands of a new chairman, William McDonough, the former president of the Federal Reserve Bank of New York, my hope is that investors will soon understand why the word "public" appears in the CPA title.

Investors have wised up, too. They no longer believe that anything Internet-related will spin into gold, or that earnings don't matter. Investors are demanding an overhaul in the way companies govern themselves, and that means more transparency and more accountability from management and their boards. Even more positive changes should result once the Securities and Exchange Commission adopts proposed listing standards that all public companies must meet in order to trade their shares on the New York Stock Exchange or the Nasdaq Stock Market. Among them are requirements that a majority of directors be independent—meaning no financial or other ties to the company—and that boards must meet regularly in executive session without management present.

It would be a mistake, however, to conclude that the job is done. For the past eight months, I have traveled the country and met with thousands of angry and jaded investors. They bought a lot of New Economy snake oil in the 1990s, and they're determined not to be taken in again. Some 18 months after Enron's bankruptcy, I would like to reassure them that all the excesses of Wall Street and its corporate clients have been uncovered and wrung out. But though most of the changes I advocated during my SEC tenure from 1992 to 2001 are now law, evidence remains that too many corporate managers, auditors, and directors just don't get it.

HealthSouth Corp., for example, revealed in April 2003 that it had overstated profits by $2.5 billion since 1997, in part by brazenly falsifying the value of assets, the amount of equipment in inventory, and even the amount of cash on hand. Just weeks earlier, the U.S. Foodservice division of Dutch supermarket giant Ahold N.V. revealed that it overstated earnings by $500 million in the past two years. In these and other cases, some of the same shortcomings that plagued Enron Corp. and WorldCom Inc. were at work: boards of directors, and especially their audit committees, were not paying attention. And auditors had adopted a "see no evil" attitude, missing clearly visible signs of possibly fraudulent activity.

Regulators in Washington have also been slow, at times, in helping to convince investors that the markets are fair. For months, the SEC fumbled in naming a chairman for the new accounting oversight board, which both delayed its start-up and the promise the board holds out for restoring the credibility of company financial statements.

Sensing a regulatory vacuum, New York Attorney General Eliot Spitzer won a $100 million settlement in May 2002 from Merrill Lynch for issuing research reports that puffed up the prospects of investment banking clients—but that its own analysts disavowed.

Spitzer and fellow state regulators then moved on to investigate ten other Wall Street firms' research operations. Those probes, eventually joined by regulators at the SEC, the National Association of Securities Dealers, and the New York Stock Exchange, were settled in April 2003, when the firms agreed to pay $1.4 billion in fines, fund investor education programs, and make independent research available to investors. Now the ball is in the SEC's court to issue rules that would make the settlement permanent—and effective nationwide.

Within the auditing profession, change is coming, but the pace is glacial. Most accountants understand that, unless they want to remain the butt of jokes by late-night comics, they must do something to restore the integrity of their audits. But the firms themselves and their trade group, the American Institute of Certified Public Accountants, seem not to have gotten the message. The CPA group weakened its own hand by stubbornly opposing the Sarbanes-Oxley law, which transferred regulation of accounting to a new Public Company Accounting Oversight Board. With the oversight board's April 2003 vote to write its own audit standards, rather than adopt those of the AICPA, the trade group's fate is sealed: With no self-regulatory role, and lacking the power to set standards, it is now reduced to a mere membership organization.

Today, accountants' dual role as auditor and consultant to the same client—a practice that I have long opposed and that I believe led auditors to wear blinders as they prepared corporate financial statements—is on the decline, but not fast enough. And the large audit firms continue to drag their feet when it comes to reform. As I write this, the firms are resisting new rules by the oversight board that would require them to register all the accountants they employ, and reveal any legal proceedings against them over the past ten years.

Despite billions in investor losses, Congress has been somewhat of a disappointment. It has reverted to its natural state by paying greater heed to the special pleadings of lobbyists for Wall Street firms and corporations than to the interests of individual investors, who have no lobbyists. In March 2003, the House of Representatives voted to lift a 205-year-old bankruptcy law prohibition against interested parties' advising bankrupt companies. This means that lawmakers would let the very bankers who helped Enron hide failed ventures in secretive, off-the-books partnerships turn around and sell advice to the bankrupt company. It makes me wonder what planet House members have been living on for the past two years.

Restoring investor confidence can't be done by passing laws alone. As tough as it is, the Sarbanes-Oxley law relies on mechanical fixes, such as tougher jail terms and a requirement that chief executives certify the accuracy of company financial statements. What's needed now are more far-reaching, immeasurable changes, such as more skeptical auditors, more trustworthy managers, more quizzical boards, and more vigilant investors. We need boards that instinctively act on behalf of shareholders, not management. We need auditors who instinctively protect investor interests, not the corporate client. We need audit committees that understand their unique role as the last line of defense for investors.

Still, it's my hope that the new law and new rules will serve as good vehicles with which to keep moving the reform agenda ahead. Indeed, there have been many positive developments in the past year. I have seen a shift in power away from the imperial CEO to outside directors, many of whom now take their responsibilities more seriously than in years past. Directors are deciding who the next CEO will be, which audit firm to hire, whether auditors can perform any consulting services, and how best to compensate managers for meeting performance milestones.

Corporate managers, too, are seeing the light. More and more companies are following Intel Corp. and others who have split the job of board chairman from chief executive, as recommended by the Conference Board's Blue Ribbon Commission on Public Trust & Private Enterprise, on which I served. At General Electric, two veteran directors were asked to resign to reduce the number of board insiders. Motorola has named a governance executive, and added two independent board members principally because of their financial expertise.

An especially heartening development for me was the April 22,

2003, vote by the Financial Accounting Standards Board to require companies to treat the cost of stock options as an expense on the income statement. It may take the FASB another year to iron out many details, especially how companies are to measure the value of those options. But I take comfort knowing that the FASB voted unanimously to proceed down this path, and that it had the gumption to ignore strong opposition from the technology industry and its champions in Congress.

Another positive sign: organized labor, shareholder activists, and pension funds are flexing their muscles. In 2003, they offered nearly 1,000 shareholder resolutions, to be voted on at company annual meetings, to limit executive pay and require companies to subtract the value of stock options from earnings. At Hewlett-Packard Co., for example, shareholders rebuffed management's recommendation and voted in favor of a resolution that urges directors to submit large executive compensation packages to a shareholder vote.

The SEC is also on the mend after years of neglect by Congress. Having been placed on a starvation budget for the three years between 1998 and 2001, one-third of the SEC's professional staff had jumped ship to find better-paying jobs elsewhere. Now the agency has a fiscal 2003 appropriation of $712 million, well above the $567 million President Bush's budget requested, and a giant step up from the $412 million that Congress allotted in 2001, my final year at the SEC helm.

What have we learned? It took the Enron and WorldCom bombs, and the two years of scandal that followed, to teach us that strong regulation of the financial markets will always be needed. Arguments that self-regulation will keep accountants, stock exchanges, and brokerage firms working in investors' best interests have been proven naive. Starving the SEC of the funds it needs to review company filings and enforce the securities laws results in a weak watchdog—and encourages companies to cheat. And when investors withdraw because they sense that the playing field is tilted, it takes a long time to convince them to come back. Efforts by regulators, prosecutors, and lawmakers to reform the system and put corporate criminals behind bars have failed to quell the anger I sense when I meet with investors. Three years after the pricking of the stock market bubble, the Standard & Poor's 500 index is down 40 percent from its peak, while the Nasdaq is off 70 percent. Investors have lost $7 trillion in stock market value. It's no wonder they remain on the sidelines. We've come a long way, but self-dealing, conflicts of interest, and lack of accountability are still in evidence. We can't afford to rest.

Arthur Levitt
May 2003

TAKE ON THE STREET

INTRODUCTION

When I first became a broker in 1963, and for many years after, my mother, Dorothy Levitt, was my most difficult client. For thirty-eight years she taught second grade at P.S. 156 in Brooklyn, New York. Like so many of her generation who grew up during the Great Depression, her mistrust of the stock market was visceral. So she invested in municipal bonds, because of their safety but also because "they charged no commissions," she would often say. I could never get her to understand that a bond purchased from the inventory of a brokerage firm included a markup that was usually far greater than an ordinary commission. In the hands of any other broker, my mother might have been easy prey. She was not unlike many investors who, even today, don't understand how brokers are paid or why they recommend certain stocks and bonds over others.

I grew up in the Crown Heights section of Brooklyn, where I lived in a modest brownstone with my parents and Orthodox Jewish immigrant grandparents. Nearly all our meals took place at an oilcloth-covered, metal kitchen table. The dinner talk focused on low finance—the comparative cost of milk or lettuce at Kushner's Troy Avenue grocery store as opposed to Waldbaum's on Albany Avenue. But often we veered into politics. The views of my grandfather, Pops, were mostly diatribes leveled, in equal measure, at the "rotten socialists" and "crooked politicians." Pops amused me, but it was my father's less strident observations that made a bigger impression.

The politics of my father, Arthur Levitt, Sr., were nominally Democratic, with a fiscal conservative streak. Six times he was elected New York State comptroller as a Democrat, but otherwise he had little to do with party politics. For twenty-four years he was the sole custodian of the multibillion-dollar pension fund of thousands of New York public employees, including teachers like my mother. The rights of the small pensioner and efforts by politicians in both parties to raid the state pension funds dominated our discussions. My father fiercely defended his independence, whether he worked with a Democratic or Republican governor, and placed the well-being of New York retirees above all other considerations.

I shall never forget the day when he encountered New York City mayor Ed Koch in the halls of the state capitol building in Albany. It was 1978, and the city, having barely avoided bankruptcy three years earlier, was facing another fiscal crisis. To Mayor Koch, tapping the state retirement funds appeared to be the only way out. But the comptroller had refused to give his approval. As Mayor Koch approached, he pointed at my father and said menacingly: "If New York City fails, it will be your fault." This confrontation upset my father so much that, moments later, he suffered a minor stroke, which left him unable to speak for several hours. Only his closest staff was aware of this episode, from which he thankfully recovered. Unable to overcome my father's tenacious protection of the pension funds, the city secured the financing it needed when the federal government agreed to guarantee the city's bonds. I learned that when it comes to protecting investors, no political party has an edge over the conscience of an honest public servant.

My first exposure to high finance and politics came in the late 1950s and early '60s, when I sold cattle and ranches to wealthy people who needed tax shelters. When the Internal Revenue Service tried to do away with the tax shelter benefits in 1960, I joined forces with the National Cattlemen's Association to try to protect the subsidy. At a House Ways and Means Committee hearing, I recall arguing before Representative Wilbur Mills, the powerful committee chairman, that reducing this tax benefit would result in farmers' producing fewer breeding cattle, which in turn would raise beef prices and irreparably harm America's consumers. In retrospect, it was a specious argument. But I learned that one of the Washington lobbyist's most common tools is to cloak business benefits in the garb of some supposed public good, and was always alert for it thereafter.

My life changed dramatically when one of the prospects I called upon, M. Peter Schweitzer, then a top official of Kimberly-Clark, said to me, "Arthur, if you can sell cows, chances are you'd be good at selling stock." He told me his son-in-law, Arthur Carter, was starting up a brokerage firm with a group of friends and that they were looking for suitable partners. I met with Carter and signed on with his tiny firm.

My partners were Carter, today the owner of the *New York Observer* newspaper; Roger Berlind, now a successful Broadway producer; and Sandy Weill, the current chairman of Citigroup. We were young, ambitious Jewish boys of middle-class origins fighting for recognition in a white-shoe industry. Initially I worked with retail clients, sought underwriting business, and learned the ins and outs of building a Wall Street firm. It was during these years that I dealt with thousands of retail investors—first as a broker and then as president of Shearson Hayden Stone, which our firm came to be called after a series of acquisitions. By the time I left in 1978, the firm was one of the nation's largest brokerages, and would ultimately become part of Citigroup.

I embraced the craft of the broker, endeavoring to help my clients, but always mindful of how a buy or sell transaction might help our profits. Most of the brokers I encountered were good, honest, and intelligent businesspeople, but their primary motivation came from a compensation system that rewarded them for the number of transactions they executed, not on how well client portfolios performed. Even when the best course of action was to do nothing in a client's account, the commission system encouraged brokers to recommend sometimes questionable trades.

We knew, for example, that we would get five times the normal commission by placing secondary offerings—shares issued by companies that had already gone public but needed more capital—with our customers. One hundred shares of AT&T, for example, at $40 a share paid a 1 percent commission for a total of $40. But the commission on 100 shares in a secondary offering of the same AT&T stock was 5 percent, or $200. We could have purchased the same shares a month, or even a week, earlier had we thought it a good investment. Why did we suddenly find AT&T attractive one day, when we weren't recommending the stock the day before? Our motivation was self-interest, pure and simple.

As our firm struggled to develop new lines of business, it was my job to call on state agencies and communities around the country to secure the lucrative franchise of managing the issuance of, or underwriting, their municipal bonds. Many times I was told that the quid pro quo of "getting on the list" of potential underwriters was to buy a table of tickets at the mayor's or governor's campaign fundraiser. This experience provided the origins of my determination in 1994 to eliminate "pay-to-play" from the municipal bond business.

When I solicited investment banking business from companies considering a public offering, I spoke of our "retail distribution" as well as the fact that our "analyst's coverage" would be vital to "getting their story out." Retail distribution meant that our sales managers would pressure our salespeople to sell these underwritings. Often, the local manager's bonus depended upon his ability to market our merchandise, and future allocations of "hot issues" were based on the salesperson's ability to place all new issues we brought to market. Analyst's coverage, of course, was always favorable; I can recall no sell recommendations (there must have been some) during my years with the firm.

I also came to understand the motivations of CEOs who cared only about the price of their stock—often to the exclusion of any long-term vision for their company. To persuade our brokers to place more of their securities in customer accounts, corporate heads conveyed important company information to our sales and research departments that was not yet available to the investing public.

At the same time, I heard from many, many retail clients that "the big guys get information before the general public" and that "the small investor will always play second fiddle to large institutions and people in the know." What I witnessed was just the tip of the iceberg. The web of dysfunctional relationships among analysts, brokers, and corporations would grow increasingly worse over the coming decades, and ending it would be one of my primary goals at the Securities and Exchange Commission (SEC).

While I am proud of helping to build one of America's largest and most distinguished brokerage and investment banking firms—and remain friendly with most of my partners and coworkers—I grew uncomfortable with practices and attitudes that were misleading and sometimes deceptive. I first spoke out against them in a 1972 speech called "Profits and Professionalism." Over my partners' protests, I called on the industry to think quality over quantity—to pay brokers on the returns their clients received, not on the number of transactions in their accounts. It caused a minor stir, but was soon forgotten. Over the next twenty years, these issues would continue to nag at me. I had an agenda but not a forum.

The ideal forum would be the SEC chairmanship, which if offered, I would have accepted without hesitation. By the time Bill Clinton tapped me for the post in 1992, almost six months after he became president, I had spent sixteen years as an executive of a brokerage firm, twelve years at the American Stock Exchange, and four years as the publisher of a newspaper about Congress. I'd like to think my Wall Street and Washington experience recommended me. But I suppose the $750,000 I raised as one of twenty-two cochairmen of a New York dinner for Clinton just before the 1992 nominating convention was not lost on the new president's inner circle. I first heard that I was under consideration, not from anyone in the White House, but from a *Wall Street Journal* story. No Clinton insider had ever interviewed me about my policy ideas, or asked me if I was interested in the job.

From the day President Clinton nominated me, I knew I wanted the individual investor to be my passion, and I wanted to pursue change in a nonpartisan way. I had spent twenty-eight years on Wall Street, and I understood the culture. Actually, there were two conflicting cultures. One rewarded professionalism, honesty, and entrepreneurship. This culture recognized that without individual investors, the markets could not work. The other culture was driven by conflicts of interest, self-dealing, and hype. It put Wall Street's short-term interests over investor interests. This culture, regrettably, often overshadowed the other.

When I arrived at the SEC in July 1993, we were in the third year of a bull market, which would run for another seven years. Individual investors were buying stocks as never before. On the surface, everything seemed fine. But there was much about Wall Street and corporate America that made me uneasy. For instance, many CEOs were paying more attention to managing their share price than to managing their business. Companies technically were following accounting rules, while in reality revealing as little as possible about their actual performance. The supposedly independent accounting firms were working hand in glove with corporate clients to try to water down accounting standards. When that wasn't enough, they were willing accomplices—helping companies disguise the true story behind the numbers. With one-third of accounting firm revenues coming from management consulting in 1993—that proportion would balloon to 51 percent within six years—it was hard not to conclude that auditors had become partners with corporate management rather than the independent watchdogs they were meant to be.

CEOs and their finance chiefs had learned they could indirectly control their stock price by currying favor with research analysts. Some were trading important information about earnings and product development with selected analysts, who in return were writing glowing reports. Such selective disclosures got passed on to powerful institutional investors—mutual funds and pension funds—and to brokers who could be counted on to place a substantial number of shares in the accounts of individual clients. Analysts were often paid more to help their firms win investment banking deals than for the quality of their research. This unholy alliance was producing revenue for the analyst's firm but hardly any benefits for most of their clients.

Mutual funds and pension funds were getting far better information, and a lot earlier, than retail investors. Because of their muscle, they were also getting superior service and better prices when they bought or sold securities. Mutual funds were very successful at passing themselves off as investor-friendly, but they had their own, more subtle, ways of taking investors' money through a confusing array of fees. Fund companies were spending billions advertising past results rather than informing investors of more important factors, such as the effect that fees, taxes, and portfolio turnover had on returns.

From my twelve years as chairman of the American Stock Exchange, I knew that investors were almost totally in the dark about how the stock markets worked. Collusive practices among Nasdaq dealers were costing investors billions of dollars a year. At the New York Stock Exchange (NYSE), floor brokers, specialists, and listed companies set the agenda, one that protected their franchise, sometimes at the expense of investor interests. The New York Stock Exchange was also resisting a truly competitive national market system that linked all the markets, as Congress had directed years earlier.

Individual investors were unaware of this side of Wall Street. And yet they were the victims of these long-standing conflicts. I wasn't alone in my observations, either. Frank Zarb, with whom I worked at Shearson Hayden Stone and who would later become head of the National Association of Securities Dealers (NASD) and the Nasdaq Stock Market, first urged me to attack pay-to-play in the municipal bond market. I discussed with Merrill Lynch chairman Dan Tully the problems I saw with broker compensation long before I got to the SEC. Shortly after my confirmation, several CEOs pleaded with me to end the unseemly practice of leaking corporate information to analysts. And analysts sent me confidential letters exposing how selective disclosure had become routine on Wall Street. They wanted me to stop it, even though they were beneficiaries. I would spend nearly eight years at the SEC trying to correct these imbalances.

I would soon learn that many people harbored doubts about me. Within the agency, the senior staff viewed me as a wealthy New Yorker who got the job by raising lots of money for Clinton. They thought I would be a shill for the industry. On Capitol Hill, pro-consumer lawmakers who considered the SEC part of their turf were also wary. When I made a courtesy call on Representative John Dingell, the Michigan Democrat whose committee oversaw the SEC, his parting comment was "Arthur, I worry you're not tough enough for these bastards."

Within the financial services industry, my appointment was welcome news, but for the wrong reason. Somehow my reputation was that of a consensus builder—someone who looked for solutions in the safety of the middle ground and didn't stick his neck out too far. My guess is that they thought they could control me.

I now had an agenda and a forum. But that didn't mean I could do what I wanted. I first had to build up political capital. Many businessmen fail to make the transition from CEO to Washington official, leaving town after a couple of miserable years without achieving much. I was determined not to let that happen to me.

I had several advantages over the typical CEO type. At the American Stock Exchange, I formed the American Business Conference, a research and lobbying group made up of the CEOs of high-growth companies. Amex companies were prominent among the founding members. I often led the group when it traveled to Washington to meet with members of Congress and cabinet officials, and once a year with the president. The organization was nonpartisan, and it became influential in both Democratic and Republican administrations.

The experience taught me much about the symbiotic nature of Washington. For the CEOs, the ability to have access to and rub shoulders with well-known people who represented America's political elite had an addictive allure. The politicians, in turn, used these meetings as an opportunity to raise funds. And White House officials saw their chance to lobby the business community to push their own policy goals.

I also knew the Washington ropes from my four-year ownership of *Roll Call,* the only newspaper that exclusively covered Capitol Hill. *Roll Call* allowed me to meet numerous legislators and their aides. I would interact with many of them later at the SEC. More importantly, *Roll Call* taught me how to work the legislative process—where to apply the pressure and how to find common ground with lawmakers, regardless of political party.

When I came to Washington, I had a pretty clear understanding of how the main power centers worked. Once I began pursuing my agenda, however, I saw a dynamic I hadn't fully witnessed before: the ability of Wall Street and corporate America to combine their considerable forces to stymie reform efforts. Working with a largely sympathetic, Republican-controlled Congress, the two interest groups first sought to co-opt me. When that didn't work, they turned their guns on me.

I first saw it happen on the issue of stock options. I spent nearly one-third of my first year at the commission meeting with business leaders who opposed a Financial Accounting Standards Board (FASB) proposal that, if adopted as a final rule, would have required companies to count their stock options as an expense on the income statement. The rule would have crimped earnings and hurt the share price of many companies, but it also would have revealed the true cost of stock options to unsuspecting investors. Dozens of CEOs and Washington's most skillful lobbyists came to my office to urge me not to allow this proposal to move forward. At the same time, they flooded Capitol Hill and won the support of lawmakers who didn't take the time to understand the complexities of the issue and the proposed solution. Fearful of an overwhelming override of the proposal, I advised the FASB to back down. I regard this as my single biggest mistake during my years of service.

From there, I skirmished many times with the business community and Wall Street. During this period the stock market rose to incredible heights. Online trading became cool, luring millions of middle-class savers into believing that investing was a no-lose game. They traded impulsively, many basing their decisions on recommendations they heard on financial news shows, which were almost always "buy." Day traders gathered in offices that provided terminals and trading techniques that more resembled a crap game than an investment stategy. Some investors were even trading stocks on the basis of postings in Internet chat rooms—information that is as reliable as the graffiti on a bathroom stall. Investors snapped up initial public offerings of companies about which they knew very little, except that an analyst told them it was the "next new thing." But what investors didn't know was that many analysts were plugging companies that had banking relationships with the analyst's firm. For corporate executives, managing short-term earnings to meet the market's expectations became all-consuming, along with keeping the share price high so they could reap big rewards by cashing in their stock options.

Business's clout was evident as we tried to stop the gamesmanship. Our cause was not helped by the fact that the economy was growing fast, the market was shooting upward, and investors were pleased by the plump returns their mutual funds and online trades were getting. My message—that the bull market would not last forever, and that it was covering up a multitude of sins—did not go over well. Wall Street saw me as Chicken Little; lawmakers either didn't believe me or didn't want to hear what I was saying. Some were downright hostile.

I came to recognize certain behavioral patterns when business groups became concerned about commission actions. The first indication of trouble was often a staff discussion between one of the SEC division heads and an aide at one of our Congressional overseers' offices. A gentle letter from the committee chairman signaled the start of a skirmish. Face-to-face visits were next followed by hearings, press releases, and ultimately a drawn-out, costly battle.

When the FASB, for example, tried to stop abusive practices in the way that many companies accounted for mergers, two of Silicon Valley's VIPs, Cisco Systems Inc. CEO John Chambers and venture capitalist John Doerr, tried to persuade me to rein in the standard-setters. When I refused, they threatened to get "friends" in the White House and on Capitol Hill to make me bend. When we proposed new rules to make sure that auditors were truly independent of corporate clients, some fifty members of Congress promptly wrote stinging letters in rebuke. In the final days of negotiation with the Big Five accounting firms (PricewaterhouseCoopers, Deloitte & Touche, KPMG, Ernst & Young, and Arthur Andersen) over new independence rules, I was constantly on the phone with lawmakers who were trying to push the talks toward a certain conclusion, or threatening me if they didn't like the outcome. In particular, Representative Billy Tauzin, the Louisiana Republican, became a self-appointed player, negotiating on behalf of the accountants. And when we began investigating possible price-fixing by Nasdaq dealers, Representative Tom Bliley called to say I was going too far. The Virginia Republican held great sway as chairman of the House Commerce Committee, which oversees the SEC, but he backed off once I told him that the Nasdaq matter could become a criminal case.

The odds against the public interest were narrowed somewhat by the press. One of the only ways to alter the business–public interest balance was to see to it that the media understood an issue and wrote about it. Without an informed press, SEC cases against the NASD, the NYSE, and the municipal bond market would not have succeeded. Nor would the commission have been able to adopt new rules to improve auditor independence or ban selective disclosure. I can recall many instances when investigative reporters broke stories about unseemly industry practices that changed behavior by virtue of public exposure.

The vast and growing number of individual investors, however, lacked focus, direction, or leadership to make much of an impression on Washington policy makers. I often wondered how to empower this expanding group that cut across economic, ethnic, and political lines. I knew that politicians, no matter where they were located on the political spectrum, understood the power of the people and would respond favorably to policy proposals if millions of investors supported them. Promoting the interests of the average investor made good policy sense, but it also made political sense.

I decided to interact personally with individual investors through town hall meetings, went into communities and talked about current SEC projects, gave basic investment advice, and allowed attendees to ask questions. I brought along representatives from the mutual fund industry and other trade groups so they could learn what was on investors' minds. In the end, I held forty-three such meetings, often in the home states or districts of lawmakers who sat on committees that were important to the SEC, making sure to include in the forum the senator or House member whose vote or support I needed.

The SEC's first Office of Investor Education provided useful information, such as the dangers of buying stock on margin, or how to calculate the effect of mutual fund expenses on investment returns. Early on, we pursued an initiative, called Plain English, to help investors understand the dense jargon used by companies in their SEC filings. And I didn't hesitate to use the bully pulpit to explain, prod, and sometimes even embarrass companies or Wall Street firms into stopping practices that hurt investors.

When I left the SEC, much work remained to be done, but I thought Wall Street and the individual investor had at least come to understand their responsibilities and rights better. And I thought I had made progress by clamping down on some of the worst abuses. Then along came a wave of corporate accounting scandals, beginning with Enron Corp. In many ways, Enron's collapse was brought on by the collision of all the unhealthy attitudes, practices, and conflicts of Wall Street and corporate America that I tried to address at the SEC. It was as if everything I feared might happen did happen— within one company.

Enron used accounting tricks to remove debt from the books, hide troublesome assets, and pump up earnings. Instead of revealing the true nature of the risks it had taken on, Enron's financial statements were absurdly opaque. Auditors went along with the fiction, blessing the off-the-books entities that brought the company down. Most analysts also played along, recommending Enron's stock even though they couldn't decipher the numbers. Analysts were foils for their firms' investment banking divisions, which had been seduced by the huge fees Enron was paying them to sell its debt and equity offerings.

Enron's smooth-talking management pushed the stock price ever higher, enabling them to make millions from their stock options. Brokers working on commission sold Enron shares to unsuspecting clients, who lost billions when Enron declared bankruptcy.

Throughout it all, Enron's sleepy board of directors, and an especially inattentive audit committee, failed to ask the right questions.

Eight months after Enron's explosion, long-distance supplier WorldCom Inc. revealed that it had improperly accounted for nearly $4 billion in expenses, topping off a string of sordid revelations about alleged accounting misdeeds at companies ranging from Adelphia Communications to Global Crossing to Tyco International. A slew of recommendations for new laws, SEC rules, and ethics codes emerged to address what looked like a massive outbreak of corporate crime. The biggest casualty was investor confidence. By mid-July 2002, the Dow Jones Industrial Average had declined 28 percent from its 2000 high-water mark, while the Nasdaq was off an astounding 70 percent. Accounting lobbyists at first tried to impede reforms, but Congress had no choice but to act. In the summer of 2002, lawmakers created a new accounting oversight body to set audit standards and investigate and discipline audit firms. Despite Congress's belated lurch toward reform, only a few lawmakers truly care more about individual investors than about their corporate patrons. The Congress that enacted the landmark investor protection statute—the Securities Act of 1933—in response to the 1929 stock market crash bears little resemblance to recent legislatures that have shortchanged the SEC.

Serious failures of corporate governance remain to be addressed, and that means a stronger role for independent directors, especially those who sit on committees that determine executive compensation and oversee the performance of the audit. Corporate audit committees are especially critical as the last line of protection for investors. They must ask more questions, test the company's disclosures and financial reports for accuracy, and hire their own experts if necessary. Audit committees also must strictly limit the amount and type of consulting work done for the company by their auditors. This is the surest way to reduce the conflicts of interest that inevitably occur when a company pays an accounting firm consulting fees that far outweigh the audit fee.

The good news is that many positive changes have occurred, post-Enron. The stock exchanges have tightened their listing standards to require company managers to be more accountable to shareholders. The SEC has proposed new rules that should result in shareholders getting more timely and reliable information. The accountants' trade group, the American Institute of Certified Public Accountants, thankfully is no longer the industry's self-regulator. The most positive changes have come at investors' behest, not as the result of new laws or rules. Under pressure from pension and mutual funds, companies are disclosing more detail in their earnings reports—though it's not nearly enough—and letting shareholders vote on stock option plans. Some companies have decided not to use their auditors as consultants any longer. And many investors are avoiding the stock of companies with aggressive accounting, especially the kinds of off-balance-sheet devices that destroyed Enron.

The farmer in Des Moines, the teacher in Coral Gables, and the truck driver in Syracuse all have a common interest in full disclosure, reliable numbers, clearly written documents, and a vigilant regulatory system. But no regulator can provide total protection against fraud. No law has been devised to anticipate the deceptions and distortions that are inevitable in markets fueled by hype and hope. America's markets operate by a set of rules that are half written and half custom. That makes the individual's responsibility to discern hidden motivations and conflicts of interest as important as any law or regulation.

But there's another reason why individual investors must be vigilant of their own interests. Investor protection is supposed to be the responsibility of three institutions: the SEC, the stock exchanges, and the courts. Yet over the past several years, the effectiveness of each has eroded. The increasing power and sophistication of special interests through Congress have thwarted the SEC. Conflicts plague the self-regulatory organizations—the New York Stock Exchange and the National Association of Securities Dealers—whose revenues come from the companies they list and the order flow of brokerage firms, the very groups the exchanges are supposed to oversee. Adverse legislation and court decisions have limited aggrieved investors' access to the judicial system.

This book is intended to give investors a guide to avoiding

pitfalls they never knew existed. I hope it helps investors understand the essential role they play in protecting their own financial future. By learning about conflicts, motivations, and political favoritism, investors can become more discerning in how they use the power of their money and the power of their shareholder vote. I hope this book makes you a more informed, skeptical, diligent, and successful investor.

CHAPTER ONE

HOW TO SLEEP
AS WELL AS YOUR BROKER

I f they have it, sell it. If they don't, buy it. That was the whispered joke on Wall Street in 1963 when I joined the brokerage firm of Carter, Berlind & Weill. It was only half in jest. It betrayed the callous attitude many brokers had toward their clients. Brokers are supposed to advise you on which securities to buy and sell, depending on your financial resources and your investment objectives. They offer garden-variety stocks, bonds, and mutual funds, or such exotic instruments as convertible debentures and single-stock futures, to help you shape a portfolio that fits your needs. Brokers may seem like clever financial experts, but they are first and foremost salespeople. Many brokers are paid a commission, or a service fee, on every transaction in accounts they manage. They want you to buy stocks you don't own and sell the ones you do, because that's how they make money for themselves and their firms. They earn commissions even when you lose money.

Commissions can take many forms. On a stock trade, the commission is a percentage of the total value of the shares. For some mutual funds there are up-front commissions, or sales loads, which are paid when you make an investment. There also may be back-end commissions, or deferred loads, which are paid when you take your money out. On bonds, brokers don't charge commissions. Instead, they make their money off the "spread," or the difference between what the firm paid to buy the bond and the price at which the firm sells the bond to you.

Warren Buffett, the chairman and CEO of Berkshire Hathaway

Inc. and one of the smartest investors I've ever met, knows all about broker conflicts. He likes to point out that any broker who recommended buying and holding Berkshire Hathaway stock from 1965 to now would have made his clients fabulously wealthy. A single share of Berkshire Hathaway purchased for $12 in 1965 would be worth $71,000 as of April 2002. But any broker who did so would have starved to death. While working in the early 1950s for his father's brokerage firm in Omaha, Neb., Buffett says he learned that "the broker is not your friend. He's more like a doctor who charges patients on how often they change medicines. And he gets paid far more for the stuff the house is promoting than the stuff that will make you better." I couldn't agree more. In sixteen years as a Wall Street broker, I felt the pressures; I saw the abuses.

"Levitt, is that all you can do?" Those stinging words rang in my ears at the end of many a week as I struggled to join the ranks of successful Wall Street brokers at Carter, Berlind & Weill. Eleven of us worked out of an 800-square-foot office on 60 Broad Street, in the shadow of the New York Stock Exchange. I divided my time between buying and selling stock and scouting for companies that might want to go public.

When I joined the firm, America was riding high. A postwar economic boom that began in the 1950s marched onward through most of the 1960s, encouraging companies to look to Wall Street to finance their expansion. The growth in jobs and overall prosperity produced much wealth, and people flocked to the stock market in search of easy money. It was a heady time, and I wanted to be a part of it. I was thirty-two, and though I had no Wall Street experience whatsoever, I started calling potential clients right away.

The competition among the partners was intense. We shared one large office so we could keep a watchful eye on one another. Arthur Carter kept a green loose-leaf binder on his desk, and in it he recorded how much gross—the total amount of sales—each of us was responsible for each week. Every Monday morning I stared, terrified, at an empty calendar page, worrying how I was going to generate a respectable $5,000 in sales. When we reviewed the results on Friday, there would be much scolding and finger-pointing. If I wasn't the lowest producer, I joined the others in berating the one who was.

Our mandate was to grind out the gross and recruit new brokers with a proven knack for selling. But on the Wall Street I knew in the 1960s and '70s, the training of new brokers was almost nonexistent. Brokers were hired one day and put to work the next cold-calling customers. At all but a few firms, research was primitive. Starting salaries were a pittance, forcing brokers to learn at a young age that they had to sell aggressively to survive in the business. The drive for commissions sometimes motivated supervisors to look the other way when aggressive upstarts bent the rules.

Today the brokerage industry is a lot more sophisticated. Nowadays brokers sell dozens of savings, retirement, and investment products, and insurance, real estate, and hedging instruments to reduce risk. But with half of all American households invested in the stock market, brokers' responsibility to the individual investor is greater than ever.

Good People in a Bad System

Sadly, the brokerage industry still has numerous flaws. That's not to say that all brokers are commission-hungry wolves on the prowl for naive investors. Some are; others are just inept. Most are honest professionals. They are good people stuck in a bad system, whose problems remain fourfold. First, some brokers are not trained well enough for the enormous tasks they are expected to carry out. Second, the system in which brokers operate is still geared toward volume selling, not giving objective advice. Third, to increase sales, firms use contests to get brokers to sell securities that investors may not need. Most brokers rarely, if ever, disclose to their clients how they are paid or how their bonuses are structured, even though such disclosures would go a long way to resolving the conflict-of-interest problem. Fourth, branch-office managers and other supervisors, who are paid commissions just like their brokers, have an incentive to push everyone to sell more and to turn a blind eye to questionable practices.

Brokers come in many stripes. There is the full-service variety, employed by the large brokerage houses advertised on television: UBS PaineWebber (part of Swiss bank UBS), Morgan Stanley, and Salomon Smith Barney (part of Citigroup). The largest of the full-service firms is Merrill Lynch & Co., which employs roughly 14,000 brokers in 500 or so U.S. locations. Merrill calls its brokers "financial advisors." They manage more than 9 million customer accounts worth $1.3 trillion. Not only do they help clients determine their investment goals and pass on customer orders to their trading desks for execution, but they also provide research from in-house analysts and give advice on a wide range of securities. For these extras, customers pay more. The average commission paid to a Merrill Lynch broker in 2000 was about $200 per transaction.

Then there are the discount houses, which give minimal advice or none at all. Many do not provide proprietary research, although they may make available research produced by other firms. Investors are charged a moderate commission or pay a flat fee for each trade.

Online brokers can be either full-service or discount, though most are discounters. For a flat fee of $9.95, one leading online broker lets customers order up to 5,000 shares. Research and advice were not on the menu when online trading first began, but some online brokers, such as Charles Schwab Corp., have moved upstream into the full-service realm by offering research and advice to customers who maintain a minimum balance.

There's a saying that compensation determines behavior. Firms never seem to run out of novel ways to use commissions to motivate their brokers—and take more money out of your pocket. One popular system is the grid. Typically, brokers receive a percentage of the commissions that they generate, ranging from 33 percent to 45 percent. As their commission sales increase, they can jump to a higher payout level on the grid. Imagine it's December 27. Your broker's payout rate is 33 percent. He has generated $470,000 in commissions so far this year. But if he gets to $500,000 by December 31, his payout rate jumps to 40 percent, applied retroactively. This means your broker can earn a windfall of $44,900 in additional compensation just by generating $30,000 in commission sales in four days. Unless a firm's ethical culture is impeccable, the temptation to sell anything to anyone, no matter how inappropriate, is overwhelming.

It's also common practice for firms to pay large, up-front bonuses to lure a star broker away from his employer. Such bonuses can equal or exceed an entire year's pay. This sum is paid on the presumption that the broker will bring his customers with him to the new firm by telling them "the big lie"—that his new firm offers better customer service and more sophisticated research. The broker, of course, never reveals that the new firm is paying him a huge bundle to move. In such cases, customer accounts are bargaining chips that brokers use to increase their personal wealth, not their customers'. Once a broker moves to a new firm, he must produce. And that means the broker is more likely to push unwanted or unneeded products, especially those paying higher commissions.

Instead of, or in addition to, an up-front bonus, brokers sometimes get what is known as an accelerated payout. This means that instead of the normal 33 percent to 45 percent of the gross commission on every trade, the broker receives 60 percent or more of the commission for several months, or even several years. The justification for enriched payouts is that brokers who jump to a new firm will be preoccupied for months with administrative details involved in account transfers and helping to orient clients at the new firm, leaving little time for salesmanship. But the reality is that such payouts boost the broker's incentive to meddle in client accounts and increase the volume of trading activity.

Commissions distort brokers' recommendations in many other ways. Some firms, for example, have special arrangements to sell mutual funds in exchange for above-average commissions. If a Merrill Lynch broker knows he'll get 25 percent more money for selling a Putnam mutual fund over an American Century fund, guess which fund the broker will try to sell you? Most large brokerage firms today sponsor their own funds, and may try to steer you to one of those. That way, the fee you pay to the manager of the mutual fund remains in-house and adds to the firm's profits. The problem is that brokerage firm funds don't necessarily perform better than, or even as well as, independent funds. According to

Morningstar Inc., a fund research company, as of June 30, 2001, the five-year annualized returns of independent funds were up 8.28 percent, and for broker-sponsored funds only 6.92 percent.

One of the worst cases of broker abuse I ever saw took place at Olde Discount Corp., a Detroit-based firm that is now owned by H&R Block. At its height in the mid-1990s, Olde had 1,185 brokers in 160 branches. In 1998, Olde and its senior management, including founder Ernest J. Olde, without admitting or denying guilt, paid $7 million in fines to settle charges by the Securities and Exchange Commission and the NASD. The regulators accused Olde managers of creating an environment that encouraged brokers to make trades in customer accounts without the customers' permission, sell stocks and bonds that were not suitable to client needs, and falsify customer records. The company often hired recent college grads to flog stocks that the firm had placed on a carefully chosen "special ventures" list. These stocks were picked, not because they suited the investment needs of clients, but because Olde held the shares, many of them highly speculative, in its inventory. Olde then marked them up in price and made a profit off the spread between what it paid and the price at which it sold the stock.

The SEC found that Olde's compensation structure paid brokers substantially more if they sold stocks from this select list; brokers who did not meet a quota of select stock sales were sent packing. If customers said they could not afford to buy the recommended stocks, Olde brokers were trained to persuade the client to use margin, which involves borrowing money from the brokerage firm to purchase shares. The firm's two-page account-opening forms included a margin agreement, but many customers didn't understand that they were requesting a margin account.

WHY YOU SHOULD AVOID BUYING ON MARGIN

Your broker may recommend that you buy shares with money borrowed from his firm at a fixed interest rate and using your shares as collateral. He may argue that trading stocks "on margin" lets you use the power of leverage to amplify your stock-picking prowess, the way professionals do. Tell your broker you are not interested. Margin borrowing is very risky and, for an individual investor like you, should be avoided at all costs.

Margin simply means buying assets with borrowed money. Such loans are highly profitable to the brokerage firm. They are marketed on the premise that if you invest more without fully paying for the securities, you can lift your returns beyond what you'd otherwise get.

Leverage is a wonderful tool in a rising market. Here's how it works. Say you buy 100 shares of a stock at $50 a share. Normally, you would have to pay your broker $5,000, plus commissions. With a margin loan, you could borrow up to half that amount, and pay only $2,500, borrowing the other $2,500 from your broker. If the stock price rises to $75, and you decide to sell, you get $7,500 ($75 × 100 = $7,500). Of course, you have to repay the $2,500 loan, plus interest. But you have gained $5,000 with an initial investment of only $2,500.

Sounds good, except that the process moves swiftly in reverse in a declining market. You could be required to sell your stock to cover the loan or, worse, your broker could sell your stock without consulting you in order to pay off the loan before the market declines further. In the market plunges of 2000 and 2001, many leveraged investors could not raise enough money from the sale of their stock to repay their loans. Again, say you buy 100 shares of a stock at $50 a share, putting up $2,500 and borrowing the other $2,500 from your broker. But the value of your shares declines to $25, or $2,500 for 100 shares. You have now lost all your initial investment of $2,500, and you still owe your broker interest on the loan.

And there's another twist you must keep in mind with margin buying. By regulation, your broker must tap you for additional money if your equity—the value of your securities minus the amount you owe—goes below 25 percent. This 25 percent is called a "maintenance" margin, and today most brokers have imposed their own, stricter maintenance margins of 30 percent to even 50 percent on riskier stocks. Again, say you have borrowed $2,500 to buy 100 shares of a $50 stock, and your broker requires a 30 percent maintenance margin. If the shares fall to $40, your equity has dropped from $2,500 (the amount of your original investment) to $1,500 (100 shares × $40 minus your $2,500 loan = $1,500). That $1,500 in equity meets the broker's 30 percent maintenance margin requirement (30 percent of $4,000 = $1,200).

But if the value of your shares falls to $25, your equity has evaporated altogether (100 shares × $25 minus your $2,500 loan = 0). Your broker will make what is known as a margin call, demanding additional payment of cash or other securities into your account within two or three days. If you are unable to pay, the firm will sell your shares. You may have to take heavy losses, even if you wanted to stick with your investment in the hope that the share price rebounds.

One of Olde's victims was a married couple with five children, the eldest of whom had Down's syndrome. In March 1993 they opened an account at Olde's Clearwater, Fla., office. The wife had been in an auto accident that left her disabled, and had received an insurance settlement. The couple wanted to invest some of her settlement in a mutual fund and a money market account—nothing very risky. But within a month, the SEC found, the broker had executed fifty trades in their account, using margin to cover half the cost. The couple was unaware that they had even signed a margin agreement. By the end of July, the couple's money had all but disappeared. Their Olde broker had executed more than two hundred trades from the select list without their knowledge.

Profits and Professionalism

In the 1970s, when I oversaw the retail business of our firm, after numerous acquisitions now called Shearson Hayden Stone, part of my job was to hire and train new brokers. While we sought those with proven ability to generate fat commissions, it bothered me that we sometimes overlooked their previous ethical shortcomings, as reflected in numerous customer complaints. The more I felt pressured to hire superbrokers who bounced from firm to firm because of regulatory infractions, but who could generate $1 million a year in gross, the more I felt the need to speak out.

In a 1972 speech called "Profits and Professionalism," given at Columbia University, I lamented, "How can a broker view himself as a professional—as a counselor who considers his client's interest before his own—when his livelihood is dependent upon him taking an action which may not be appropriate or timely to take?" I then called on the industry to develop some way to pay brokers on how well their clients' investments performed, rather than on volume of transactions.

My partner, Sandy Weill—who as Citigroup chairman today oversees Salomon Smith Barney, one of the nation's largest brokerage firms—read the speech and said, "This is ridiculous. I can't stop you from doing this, but I certainly don't agree." Likewise, Hardwick Simmons, our marketing manager at the time and now CEO of the Nasdaq Stock Market, said I just didn't understand the business, and suggested that I stop tilting at windmills.

In the thirty years since that speech, nearly every firm in the industry continues to pay its brokers at least partially on a commission basis. Why so little progress? Resistance from top industry leaders. At a late 1993 dinner at the River Club in New York City, a dozen or so top executives gathered to hear my analysis of what was wrong with broker compensation. I made it clear that I thought there was a problem, and that, as SEC chairman, I expected the industry to do something about it, especially now that millions of individual investors for the first time were pouring into the market and risking their life's savings. I later learned that some of the CEOs left the dinner shaking their heads, grumbling about my "holier-than-thou" views.

In early 1994, I set up a blue-ribbon panel led by Dan Tully, then the chairman and CEO of Merrill Lynch. The panel's orders were to recommend ways to reduce conflicts between investors and brokers by changing the broker compensation system. After a year of study, the Tully Commission produced a code of industry "best practices." These were not pie-in-the-sky proposals but field-tested practices that some brokerage firms were already using. While I was only partly successful in persuading the industry to adopt the best practices, the most enduring achievement of the Tully Commission was getting industry leaders to acknowledge the existence of conflicts.

The panel's work and the way in which some industry leaders opposed it are instructive. Only two of the panel's five members came from the industry. Tully was one, and Chip Mason, chairman and CEO of the Baltimore-based investment bank Legg Mason Inc., was the other. Warren Buffett, who had recently led the investment banking firm of Salomon Brothers while it was dealing with the consequences of serious legal and ethical lapses in acquiring U.S. Treasury securities, agreed to join the panel. So did Samuel Hayes III, a Harvard business school professor, and Thomas O'Hara, chairman of the National Association of Investors Corp., a group representing investment clubs.

I gave the industry the impression that if it did not act, I would seek to impose stiff rules. But I was playing regulatory poker: If I pushed new rules, Republicans in Congress would almost certainly accuse me of overkill and tie my hands, so regulation was out of the question. Having only moral suasion at my command, I solicited the support of ordinary investors by holding town hall meetings throughout the country. When reporters began writing negative stories about some of the more odious compensation schemes, the firms had little choice but to denounce the practices in public. Secretly, however, they were perpetuating them. Tully knew, for example, that some brokerage firm leaders were looking me in the eye and insisting that they were not offering up-front bonuses, when they were. One firm, at that moment, was offering $1 million for Merrill's top producers.

The heightened scrutiny caused firm executives to examine their own houses. Many discovered that their branches were taking part in sales contests, or that brokers were being pressured into making cold calls using a mechanical script, having little or no familiarity with the products they were peddling. Even Tully says he learned that unbeknown to him, some of his branch offices were using contests to jack up sales.

Most major brokerage firms agreed to play ball with the SEC, saying they would commit to the Tully Commission's code of best practices, which included: ending product-specific sales contests; paying brokers a fee based on the percentage of client assets in an account, instead of on commissions alone; and banning higher commissions for in-house, or proprietary, products.

Some firms resisted. Phil Purcell, CEO of Dean Witter Reynolds Inc. (now part of Morgan Stanley), at first refused to jettison a policy of paying higher commissions for in-house products. Dean Witter was especially vulnerable on this point. The percentage of house-brand mutual funds sold by Dean Witter brokers was the industry's highest at 75 percent. At Merrill Lynch the figure was around 50 percent, and at Smith Barney only 30 percent. That meant that three out of every four Dean Witter customers who expressed interest in a mutual fund were steered to a Dean Witter fund, which carried an up-front fee, or load, that supposedly compensated the broker for his objective advice. Dean Witter brokers were getting up to 15 percent more commission for selling in-house funds. According to mutual fund rating firm Morningstar Inc., these funds at the time were not stellar performers, ranking below those of the five largest independent fund groups. When we shared with Purcell the data on how often Dean Witter brokers funneled customers into proprietary funds of subpar performance, he agreed not to resist the recommendation against higher payouts for in-house products.

Surprisingly, Merrill Lynch was also one of the resisters. Tully says he took the blue-ribbon committee job because Merrill had already switched from a compensation system that rewarded brokers for the number of trades they did to one that encouraged brokers to increase the amount of assets they had under management. Today, commissions make up only 25 percent of Merrill's.$22 billion in revenues. Tully believed the rest of the industry should follow Merrill's lead. Still, Merrill couldn't hold itself out as a paragon. One of the Tully Commission's most contentious recommendations was to end up-front bonuses. But Launny Steffens, then head of Merrill's retail broker business, balked at ending or even limiting the practice. Steffens, who retired from Merrill Lynch in May 2001, was a highly influential figure in the company. His army of brokers was the backbone of the firm and responsible for about half its profits. But Merrill's Achilles' heel was the very same well-developed system of branch office brokers: every other firm jealously eyed Merrill's brokers, and often tried to recruit them. It was not uncommon for Merrill trainees to get lucrative employment offers within weeks of completing a six-month course, which saved the hiring firm $100,000 (Merrill paid its trainees salaries of $40,000 for six months, and its training program cost an additional $60,000 per person).

Steffens simply would not disarm, and Tully, his boss, refused to pull rank and force him to back down. "I don't think Launny was wrong," Tully says now. "The SEC had its point of view. But Launny lived in the real world, not in a test tube. He understood what the competition was doing, and if he let that happen, he'd lose money and talent." Today, Merrill Lynch continues to pay up-front bonuses, as do most firms in the industry. Recruitment bonuses for top performers are now as high as the signing bonuses some professional sports teams pay for star athletes.

In the end, I failed to persuade all the firms to adopt certain key provisions of the code, and some have since backed away from their pledges. "In all honesty," Buffett told me later, "Dan Tully probably didn't want to change the system much. The system works too well. Merrill Lynch would be in terrible shape if it weren't for investors turning over their portfolios." How serious are the conflicts between broker and investor? Serious enough that a former top official of a major brokerage firm confessed to me privately that he would not send his mother to a full-service broker.

In recent times Wall Street firms have increasingly been using their analysts as glorified salespeople. The analysts make pitches for investment banking deals by promising to write glowing reports on companies if they hire the firm for an initial public offering or a debt issue.

When analysts write reports that gloss over problems in a company, brokers feed that information to investors, who are misled into buying the shares. And when analysts fail to warn that a company is in trouble, even keeping a "buy" recommendation on a stock that has lost most of its value, retail investors are left holding shares long after the pros have ditched them. At times, brokers have unloaded on their retail clients unwanted stock from their firms' inventory. They have even told clients to buy stock that their own analysts are shorting, a speculative ploy that involves borrowing shares in the expectation that they will decline in value. In the great stock market sell-off that began in March 2000 and continued well into 2002, some $7 trillion in market capitalization (the price of all publicly traded shares multiplied by the number of shares outstanding) was lost, much of it by retail investors.

Beware the Online Broker

The explosion in online trading is a direct outgrowth of the high cost of commissions and the lack of trust by many investors in their full-service broker. Companies such as E*Trade and Ameritrade are electronic brokers that use the Internet to gather retail investors' orders. This new twist in investing caught fire in the mid-1990s, when the bull market was in full swing. Anyone could open an account and begin buying and selling up to 5,000 shares for as little as $8. In most cases, trades are executed within ten seconds. Some online brokers also offer vast amounts of information for free, including research, streaming market data, and news. The ease and low cost of online trading lured 10 million Americans into opening online accounts between 1996 and 2000.

Alongside the online trading revolution came powerful new computer networks, called electronic communications networks, or ECNs, that act much like electronic stock exchanges. They match up buyers and sellers in a split second, and because they involve no human intervention, they do so at a fraction of the cost of the New York Stock Exchange or the Nasdaq Stock Market.

But the online trading revolution comes with its own hidden dangers that investors must know about and avoid. One is "payment for order flow," which involves a rebate to the brokerage firm for every order it funnels to a market-maker. Market-makers are middlemen who post prices at which they will buy and sell stocks for their own accounts and for others.

Online trading is a misnomer. When you place an order with an online broker, you are not trading directly with a stock exchange. Instead, your order is routed to the market of the online broker's choice. Because market-makers will pay a small fee for your order, the chances are pretty good that your buy order will not be executed at an exchange, but will be matched against someone else's sell order, and only the transaction is reported to the exchange.

The problem with payment for order flow is that your buy order may not be exposed to a large number of sell orders, and that may deprive you of a better price. The concept of getting the best possible price in the shortest amount of time is known as "best execution." Under SEC rules, your broker is obligated to get the best execution available for your order. If your broker is funneling orders to the highest bidder and ignoring his best-execution duty, you may be paying a lot more for shares than is necessary.

Now that share prices are quoted in decimals instead of fractions, spreads between buy and sell prices have narrowed, thus reducing the profit that market-makers and others make from spreads. And that, in turn, has made payment for order flow less attractive. But even though payments are declining, the practice persists today.

Say you place an order for 1,000 shares with an online broker, which then routes your order to a market-maker, who then "rebates" the broker a penny for every order it gets at the market price. But another market-maker or exchange not paying for order flow might be able to improve the price by 5 cents, saving you $50 ($.05 × 1,000 shares = $50). That's five times what most online brokers charge in commissions. The moral is: don't be fooled into saving $5 in commission charges, only to pay far more in hidden trading costs.

Another hidden trip wire for investors is internalization, which happens when a brokerage firm passes on orders to its own market-making subsidiary that matches buys with sells. Economically, internalization is just like payment for order flow, except that the parent company gets to keep all the payments. For the investor, the problem is the same: a buy order that doesn't meet up with a larger universe of sell orders may get executed at a higher price than the best available price the broader market is offering. Charles Schwab & Co. is the king of internalization. Its wholly owned market-making company, Schwab Capital Markets (formerly known as Mayer & Schweitzer), matches thirty-six percent of orders placed with Schwab brokers or received online. That means many Schwab orders are exposed only to other Schwab customers' orders. The company fulfills its best execution obligation by making sure that customers get the best available price that other markets may be advertising.

New SEC rules, which took effect in 2001, can help you avoid brokers that steer your order to an execution facility for their benefit, not yours. The rules require brokers, each quarter, to reveal where they send orders, and whether they received a rebate. Exchanges, ECNs, and market-makers must also reveal, each month, how well they execute customer orders, and how often they improve prices, on a stock-by-stock basis. These data can help you decide if you want to sacrifice speed for a better price—data that were not available prior to the SEC rule. If you don't like the way your online broker is routing your orders, you can switch to another broker with a better record.

In many ways, brokers are inevitable. If you walked onto the floor of the New York Stock Exchange, you would not be able to buy a single share without placing your order through a broker. If you buy and sell stocks through an online trading firm, you're still accessing the market through a broker, albeit an electronic one.

Fire Your Broker

If you have less than $50,000 to invest, you don't need a broker. The strategy that makes the most sense is investing in low-cost mutual funds, especially index funds that match the performance of a stock index. You could start off with a fund that follows the Wilshire 5000, which includes virtually all U.S. stocks, or the Standard & Poor's 500, which mimics the shares of 500 large U.S. companies. As you become more comfortable investing in mutual funds, and as your assets grow, you can move into index funds that track small, medium, and large companies. Or you can buy funds that track fast-growing companies or undervalued ones. As most experts suggest, put a small amount of your assets into an international fund and a Real Estate Investment Trust, which is like a mutual fund but it invests only in real estate. And for diversification, consider a corporate or government bond fund. Bonds are less risky than stocks, but historically stocks have outperformed bonds.

Even three years into the bear market that started in March 2000, it's still smart to invest in stocks. Indeed, you should consider bear markets, which drive share prices down, as a good time to buy.

If you have more than $50,000 to invest, you should fire your broker and find an investment adviser. Brokerage firms would like you to think that they perform the same functions as investment advisers. Many brokers call themselves "financial consultants" or "financial advisers." But they're not the same as independent investment advisers.

Like a broker, an investment adviser can help you create an investment plan that conforms to your lifestyle, income level, and investment goals. Also like a broker, an adviser will help you allocate the correct percentages of your assets into stocks, bonds, and cash, and rebalance your portfolio over time as the various pieces grow or shrink. But many brokers do not have a fiduciary duty—a legal obligation—to put your interests above his or the firm's. True, a broker has to recommend investments that are suitable to your financial status and tolerance for risk, as well as a duty to get you the best execution possible for your trades, as we discussed earlier. But an investment adviser's fiduciary duty is on a higher plane, like that of a lawyer, a trustee, or the executor of an estate.

Investment advice is a big business, and the huge array of advice-givers can be confusing, so let's go over the basics. There are different kinds of investment advisers, depending on their qualifications and how they are paid. Most investment advisers charge fees, which can be an hourly rate, an annual figure, a percentage of your assets, or a fee-plus-commissions. I recommend you find a certified financial planner (CFP)—someone who takes a holistic approach to your finances—if you want your adviser to consider your retirement, insurance, tax, and estate-planning needs. You can obtain a list of CFPs near you through the Financial Planning Association (*www. fpanet.org/plannersearch*). Members must pass a proficiency test and keep up with continuing education requirements. Financial planners who are members of the National Association of Personal Financial Advisors (*www.napfa.org*) also must pass an exam, but in addition they submit their work to peer review and are not supposed to charge anything but a fee. In either case, be sure to verify a financial planner's certification. If you don't understand what a credential means, ask what the planner did to earn it.

You will need to decide how you want to pay for advice before choosing an investment adviser. A financial planner's fee can be an hourly rate (you should expect to pay at least $100 per hour but $200 is not unusual for an experienced CFP); a percentage of the assets you are investing (usually 1 percent but could go as high as 2 percent); or a flat fee for a set number of visits (a typical rate might be $2,500 for up to five visits) and unlimited telephone access. Some advisers will charge you a fee as well as the commissions that a brokerage firm will charge to execute trades on your behalf or sell you a mutual fund.

Which is the best payment option? That depends on you. I like the hourly fee or the flat rate. Both are fully disclosed, there are no hidden charges, and the adviser's interests won't conflict with yours. If you spend many hours a month managing your money, then you're probably better off paying an adviser's hourly fee. Chances are, you won't be taking up a lot of an adviser's time, so you needn't worry about the ticking clock. On the other hand, if you expect lots of hand-holding because you're just starting out as an investor, don't have the time to manage your finances, or are about to retire and have numerous questions, then you're probably better off paying a flat fee. Look for an adviser who will give you a number of in-person visits plus unlimited telephone access. In the long run, you'll probably pay less than the hourly rate.

Like commissioned brokers, investment advisers can have conflicts. So don't forget to ask: how are you getting paid? Some advisers receive a commission for referring you to a specific tax accountant, for example, or for selling you a certain mutual fund. Or an adviser may have a fee-splitting arrangement that rewards him for sending your trades through a certain brokerage firm. Such fees may signal that the advice you're getting isn't exactly independent. Some advisers can sell only their firm's product line. If so, you may want to find an adviser who can offer you a wider array of investments.

One more important point: investment advice is not a highly regulated business. A loose patchwork of federal and state agencies oversees the industry. It's up to you to protect yourself by checking an adviser's registration and disciplinary records. The SEC requires investment advisory firms, but not individuals, with more than $25 million under management to file Form ADV, which explains investment strategy, fee schedule, ownership, potential conflicts, disciplinary record, and much more. But the SEC has no competency requirements; firms need only fill out the form and pay a fee. Firms that manage less than $25 million must file with their respective states, some of which also regulate individual advisers. You can check out state-registered advisers by contacting the North American Securities Administrators Association (*www.nasaa.org*).

It would be helpful if Congress and the SEC created a uniform regulatory regime for all "advice givers," be they brokers or financial planners, large or small firms, or subject to state or federal oversight. In late 2001, the SEC, with the help of NASAA, eliminated some of the confusion when it launched a Web site (*www.adviserinfo.sec.gov*) to help investors find an appropriate adviser. The site contains the Form ADVs of more than 7,000 SEC-registered and 1,700 state-registered investment advisers. The SEC plans to add the remaining 16,000 state-registered advisers over the coming years to complete the database.

Be Careful, Even If Your Broker Is Fee-Based

If you decide to stick with a broker, it's best to find one whose compensation is fee-based. To its credit, the brokerage industry increasingly is replacing commissions with fee-based accounts. But even these pose conflict-of-interest issues that investors must weigh carefully.

Also called special accounts or managed accounts, fee-based accounts allow investors to custom-tailor a portfolio. Brokerage firms often team up with money managers to create personalized portfolios of stocks and bonds, much like a mutual fund except the individual investor owns the securities. The broker gives an expert in, say, technology stocks or municipal bonds a percentage of your money to manage, depending on how you and your broker have decided to allocate your assets. You won't pay commissions, but fees can be very high, ranging between 1 percent and 3 percent of the portfolio's value, of which the broker typically gets 60 percent and the money manager 40 percent. Most brokerages require at least $100,000 to open such an account, but that minimum is declining as firms aggressively market these accounts.

Brokerage firms like fee-based accounts because they get a steady stream of income whether or not you trade, in place of the sporadic revenues that trading commissions produce. The accounts appeal to investors who want to avoid the capital gains taxes of mutual funds and like the individualized treatment. Your broker may also claim that this method aligns your interests with his and a money manager's, since there are no commissions.

But you should think twice before you choose this type of account. Managed account fees seem sky-high in comparison to the 0.5 percent of assets or less that most index mutual funds charge. And unless you are an active trader, you may be better off paying commissions. If your account has $100,000 in it, and you are paying your broker a 1.5 percent annual fee, you are giving up $1,500 a year. Is it worth it? It is only if you anticipate paying trading commissions of that amount.

Fee-based brokers can be hazardous to your financial well-being in other ways. Because you are paying your broker an annual fee no matter how much activity takes place in your account, he may not pay adequate attention to your portfolio. The burden is on you to make sure this doesn't happen. And many brokerage firms require outside advisers to execute trades through them. If an adviser hopes to get more referrals from the brokerage firm, it's in his interest to give the firm's trading desk as much business as possible. This tying relationship reintroduces the very conflict that fee-based accounts were designed to avoid.

Of course, there are exceptions to my "fire your broker" admonition. One is the broker network of St. Louis–based Edward Jones, whose 7,500 branch offices dot just about every Main Street in America. If you are among the 5.4 million customers of this regional brokerage firm, and are satisfied with the service you are getting, then relax. The 8,000 brokers at Edward Jones work on commission, but they are trained to teach their customers to invest for the long term—that is, to buy and hold for at least ten, and up to twenty, years when possible. Managing Partner John Bachmann says the typical Edward Jones customer holds the same mutual fund for twenty years, against an industry average of four years. That tells me his brokers aren't putting their financial interests ahead of their clients'.

Edward Jones differs in several other important ways. It does no investment banking, so there is no danger that an Edward Jones "buy" recommendation is influenced by a desire to win a stock-underwriting deal. Because the firm caters to the serious, long-term investor, it does not offer Internet trading and it does not sell exotic or high-risk products such as options, commodities, and penny stocks. It does not peddle in-house mutual funds, and thus avoids the conflicts of interest inherent when a firm promotes its own, more profitable products. The firm also has a policy of not paying up-front bonuses to attract star brokers, and it sends every newly hired broker to a four-month training program. A company's culture does matter, and the culture of most brokerage firms encourages transactions. Edward Jones's culture does not.

Look Your Broker in the Eye

If you choose to invest through a broker, don't let him do anything until you have a chance to meet face-to-face. Try to establish a rapport, and keep in constant touch. When I was managing accounts for clients, I noticed that a few of them consistently outperformed the others. They happened to be the ones who nagged me the most, always asking why I bought this bond or why I didn't buy that stock.

Make sure you and your broker map out an investment strategy—and stick with it. Good brokers will suggest investments that match your financial wherewithal and future goals, and help you develop a road map to get there. The two of you should write all this down and periodically review it. Remember that your broker is a salesperson, and while he wants you to succeed, he also wants to earn commissions.

When shopping for a broker, here is a checklist of questions to ask, so you can decide if this is the right broker for you:

- Does your firm emphasize in-house products over the products of other companies? What percent of in-house products (e.g., mutual funds) does your firm sell, versus products originated by other firms?
- Will the firm allow me to pay a fee, based on the total assets in my account, instead of commissions?
- Does the firm have a training program that pays brokers a salary for a year, instead of a two-month training program, after which the broker is paid a commission?
- Does the firm ever pay up-front bonuses to recruit brokers away from other firms?
- Does the firm hold sales contests to induce brokers to sell more of a certain product, whether in-house or not?
- What is your experience and training? How many brokerage firms have you worked for?
- Where do you get your stock and bond recommendations?
- If you recently changed firms, are you receiving special compensation for having switched firms, or any other kind of bonus plan?

- How many clients do you currently serve?
- Have you ever been disciplined for a violation of the securities laws? You can check the answer by calling the NASD's public disclosure hotline, 1-800-289-9999.
- Can you supply references?

Once your broker does make a recommendation, you should ask: How does this stock, bond, or mutual fund meet the investment goals we outlined? Why are you suggesting this over other options? Is this the best course of action for me, or just one of many possibilities? Does your firm have a business relationship with any of the companies whose shares you are recommending? For example, make sure you know if the broker's firm has helped the company with an initial public offering of stock or a debt offering anytime in the past two years. If your broker recommends a mutual fund, be sure there is a good reason for buying it, beyond that the broker gets a higher payout from that fund company over others.

And don't forget to ask about the risk involved in the securities your broker is recommending. One way to help you understand risk is to ask your broker to describe the worst-case scenario, the best possible outcome, and the most likely result of this investment. It's also good to know how easy or difficult it would be to liquidate, or sell, the investment. Some investments are difficult to unload, and you should know that beforehand.

Of course, you will also want to know what the commission on each transaction will be. Will there be any other ongoing costs? Is the commission negotiable? Remember that commissions reduce the value of your initial investment and thus reduce the returns you get over time. Brokers have an incentive to steer you toward products that pay them a higher commission rather than products that may be more suitable for you but that pay a lower commission. Low-risk investments, in general, pay out lower commissions.

You also have a right to know if your broker is participating in any kind of contest or promotion that rewards him for selling certain products. While less common in the business today, contests still exist at some firms. Contests reward a broker, who accumulates points toward a prize, such as a vacation or a stereo. But the prize can skew the broker's advice, especially if he is close to winning the big prize.

Once you make an investment, you will get a piece of mail known as a confirmation slip. Be sure to read it, and then file it. This is the notice that your order has been completed; it will include the price you paid and the commission charged. Sometimes the commission will read "zero," but that doesn't mean the broker isn't getting a fee to sell the product. Sometimes the commission is paid by the company issuing the shares, or by the mutual fund. And sometimes securities are sold to you out of the brokerage firm's own inventory. In that case, the broker gets a piece of the markup.

Keep Up with the Chores

As an investor, you have responsibilities, too. The more you understand these, the more rewarding your investment experience will be.

First, do nothing until you have a strategy. This involves creating a financial plan with your adviser, whether that person is a certified financial planner, investment adviser, or broker. This plan should state your investment goals, such as having enough money to buy a new house or boat, put your children through college, or live comfortably in retirement. The plan should contain a personal balance sheet, or description of all your assets, such as your home and money in bank accounts, and all your liabilities, such as your home mortgage and any personal loans. Finally, the plan should state how much you are willing to set aside each month.

Once you have calculated your net worth and determined how much you want to invest and what you want your investments to help you achieve, there is one more important decision to make: how much risk are you willing to accept? This is a vital question that you and your adviser should talk over. Don't be shy—your adviser needs to know as much as possible about your financial condition and goals, and also needs to know how conservatively or aggressively you expect your portfolio to perform. How would you feel if you lost 10 percent of your initial investment? What about 25 percent? If losses of any kind make you sick to your stomach, you should stick to low-risk investments, such as stocks and bonds of the blue-chip companies—the large, more reliably profitable corporations. But if you can lose 10 percent or 25 percent and take it in stride—hoping that the market will bounce back as it has done historically—then your appetite for risk is greater and you should consider investing a portion of your funds in smaller, fast-growing companies. Brokers also use this information to make sure they are complying with NASD "suitability" rules. These require brokers to recommend only securities that are suitable for your risk tolerance, financial situation, and investment objectives.

In general, the higher the risk, the greater the potential for reward and for losses. Shares of start-up companies, or of companies in emerging markets such as Asia and Latin America, are considered high-risk. Low-risk investments, such as government bonds, are guaranteed to return a steady stream of interest, plus your initial investment. Government bonds, and many corporate bonds, are thus useful for those approaching or already in retirement as a steady source of income. But inflation could eat into your returns, eroding the purchasing power of your income.

You and your adviser should also discuss diversification, or not putting all your eggs into one basket. If one sector of the economy is booming, and you pile all your funds into that sector, you won't be able to offset your losses if the sector goes bust. In 2000 and 2001, many investors learned this lesson the hard way when the bottom fell out of technology stocks. A portfolio with a mix of stocks or stock mutual funds and bonds, plus some money that you can easily convert to cash, such as a money market account, is considered diversified. If your company has a profit-sharing plan or retirement plan that makes contributions in company stock, make sure you balance that with stock in companies that specialize in different sectors of the economy.

To be a responsible investor, you should also keep up with the chores: Keep all correspondence that your investments generate. There will be quarterly statements, annual reports, prospectuses, confirmation slips, and more. Read them and file them. Even if you are prone to stuffing everything into one huge folder, keep it all. You should check every confirmation slip to make sure it matches what your own notes say you bought or sold, and what you were told the commission would be. If you ever have a dispute with your broker, you will need those confirmation slips. Or you may need to pay taxes because your mutual fund sold some of its holdings. If you sell shares of stock, and you owe capital gains taxes on the increase in value between the time you first bought it and when you sold it, you can deduct the cost of commissions from the proceeds of the sale. Any of this valuable information could arrive in the mail throughout the year, and not just when it's time to prepare your taxes.

Reading your financial mail and staying abreast of financial news are important chores, too. It's smart to compare your portfolio each quarter with an appropriate index, such as the S&P 500 if you are holding domestic equities. But don't pay too much heed to the cascade of financial information available to you on television, in the financial press, and over the Internet. You need not watch CNBC all day or scour the business pages of your daily newspaper. It's probably not even a good idea to track the daily ups and downs of your stock holdings. Unless you plan to retire soon, you should view your investment as long-term, with a ten-to-twenty-year horizon. A regular perusal of the financial pages of a newspaper or a business magazine at week's end should keep you informed enough to understand the major trends that affect the overall economy and the particular companies you have invested in.

That's not to say you shouldn't read and learn about the major events that affect your finances. You should. But if you have a strategy and stick with it, and if you occasionally keep track of how well your investments are doing and talk over their progress with your adviser, you won't need to spend a lot of valuable free time monitoring the stock market and the Internet. Remember: trust your own instincts. No expert, stock market guru, or financial columnist knows what you should invest in better than you.

CHAPTER TWO

THE SEVEN DEADLY SINS
OF MUTUAL FUNDS

As I prepared to join the Securities and Exchange Commission in 1993, I knew I had to sell all my stocks and bonds to avoid even the appearance of a conflict of interest. No SEC chairman can sit in judgment of a company in which he owns stock, so I had already begun exploring my options. I could buy either government bonds or mutual funds. With the help of an investment adviser, I decided it would be best to put my money into mutual funds. I had never owned a mutual fund, only stocks and bonds that I had picked myself, or that an adviser had picked for me.

As I pored over fund prospectuses, what really got under my skin was that the documents were impossible to understand. At first I was embarrassed. Then it hit me: if someone with twenty-five years in the securities business couldn't decipher the jargon, imagine the frustration for the average investor. Mutual fund prospectuses were written in impenetrable legalese, by and for securities lawyers. I would soon discover that this was but one of many troubling practices in the mutual fund industry.

Mutual funds have been wildly successful marketing themselves as the investor's best friend. They offer hassle-free, professional portfolio management and a wide array of fund choices. In 1980 Americans invested $100 billion in some 500 funds. But by 1993, those numbers had ballooned to $1.6 trillion and more than 3,800 funds. A decade later, at the end of February 2003, the number of funds had more than doubled to 8,200 and the amount invested in them had quadrupled to $6.3 trillion—more than the $6 trillion in bank accounts. Today there are more mutual funds than there are public companies.

THE TAIL WAGGING THE DOG?

Why have mutual funds grown so fast over the past two decades? The creation of the Individual Retirement Account fueled the early boom years by allowing investors to put their retirement savings into tax-protected mutual funds. When corporate 401(k) pension plans in the late 1980s began offering employees a menu of mutual funds in which to invest, millions more jumped aboard. Today about 38 percent of mutual fund assets comes from 401(k)s. Brokerage firms, looking to get in on the action, developed mutual fund products and began aggressively selling them through their broker networks. But the bull market in stocks in the 1990s really broke the dam.

As the amount of money in mutual funds, part of what Wall Streeters call the "buy side," has grown, so has the industry's clout. Today, funds own 20 percent of all publicly traded shares.

Is that too much power? Most experts say mutual funds aren't the tail wagging the dog—yet. According to fund research company Lipper Inc., when the S&P 500 plummeted in March 2001, fund investors redeemed $20 billion of their money over the entire month, or a mere 0.5 percent of all the assets of stock mutual funds.

But others warn that funds' collective actions may increase volatility, or price swings. For example, D. Deon Strickland, an SEC economist who studied mutual fund behavior as an assistant professor at Ohio State University, says mutual funds sometimes exaggerate market swings by pushing prices farther in the direction in which they are already moving. The danger is that mutual funds, which tend to act like a herd, could turn a routine market correction into a steep decline.

At the SEC I met regularly with top mutual fund executives who loved to extol the virtues of their clean industry. They were right to a degree: it has been free from major scandal for decades. But the industry has a lot to answer for, and it has been slow to respond to criticism. The way that funds are sold and managed reveals a culture that thrives on hype, promotes short-term trading, and withholds important information. The industry misleads investors into buying funds on the basis of past performance, which should be only one of several factors to consider. Some funds are able to get away with overly high fees because investors don't realize how fees can reduce their returns. The industry spends many millions of dollars a year on marketing, but does a poor job explaining the effect of annual expenses, sales loads, and taxes on investment returns. Nor does it publicize that actively managed mutual funds on average fail to perform as well as the benchmark against which they are measured. Funds resist giving out important details about their own internal operations, such as what they pay portfolio managers, and when and why managers leave. Fund directors, rather than acting like watchdogs on investors' behalf, passively approve fund management contracts year in and year out.

One of my biggest complaints is that most of the players in this highly profitable industry are reluctant to spend more than a pittance on educating fund investors. I think fund companies believe that the underinformed investor is a more profitable investor. Barry Barbash, who as head of the SEC's Division of Investment Management oversaw the mutual fund industry, told me in 1993 that he had no idea how much investors really understood about mutual funds. So we hired a polling firm to find out. After several surveys and even a few focus groups—efforts that the Investment Company Institute, the industry's trade group, derided as pseudoscientific—we realized that most investors were even more befuddled than we had imagined. This discovery spurred me to take a number of initiatives aimed at helping investors navigate the mutual fund maze.

Years earlier, the SEC had tried, with only limited success, to simplify the language in the fund prospectus. Fund documents were stilted in part because of rigid SEC rules on what a prospectus must say to comply with the Investment Company Act of 1940, which governs mutual funds. But many fund groups and their allies in the legal community were comfortable with the current rules and resisted change. They knew how to emphasize the points that put their funds in a good light and how to downplay the bad stuff without getting into hot water.

Once again, Warren Buffett, the CEO of Berkshire Hathaway, was a crucial ally, this time in a renewed attempt to make fund documents more lucid. Buffett applied some of his down-home common sense to help de-jargonize mutual fund legalese. I asked him to rewrite this turgid paragraph from a fund prospectus:

> Maturity and duration management decisions are made in the context of an intermediate maturity orientation. The maturity structure of the portfolio is adjusted in anticipation of cyclical interest rate changes. Such adjustments are not made in an effort to capture short-term, day-to-day movements in the market, but instead are implemented in anticipation of longer term, secular shifts in the levels of interest rates (i.e., shifts transcending and/or not inherent to the business cycle) . . .

Ten days later, he faxed this back to me:

> We will try to profit by correctly predicting future interest rates. When we have no strong opinion, we will generally hold intermediate-term bonds. But when we expect a major and sustained increase in rates, we will concentrate on short-term issues. And, conversely, if we expect a major shift to lower rates, we will buy long bonds. We will focus on the big picture and won't make moves based on short-term considerations.

Buffett's rewrite was a model of clarity, and it became the linchpin of an effort to simplify mutual fund prospectuses. We worked with the industry to come up with what is today called the "profile," a two-to-three-page, plain English summary of a fund's performance, investment style, and risks. While the profile is not mandatory, some fund companies have adopted it because investors have found it convenient and easier to read than the prospectus.

Mutual fund companies are eager to be seen as pro-investor, but the truth is they aren't always. At the SEC, I saw many cases of abuse by fund personnel. I saw portfolio managers line their pockets by purchasing shares for their own accounts, and later buying the same shares for the fund, thus driving up the value of their personal holdings. This scheme, called "front-running," is illegal under the securities laws. I saw fund companies inappropriately allocate initial public stock offerings (IPOs) to weaker funds that needed performance boosts, bypassing other funds to which they owed a duty. While this makes sickly funds more appealing to new investors, it hurts the interests of existing shareholders. I saw fund directors compromise their independence by accepting low-priced IPO shares from fund sponsors without disclosing the gifts. Portfolio pumping was another practice that irked me. This occurs when a portfolio manager, on the last day of a reporting period, tries to manipulate the market by buying large chunks of a security the fund already holds. If successful, the fund's value rises, and its quarterly record glows more brightly. But such results are akin to false advertising, luring unsuspecting investors into buying a fund whose recent performance has been rigged.

Many of these were not isolated acts committed by rogue fund managers. The SEC brought enforcement cases against some of the largest and most respected companies during my tenure. A mutual fund run by Van Kampen Investment Advisory Corp., for example, claimed in advertisements that it had returned 62 percent in 1996. According to fund-rating service Lipper Inc., that made it the top performer in its class, a full 20 percent ahead of the second-best-performing fund in the category. But investors weren't told that the excellent returns of the Van Kampen fund, a so-called incubator fund operating on seed money until its portfolio manager could establish a track record for marketing purposes, were on relatively tiny assets of between $200,000 and $380,000. Nor were investors told that more than half the returns came from investments in thirty-one hot IPOs. The fund, in fact, only had to buy between 100 and 400 shares of each IPO to achieve a huge magnifying effect. The 62 percent return unrealistically raised investor expectations, but it was also an unsustainable performance. When senior managers of Van Kampen decided to sell the fund to the public, some 15,000 people invested $100 million within six weeks. Without admitting or denying guilt, Van Kampen settled SEC charges that it had misled investors.

A fund run by Dreyfus Corp., owned by Mellon Financial Corp., paid almost $3 million to settle, without admitting or denying guilt, similar charges of fraudulently luring investors with unsustainable returns. Its manager claimed returns of more than 80 percent, but failed to tell investors that the fund had received a disproportionate number of IPO shares that should have been allocated to other Dreyfus funds.

And a Legg Mason portfolio manager inflated the value of notes (corporate IOUs that were sold in private placements) in two Legg Mason funds, deceiving the funds' investment advisers and her own managers from 1996 to 1998. Because she was not properly supervised, the portfolio manager was able to record fictitious numbers when reporting the daily value of the notes in the portfolios she managed. Even after the issuers of some of the notes defaulted on their interest payments and were forced into bankruptcy, she used an elaborate ruse to overstate the value of the funds, causing new investors to overpay. Legg Mason, without admitting or denying guilt, settled SEC charges that it failed to properly supervise the portfolio manager.

Maybe the fund industry should work less on image creation and more on making sure it has done everything possible to safeguard investors' money and boost their returns. The industry has become a financial powerhouse over the past twenty years. But as funds increasingly see themselves as glitzy marketing operations rather than stewards of other people's money, they risk losing investors' trust. When forced to walk a mile in the shoes of the typical retail investor after my appointment to the SEC, I learned many valuable lessons about the shortcomings of mutual funds, their Seven Deadly Sins.

High Fees Strangle Returns

The deadliest sin of all is the high cost of owning some mutual funds. Despite what many investors believe, investing in funds is not free. Funds collect more than $50 billion a year in fees from investors. Near the front of a fund's prospectus you can see a schedule of fees and expenses, with sales loads listed separately. The numbers may seem harmless, averaging 1.62 percent in 2002, but they can dramatically reduce your returns over time. Despite efforts by the industry to downplay the fee controversy, you should understand this basic fact about funds: The bite taken out of your investment by fees often determines whether you have gains or losses.

When was the last time you thought about the mutual fund fees you pay? Most people don't give them even a passing thought. That's good for the fund industry, which does an exemplary job touting the benefits of mutual funds, but prefers to gloss over what it costs you each year. To the industry, one of the greatest design features of funds is the way they artfully camouflage fees as a percentage of assets. Most people would consider a 2 percent annual fee to be quite low, and don't realize that it is really a punishing levy.

And the way fees are automatically deducted from a fund's returns—you never see an invoice and you never have to write a check—makes them all but invisible. If you invest $10,000 in a domestic stock fund with an expense ratio of 2 percent and a sales load of 3 percent, and you get annual returns of 7.5 percent for twenty years, your money would almost triple to $27,508. But you would also have lost $14,970 in fees and foregone earnings over the twenty years. Most American households would spend less than that for utilities over twenty years.

You may already know that mutual funds can be divided into two fee classes: load funds and no-load funds. A load is a one-time fee or commission. It is charged in addition to an annual management fee, which goes toward paying the investment advisers who oversee the portfolio and overhead expenses. Load funds usually take between 3 percent and 6 percent of your investment as soon as you open an account. Sometimes the load is taken when you withdraw your money, and thus is called a back-end load, or "deferred sales load."

Naturally, investors don't like it when funds skim 5 percent of their savings right off the top. So fund companies have figured out ways to hide some of the load by assessing annual fees that you pay as a percent of your assets in the fund. This is called a "distribution" fee, or a 12b-1 fee, after the Investment Company Act rule that governs such fees.

These fees are supposed to cover marketing and advertising costs. Brokers' commissions, for example, often come out of 12b-1 fees. So does the cost of a toll-free phone number. And when your mutual fund advertises on television, the cost of that expensive thirty-second ad comes out of, you guessed it, 12b-1 fees. You should avoid owning shares in a fund that charges these fees, which are no more than a levy on existing investors to help find new investors. Why should you pay to tell the rest of the world how good your fund is?

No-load mutual funds also charge fees. As with load funds, they charge management fees. Some no-loads also charge an "exit fee" when you sell your shares. Some even charge a 12b-1 fee, but it can't exceed 0.25 percent of assets or the fund loses the right to call itself a no-load.

Fees are confusing, but not impossible to figure out if you know what to look for. The best way to determine how much a fund is charging you is to read the fee table at the front of the prospectus. The table lists one-time fees such as front-end and back-end loads and recurring charges such as advisory and 12b-1 fees. One of the best ways to comparison shop is to examine the expense ratio, an important number that also appears in every prospectus. An expense ratio is simply the percent of total fund assets—your money—eaten up by annual fees. The number includes 12b-1 fees, but it does NOT include loads, which are charged only once.

An expense ratio of 1 percent means that if you invest $10,000, the fund is taking out $100 every year. Since the average expense ratio for a fund invested in U.S. stocks is 1.62 percent, $162 of every $10,000 does not get invested. The most cost-efficient fund companies manage to hold their expense ratios to less than 1 percent, with Vanguard, the leanest of all, averaging 0.27 percent. The largest fund group, Fidelity Investments, has an average expense ratio of 0.75 percent. But some funds inexplicably have expense ratios as high as 4 percent.

Expense ratios are lowest for index funds, which require little research and management expertise because the fund simply buys all or a representative sample of the securities listed in a particular index, such as the S&P 500, and tries to match its performance. Actively managed funds have higher expense ratios because they have to pay for research and stock-picking expertise. Expense ratios for small funds should be higher than for larger funds since the cost of running any fund is spread over the asset base, and as a fund grows, it can take advantage of economies of scale. The most expensive are the international funds, which have to charge more because of the need to hire experts who understand companies that follow non-U.S. accounting and disclosure rules, and the extra cost of managing foreign currency risk.

One might assume that a fund with a higher expense ratio is a better-managed fund because it's probably paying for smarter managers and advisers than the fund with a rock-bottom ratio. Like the difference between a Hyundai and a Mercedes-Benz, you get what you pay for, right? That may be true for automobiles, but the opposite is true for mutual funds. Funds with expense ratios of 1.5 percent are no better than funds with expense ratios of 0.5 percent. In fact, most researchers have concluded that funds with low expense ratios actually outperform more expensive funds. The simple reason is that the fund starting off with an expense ratio of 1.5 percent has to consistently show better returns just to stay even with the performance of a leaner fund.

Let's see how the numbers work. Say you invest $10,000 in Fund A. Assume the stock market will return 7.5 percent a year for the next twenty years, a conservative guess considering that the average return for stock funds for the past thirty years has been about 12 percent. Also assume that the fund has an expense ratio of

1 percent. Over twenty years, the investment will grow to $34,743. Now assume that Fund B has an expense ratio of 2 percent, or just a percentage point higher than Fund A, and that its portfolio managers invest in exactly the same stocks. In twenty years, Fund B will grow to only $28,359, or 18.4 percent less than Fund A. The more expensive fund is in perpetual catch-up mode.

By the way, I didn't do these calculations in my head. I used the SEC's mutual fund calculator, available at *www.sec.gov.* When you get to the site, click on "interactive tools," and then click on "mutual fund calculator." The calculator allows you to run similar numbers on bond and money market mutual funds, and to plug in any assumptions you wish. Just be careful not to compare apples with oranges, or a low-cost money market fund with a high-cost international stock fund.

Here's another trick to help you put mutual fund expenses in context. Don't look at the 1 percent or 2 percent expense ratio in isolation, but rather as a percentage of what you expect your returns to be. Here's an example: If a fund advertises its expense ratio as 1.5 percent, and you are reasonably expecting the fund to return 7.5 percent after one year, the true expense ratio is 20 percent (1.5 divided by 7.5 = 20 percent). A thriftier fund with an expense ratio of 0.5 percent eats up only 6.6 percent of your returns (0.5 divided by 7.5 = 6.6 percent).

The Investment Company Institute (ICI), the industry trade group that, naturally, defends mutual funds, claims that fees for stock funds actually declined 25 percent between 1990 and 1998. That's not exactly true. What the ICI doesn't say is that fund assets increased by 2,000 percent in that period. Anyone in the business can tell you that economies of scale rule when managing money: the more you have, the less it costs to manage. The ICI also doesn't count the high costs charged by the 5 percent of funds that go out of business every year. Nor does the ICI consider that the average fund holds between 5 percent and 7 percent of its assets in cash. That money is never invested in the stock market, yet you pay a management fee on it, and thus there is an "opportunity" cost that shows up in reduced returns. John Bogle, the founder of the Vanguard

Group and the person who pioneered index funds, calls the ICI's claim that fund costs have declined "sheer, unadulterated bologna." Bogle says the true cost of owning an equity fund is more like 2.5 percent, a long way from 1.4 percent.

Some experts, such as Don Phillips, managing director of Morningstar Inc., a Chicago company that rates mutual funds, believes funds with higher expense ratios pose special problems. As explained above, funds with above-average fees have to show above-average returns, or else their Morningstar ratings will lag behind the funds in their peer group. And that, says Phillips, induces portfolio managers to take greater risks with your money. The Milwaukee-based Heartland Group provides an example of what happens when a fund takes outsized risks with investors' money. Three Heartland bond funds invested in high-yield bonds (read: junk bonds) that were issued, but not guaranteed, by state and local governments for such projects as nursing homes and sewer systems. When the fund needed to sell some of its assets— some projects that the bonds supported defaulted on their interest payments, scaring investors into redeeming shares—the bonds were so illiquid, or thinly traded, that bond dealers demanded extremely high prices to take them off Heartland's hands. One Heartland fund lost 70 percent of its value in a single day. In March 2001 the SEC forced the funds into receivership.

The Tax Trap

The Second Deadly Sin is taxes. Big surprise, right? Well, unless your money is in a tax-deferred retirement fund, such as a company 401(k) plan or an Individual Retirement Account, you will probably have to pay taxes on your mutual fund's gains when it sells stocks in the portfolio. Even more surprising, you may have to pay taxes when your fund loses money.

To understand why, let's go back a couple of steps. By law, mutual funds don't pay taxes. Instead, they pass on those taxes to you, the shareholder. If your fund manager sells a stock for more than it cost the fund, that's called a capital gain. Capital gains are taxed at your ordinary income tax rate (between 28 percent and 38.6 percent for most investors) if the fund held the stock for less than a year. If the stock was held for more than a year, the tax is 20 percent.

Mutual funds have taxable gains for a number of reasons. One may be that the fund is doing poorly. Shareholders will redeem their shares if results slip, and that forces the fund to sell assets to repay those bailing out. Even if you're not one of them, you still have to pay your portion of the capital gains taxes.

Dividends are another reason that taxes come due. Dividends are the per-share distributions companies make out of their quarterly earnings. Many investors instruct their mutual fund to automatically reinvest their dividends. This means the fund uses the money to buy more shares in your name. But even if you reinvest and never see a penny of dividends, they are subject to tax, says the Internal Revenue Service.

A third reason you may get a tax bill is high turnover. Turnover measures the frequency with which a fund manager buys and sells shares, sometimes in search of the next high-flier or undervalued stock on the verge of taking off. According to Lipper, the average fund in 2000 showed a turnover rate of 122 percent, which means that the entire portfolio changed between January and December, and 22 percent of the replacement shares changed as well. I consider such frenzied trading excessive. Much of it is motivated by how portfolio managers are paid. Most portfolio managers are compensated on the basis of pre-tax, not after-tax, returns. If after-tax results determined their compensation, I'm certain we would see less turnover and fewer capital gains distributions.

Funds distributed a record-shattering $345 billion in capital gains to shareholders in 2000. These gains had accumulated throughout the 1990s, but once the air came out of technology stocks, portfolio managers began dumping them. While they lost some of their value, they still showed a capital gain.

When you buy into a fund, you are most likely buying into a tax liability. For example, say you buy $10,000 worth of Fund XYZ on December 20 at $10 a share. The next day, the fund calculates

that its cap gains for the entire year came to $2.00 a share. You own
1,000 shares and therefore will receive a "distribution" of $2,000—
taxable to you. Because you were a shareholder of record on December 21, you have to pay the same taxes as the guy who bought on
January 1, except that he probably paid less for his shares. In the
end, the total amount of money you have invested in the fund
remains $10,000, so you may be tempted to view all of this as a
wash. But you have now incurred a tax bill on $2,000 of your own
money. Soon you will receive a Form 1099 from the fund, which
states your share of the dividends and the short- and long-term capital gain.

One way to minimize taxes is to avoid buying shares in a fund in
December, when most funds do their year-end tax calculations.
Another is to judge funds by their after-tax, rather than pre-tax,
return. Most funds do not advertise these figures, but as of February 2002 the SEC requires mutual funds to report after-tax year-end
results in the fund prospectus.

Luckily for investors, new funds have popped up that seek to
minimize taxes. Some well-established funds, for example, are placing new shareholder money in a pool that invests in the same securities as the original fund, but that walls off the newcomers from
any capital gains liability that had built up prior to their investment.
As of December 2001, the SEC requires funds that tout themselves
as tax-efficient to include their after-tax results in advertisements.

Kickbacks, Compensation, and Clunkers

That brings me to the Third Deadly Sin, which is that some fund
operations are less than transparent. They don't want you to know
a whole lot about what goes on behind the curtain at fund headquarters. The use of so-called soft dollars is one practice that fund
companies prefer to keep secret. Soft dollars are a form of legal
kickback. Every time a portfolio manager buys or sells a stock, she
has to pay a commission to the broker who executes the trade. In
many cases, the fund is willing to pay a higher commission to a full-
service broker, rather than go through a discount broker, because

the fund gets a "rebate" in the form of soft dollars. Rebated dollars are then used to purchase research, software, and even computer equipment.

Who pays for soft dollars? You do. In recent years, the SEC estimated that soft-dollar deals exceeded $1 billion. Typically, $1 of credits accrues for every $1.60 of brokerage commissions paid. Congress made these kickbacks legal in 1975 when it passed what is called a "safe harbor" law. The legislation allows fund managers to pay more in commissions than is necessary, as long as the excess comes back in the form of services or research that benefits fund investors.

There are two problems with soft dollars. The first is that the system is opaque. As you can imagine, soft dollars can be abused. In 1998, the SEC found that some money managers were using soft dollars to pay for salaries, office rent, and even vacations. And while soft-dollar arrangements are supposed to be disclosed to investors, oftentimes they are not. The second problem is that many funds are not taking advantage of cost-saving efficiencies in order to keep the soft-dollar spigot open. Low-cost electronic trading systems, such as Archipelago and Island, can execute many trades at two cents a share. But funds are sticking with higher-priced trading desks, such as Goldman Sachs, where a trade costs about five or six cents a share, to gain access to soft-dollar benefits.

Earlier I mentioned portfolio managers' compensation, which is something else funds don't like to publicize. One recent study by executive search firm Russell Reynolds Associates found that the average compensation for a domestic stock fund manager is $436,500. How much does your fund manager make? You may never know, since the SEC does not require that figure to be revealed in the prospectus. Fund managers demand to know every last detail of the compensation package of CEOs whose stock they own, but they are loath to reveal their own compensation details to fund shareholders.

Nor do most funds tell you what managers' incentives are. Similar to brokers', fund managers' compensation structure may have built-in incentives that skew their behavior. If your fund has socked you with a capital gains tax of $1 a share, you might want to know if the manager is compensated on the basis of pre-tax returns, thus freeing her of concerns about after-tax results. Investors are the ones who bear the burden of capital gains taxes, not the fund manager, so why should she care if her fund shows capital gains?

There's another reason you might want to know your portfolio manager's compensation. In recent years, mutual funds have had to compete with hedge funds (which cater to wealthy people and are not SEC-regulated) for the best portfolio managers. Unlike mutual funds, hedge funds compensate portfolio managers by letting them keep 20 percent or more of their gains. To stop their portfolio managers from leaving for that kind of lucre, numerous fund companies have started hedge funds, and are letting their existing fund managers run them as well. But this raises conflict-of-interest issues. If a fund manager gets an allocation of shares in an initial public stock offering, for example, does the hedge fund or the mutual fund get the shares? If both funds hold shares in a company that is losing money, which fund gets first crack at getting out of a bad position? You should ask your fund to reveal the manager's compensation or, at the very least, what other funds the manager oversees that might take priority.

Another oft-used trick of the trade is hiding clunker funds. Assume a mutual fund company creates a fund that is a flat-out failure, down a significant amount in net asset value (the per-share value of a fund, after subtracting its liabilities) within a year or two of creation. How to paper over the mistake? They propose to shareholders of the failing fund that they merge into a bigger, more successful fund. Who would turn down such a deal? Shareholders of the failed fund win. So does the fund manager whose stumble is quickly forgotten, and who can now claim credit for the continuing success of the larger fund. Not a particularly transparent process for an industry that swears by its openness.

Indexed or Managed Funds?

The Fourth Deadly Sin is also the fund industry's dirty little secret: most actively managed funds never do as well as their benchmark.

Every fund compares its results against a benchmark, or a basket of stocks or bonds that the fund adviser chooses as a performance yardstick. For the year ended December 30, 2001, 47 percent of domestic stock funds did not perform as well as the S&P 500, according to Morningstar, even though the S&P lost 13.4 percent. And 2001 was one of the better years for managed funds.

For years, experts have debated whether index funds are superior to managed funds. Index-fund proponents argue that actively managed funds waste money by paying higher salaries for top-flight analysts and stock pickers to put together a winning portfolio. They also incur higher transaction costs because they engage in frequent trading. But after all that, most managed funds still can't beat the passive index funds.

On the other hand, managed-fund backers say that index funds don't always perform better, such as in the twelve months following the March 2000 technology bust. And managed-fund aficionados say index funds are, well, boring. When the market is booming, they mimic but never outshine the indices. And when the market slides, they tamely follow it over the precipice.

Both sides can claim partial victory in this ongoing debate. Don Cassidy, a senior research analyst at Lipper, says that actively managed funds outperformed index funds for twelve of the past twenty years. But when comparing returns (including expenses but not sales loads) over those twenty years, the indexes came out slightly ahead on an annual basis, showing 12.59 percent in total returns versus 12.40 percent for the managed funds. When sales loads are included, the index funds beat the managed funds by about 1.2 percent a year—a significant amount when multiplied over ten or twenty years.

Fund managers will say one reason they can't beat the index is because of an Investment Company Act requirement, called the 5 percent rule. The rule says that, for a fund to market itself as diversified (and most funds want to be diversified), no single stock can account for more than 5 percent of 75 percent of the fund's total assets. In other words, a fund can have 25 percent of its holdings in a single stock, but for the remaining three-fourths of its holdings, the fund must follow the 5 percent rule. That means a diversified fund must have at least sixteen different stocks, and if one of them zooms in value, that stock must be sold off until the rule is satisfied.

But the 5 percent rule is far less to blame than the higher fees of managed funds. It's hard to outperform index funds, let alone stay even with them, when you're wearing leg shackles. And when portfolio managers see their results start to slip, they trade more, thus digging themselves into a deeper hole.

Then there's the herd mentality of active fund managers. Most of them flock to the same familiar companies and often overlook the new, obscure companies that show great promise. But they take comfort in knowing that, even if their fund misses out on a great opportunity, most of the others in its peer group will too.

The Culture of Performance

The Fifth Deadly Sin, and a close cousin to Number Four, is that a mutual fund's past performance, which is the first feature that investors consider when choosing a fund, doesn't predict future performance. Funds buy expensive ads in newspapers and magazines to tout their performance over the past one, three, five, and ten years. I must admit, I pay attention to those alluring numbers, too. The mutual fund industry irresponsibly promotes this "culture of performance," even though it knows perfectly well that it misleads investors. When it comes to mutual funds, the past is not prologue.

If funds are in the business of helping their customers make money, why would they mislead them, you might ask? The answer is that fund managers are in a cutthroat business. Their jobs depend on their ability to attract new money, and that often depends on outperforming other funds in the sector and getting a high ranking from Morningstar. As assets grow, revenues from management fees also grow. But if the fund is at the bottom of its sector, its rating will sink, and it will cease to attract new money.

The problem with this system is that the rankings, which by necessity are based on past performance, do not tell you much of anything about a fund's future performance. It's like looking in the rearview mirror to see the road ahead. Studies have shown that if you take the top 10 percent of funds in any year, four out of five of them will not be in the top 10 percent a year later.

There are more important considerations than past performance. Two we already discussed: fees and taxes. It's also crucial to know a fund's managerial experience. Morningstar looked at fund manager performance between March 2000 and March 2001, when the stock market tumbled and almost every domestic stock fund lost money. But funds managed by teams with at least four years' tenure lost less money than both the S&P 500 and the average stock fund. In fact, as experience levels increased, the amount of losses declined.

A change in the fund's portfolio manager—the person making the day-to-day investment decisions for the fund—is also a valuable indicator. Bill Miller, the manager of the Legg Mason Value Trust Fund, is legendary for outperforming the S&P 500 for twelve consecutive years, from 1991 through 2002. But if Miller leaves the fund, his replacement may not have the same success rate. Or the manager may stay put but the investment strategy changes. You should not expect a fund whose strategy has suddenly switched to repeat last year's results.

Practice What You Preach

The Sixth Deadly Sin is that most fund managers don't practice what they preach. Most say they believe in the merits of long-term investing. They also lecture their own shareholders to stay invested in their funds for the long term, preferably ten to twenty years. But as I said earlier, the typical fund manager sells every stock in her portfolio at least once a year. If a company misses its quarterly earnings estimate, out goes the stock, even if the long-term prospects are good. Rarely is this focus on the short term revealed or explained in the fund prospectus, even though it can affect results.

Morningstar studied the effects of turnover on fund performance in 1998. It found that the lower the turnover, the better the performance, because turnover drives up trading costs, such as brokerage commissions, and trading costs reduce results. So why do managers

persist with their frenetic buying and selling? Because they are convinced that they can add value by outsmarting the market on a day-
to-day basis rather than buying and holding for the long term.
"Short-term speculation is what they're doing," gripes Vanguard
founder Bogle. "All this thrashing around hits investors with higher
transaction costs and higher taxes, but no observable improvement
in fund performance."

Too many fund managers also buy stocks when they think the
market is about to move up and sell when they believe the market is
getting ready to swoon. In other words, they try to time the market,
a strategy most experts warn is a foolish attempt at achieving the
impossible. No one is smart enough to time the market's ups and
downs.

Fund Directors: Chihuahuas, Not Dobermans

When a company's stock suffers because of management deficien-
cies, fund managers are the first to ask: Where's the board of directors? Mutual funds have led the charge in many cases against
absentee directors, and have done much to make the governance of
corporations more shareholder-friendly. The role of the mutual
fund as investor watchdog is sure to accelerate now that the SEC
has adopted a new rule, effective in April 2003, requiring funds to
disclose how they vote the proxies of corporate shares that make up
their portfolios—and why they voted for or against management.
Funds that routinely back management on such important matters
as CEO pay—either out of passivity or because the fund runs the
company's pension plan or has some other financial relationship to
protect—won't be able to keep those votes a secret any longer.
From now on, funds must vote in the interests of their own shareholders, and they must reveal, either on a Web site or by mailing the
information on request, the policies that guide such votes. This
means that, when a company nominates a director who already sits
on a dozen other boards, the fund will have to explain why it
believes that director is not just a professional board-sitter. Or if a
board has let its CEO engage the company auditor as his own

personal tax adviser, the mutual fund must explain how that does not hamper the auditor's independence. But when it comes to their own governance, mutual funds don't practice what they preach. They seem to prefer lapdogs over watchdogs. Warren Buffett likes to say that mutual funds choose their directors from the kennels of Chihuahuas, not Dobermans. One reason for this may be the lucrative pay and perks that fund directors get. The ten highest-paying fund families now compensate independent directors an average of $150,000 a year.

Another reason why mutual fund boards are passive is that they are all but invisible to investors. Until recently, you couldn't even find their names unless you requested the "Statement of Additional Information" from the fund company. As of 2002, directors' names must be listed in the fund's annual report, but that's a long way from interacting with investors, which is the only way directors can truly represent their interests. One step fund shareholders can take is to demand that directors answer two important questions in the annual report: Can you demonstrate that you looked at a number of other investment advisers, and that the one whose contract you approved is better than the others? Also, can you demonstrate that the advisory fee you've approved is the lowest possible rate you can get for me? You have the right to ask these questions. And don't settle for boilerplate answers.

The SEC sought to stiffen the backbone of fund boards by requiring, as of July 1, 2002, that a majority of directors be independent from the fund adviser, up from the previous 40 percent rule. Now, directors unaffiliated with the fund can control its machinery, such as by electing officers, scheduling meetings, and naming independent directors to replace those leaving the board.

You Can't Judge a Fund by Its Name

The Seventh Deadly Sin is that you can't judge a fund by its name. Many funds have monikers that are misleading; some are downright deceptive. In the late-1990s technology stock bubble, some portfolio managers took advantage of investors' penchant to chase the latest fad by slapping "Internet" in front of their fund names. The chances of that happening now are much lower. As of July 2002, the SEC requires funds to have at least 80 percent of their assets in the securities that their fund name implies, up from 65 percent previously. This new rule is forcing funds that called themselves something like the Americas Government Fund either to dispose of East Asian government debt if it exceeded 20 percent of fund assets, or change their names. Likewise for funds that called themselves an equity income fund but had 25 percent of assets in stocks that pay no dividends. More than five hundred funds, in fact, had to change their names because they failed the 80 percent rule. Invesco's Blue Chip Growth Fund, for example, is now called just Growth Fund, since 60 percent of its holdings are in technology stocks, and many of those can hardly be called blue chips these days.

Still, in mutual funds, a rose isn't always a rose. The 80 percent rule obviously allows a fund to invest up to 20 percent of assets in almost anything. If a fund calls itself the U.S. Government Bond Fund, investors might assume that the assets are rock-solid bonds backed by the full faith and credit of the U.S. Treasury. But that fund portfolio could hold 20 percent of its assets in high-yield bonds, also called junk bonds.

One of the collapsed Heartland funds called itself the Heartland Short Duration High-Yield Municipal Bond Fund. Investors may have been fooled by the term "municipal," which to many connotes safety and security. But few of Heartland's bonds were actually guaranteed by the government units that issued them. The Vanguard Short-Term Municipal Bond Fund has a similar name, but is invested in bonds guaranteed by local governments with high ratings.

The industry has been engaged in a lengthy debate over whether the SEC should require more frequent disclosure of a fund's portfolio holdings. Currently, funds must reveal holdings twice a year in shareholder reports. At the SEC, I agreed with the industry's point of view that more frequent disclosure would drive up fees and that most shareholders would pay little attention. And I agreed that more frequent disclosure could actually hurt funds by revealing their strategies to front-runners, professional traders who buy shares ahead of a fund in an effort to profit from the sale of the shares once the fund's bidding pushes the share price up.

But I'm now convinced that disclosure at the end of every quarter—possibly with a sixty-day lag so funds won't be hurt by front-running—makes sense. More frequent disclosure might have helped Heartland investors keep closer tabs on their bond fund. Quarterly disclosure also would help investors know whether their funds are following the investment strategy they signed on for. And financial planners would know if their clients are properly diversified. I'm pleased that the SEC seems to agree. In the spring of 2003, it proposed a rule to mandate quarterly disclosure.

Funds also leave investors' heads spinning with the many classes of shares available among the load funds. Many load funds have A, B, and C classes, each of which carries different sales charges, depending on how quickly and easily you want to withdraw your money. The holdings in a fund with multiple classes will be identical, but investors will experience a wide disparity in returns. For example, a Class A shareholder in XYZ Fund pays up-front fees of 5 percent at the time of purchase. If $10,000 is invested, that means only $9,500 is going to work for you. Most Class A shares also charge a low annual marketing fee of 0.25 percent. Class B shareholders pay no up-front fee but instead pay an annual marketing fee of about 1 percent. After six or so years, Class B shares convert to A shares and pay the lower annual fee. Brokers like to recommend Class B shares because, they tell clients, there is no up-front fee. But B shares are more expensive in the long run, and some investors are better off buying A shares.

With Class C shares, fund companies are experimenting with all kinds of fee structures to protect themselves from investors who jump in and out of funds. When investors bail out—the average investor stays in a mutual fund for four years—fund companies often lose money redeeming shares in order to pay back investors and process the paperwork. Some funds now charge up-front and back-end loads and exact permanently higher annual fees, typically around 1.85 percent to 2 percent. Prudential, for example, charges its Equity Class C shareholders an annual expense ratio of 1.62 percent, plus a 1 percent front load and a 1 percent deferred load. While Class C funds originally were designed to stabilize fund assets despite investor fickleness, their loads and expenses can be downright punitive.

Now that you know the Seven Deadly Sins, you might wonder, Why should I invest in a mutual fund at all? If you're the type of person who has the discipline and the time to pick stocks on your own, then you should do so. But if, like most people, you don't have the time to understand what drives markets and aren't inclined to read numerous corporate earnings statements, then mutual funds are a safer, more convenient investment.

But be a smart mutual fund investor. Pay attention to fees and expenses. Pick a no-load fund that charges no 12b-1 fees and has an expense ratio below 1 percent. If you can, avoid funds that brokerage firms are selling, since they will hit you with a sales load, and their in-house funds often don't do as well as the independent groups'. Many brokerage firms' in-house funds are not portable, either. That means that if you switch to a broker at another firm, you may have to cash out of your mutual fund and incur some expenses to do so.

The Shelf-Space Rat Race

It's getting a lot harder these days to find no-load funds, as more and more fund companies give up selling directly to investors in favor of selling through brokerage firms. A decade ago, most funds were no-loads; today about 80 percent of funds are sold through intermediaries, about half of whom are brokers and the other half investment advisers.

With so many funds to choose from, all but the highest-ranked funds are having trouble attracting investors on their own, and have turned to these intermediaries. Invesco Funds Group and

Credit Suisse Asset Management are two fund companies that switched most of their funds to brokerage sales in 2001.

The growing number of funds sold through intermediaries seems to say that investors want help picking the right fund. The problem is that investors must pay sales loads to compensate brokers and fee-based advisers for their time. Another problem concerns a practice, deceptively called revenue-sharing, in which brokerage firms charge fund companies fees for being placed on a preferred list of funds that brokers sell more aggressively. This practice is much like the premium that food companies pay to position their goods at eye level on supermarket shelves. According to the Boston-based consulting firm Financial Research Corp., the fund industry pays some $2 billion a year for shelf space. Because brokers can choose from among thousands of mutual funds when making client recommendations, fund companies are forced to pay these premiums, especially since payment guarantees them access to a trained retail sales force. But investors are kept in the dark. When their broker recommends a fund, they don't know enough to ask: Are you suggesting this fund because your research shows it's the best investment for me, or because your firm is paid $1 million to push it?

If your head is spinning from all of this, take the easiest and safest route and pick a low-cost index fund. Many Vanguard, Fidelity, and TIAA-CREF funds fit the criteria I outlined above. Vanguard, for example, has twenty-one no-load index funds to choose from. Start off with the boring but predictable returns of a broad-based index fund—one that tracks the S&P 500 or, to get exposure to the entire market, the Wilshire 5000—over the more alluring, but volatile, managed funds. Index funds generate less capital gains taxes and also charge lower fees and expenses. They make the most sense when you want to be invested in large-cap stocks, since it's harder for portfolio managers to beat those indices.

If you want to diversify beyond a broad-based index fund—assuming your budget allows it—you could start off with a fund that invests in small-cap companies and that tracks the Russell 2000 index. The risk is higher, but historically small-cap companies offer higher total returns. You could also put some money into a fund that mimics the S&P MidCap Index, which, as its name implies, invests in medium-sized companies. You might also want to buy a value fund, which looks for unglamorous stocks that seem cheap compared to their peer group, but offer potentially outstanding returns. And just to be ready for those years, like 2001 and 2002, when the economy turns sour, it's good to own a bond fund. Bonds tend to hold their value better than stocks when interest rates are declining and the economy is growing slowly or not at all.

If you want diversification without much fuss, try a hybrid fund, which blends stocks and bonds for a one-stop-shopping approach. You give up control over how much of your assets are invested in stocks or bonds, since hybrid fund managers have wide discretion over the ratios of each that they buy. If you like the convenience of a hybrid and don't mind letting someone else do your asset allocation, at least make sure the fund is buying tax-free bonds if your money is not in a retirement account. That way, you will be shielded from paying ordinary income taxes on the dividends that bonds pay.

You might want to try a variant to index funds called the "exchange-traded fund." ETFs are packages of shares traded on a stock exchange. They combine the simplicity of index funds with the flexibility of stocks. For example, the ETF shares that shadow the Nasdaq 100, which comprises the 100 largest Nasdaq stocks, go by the ticker symbol QQQ, and thus are called Cubes. Cubes are managed by computer software, with little human intervention, and are designed to trade in lockstep with the Nasdaq 100. Unlike a mutual fund, Cubes can be bought and sold throughout the day. Expenses are rock-bottom—less than 0.2 percent—plus a broker's commission. Another advantage of ETFs: capital gains are taxed only when an ETF is sold, like a common stock. A regular mutual fund, on the other hand, can produce capital gains that result in taxes that shareholders must pay even if they haven't cashed out. ETFs are growing in popularity: as of March 2003, 114 ETFs had assets of $93 billion.

Here are a few rules of thumb to help you avoid nasty surprises when shopping for a mutual fund.

- Whether it's a stock or a bond fund, always look for no-load funds that charge low fees.
- Avoid sector funds, such as high-tech or health care funds. Brokerage firms and fund companies sometimes push hot stock sectors. But just like the turbocharged Internet funds, "hot stock funds" tend to hit home runs one year and strike out the next.
- Avoid the cult of personality. Fund companies are attracting investors by creating funds around hotshot money managers, but most of them will flame out in a year or two.
- Read the prospectus. Before you invest, make sure the stellar results of a fund aren't the handiwork of a longtime manager who has just resigned, or were pumped up like an athlete on steroids by well-timed initial public offering purchases.
- Take the time to ask whether the fund's sponsor has had any run-ins with the SEC. If it has, you may want to stay clear. The organization may care more about hype than acting in investors' best interests.
- Don't chase fads. Behavioral researchers have noticed that investors tend to flock to funds that show superior results. But studies show that this year's high-flier won't be the top performer next year. When everybody else is signing up, remember: past performance does not guarantee future results.

CHAPTER THREE

ANALYZE THIS

In April 2003, the New York Attorney General, Securities and Exchange Commission, state securities administrators, and the stock exchanges arrived at an historic agreement. The regulators dropped year-long investigations into biased research by the biggest, most prestigious Wall Street firms. In exchange, the firms agreed to pay fines totaling $1.4 billion. More important, the firms agreed to fundamentally change the way they do business. No longer will analysts serve as sales arms to investment bankers—the brokerage firm employees who arrange stock and bond offerings to the public. Analysts will not be allowed to accompany investment bankers on so-called pitch meetings, where firms sell their banking business to corporations. Nor will analysts be able to attend road shows, in which investment bankers try to find buyers for share offerings.

The agreement doesn't end there. Investment bankers can no longer weigh in on analysts' performance reviews, or play any role in analysts' compensation. Indeed, any interaction between the two sides will now be monitored by each firm's lawyers. Brokerage firms also must obtain independent research from outside sources, and make it available to investors. And each firm must submit to supervision by an independent monitor, contribute to an investor education fund, and undergo a compliance review within 18 months. Along with the settlement agreement, regulators released exhibits consisting of e-mails and memos between analysts and investment bankers that reveal the corruption of Wall Street research. The missives are sure to serve as road maps to plaintiffs' lawyers suing on behalf of small investors. Some firms will shed their research divisions altogether. If so, independent boutiques may find it easier to grow and prosper.

What happened to the Wall Street firms that they accepted such ignominious terms? In short, the firms violated the basic tenet of their business—that the investor comes first. The world first learned this in April 2002 when New York Attorney General Eliot Spitzer released subpoenaed e-mails of analysts at Merrill Lynch. The e-mails revealed what some had long suspected: analysts often recommend shares of companies that have an investment banking relationship with their firm; yet, privately, analysts deride these same companies. Henry Blodget, Merrill's star Internet analyst, in one e-mail referred to a company as "a piece of junk." And yet he had bullishly recommended the same company to investors. Other stocks for which he issued glowing reports were called "crap" or "a dog." When Spitzer released the documents, investor outrage was palpable.

Though the firms deny it, the e-mails seem to show that analysts were using buy recommendations as bait to win business for their firm's investment bankers. The analysts also appeared to be punishing companies by downgrading their stocks if they went elsewhere for investment banking services. And the e-mails made clear that analysts knew they could boost their compensation if they helped snag banking deals.

In some respects, the e-mails were not so surprising. During the past two decades, the economics of Wall Street had shifted away from retail sales to arranging initial public offerings, which brought in billions of dollars of profit during the runaway bull market. The thinnest of lines separating investment banking from research had eroded to the point where analysts were making sales pitches to potential banking clients. Wall Street firms grew so obsessed with capturing as much of this lucrative business as possible that they viewed security analysis as an adjunct to investment banking rather than as a source of unbiased advice for retail investors.

Publicly, the firms maintained the fiction that a so-called Chinese wall existed between research and banking. I have come to believe that Chinese walls serve more often as marketing tools than a shield against conflicts. Privately, Wall Street leaders allowed, even encouraged, the two to work closely together. The Street's culture assumed it was acceptable to ignore conflicts that might harm individual investors as long as the IPO business was booming. Balancing the profit motive with the public interest had gone out of fashion.

Greed in the end clouded the business judgment of a lot of smart people. For a few billion dollars in short-term profits, brokerage firms tarnished their own brands. In an industry where trust is paramount, loss of faith among investors can't be restored by simply mounting a savvy public relations campaign. In mid-2002, the firms' share prices reflected their loss of reputation. Merrill Lynch alone lost $8 billion in market value in the four weeks after Spitzer released his findings. Private lawsuits could also cost the firms dearly, as individual investors who followed analysts' tainted advice clamor for recompense. It could take years before some of the firms regain investors' respect.

Wall Street's response to the problem was to do the bare minimum. Since the summer of 2001, the securities industry three times tried to quell the uproar over apparently biased research reports—twice before Spitzer's revelations, and once afterward—by endorsing increasingly complex rules governing what analysts must disclose, when they can own shares in companies they rate, and how they should be paid. But each time, the industry continued to insist that analyst recommendations were not influenced by a need to attract and maintain corporate clients. Although the industry's proposed rules grew superficially tougher with each iteration, they never got to the heart of the matter. Until Wall Street firms agree to a complete separation of research and investment banking, the issue will remain with us.

Sadly, the damage is all self-inflicted. Wall Street could have avoided this scandal as far back as the spring of 2000, when I first tried to convince the stock exchanges (as self-regulatory organizations, they oversee the conduct of brokers, analysts, and investment bankers) to issue rules that would require disclosure of conflicts of interest. But the exchanges, whose governing boards are heavily influenced by the heads of the major Wall Street firms, have deep-seated conflicts of their own and refused even to get the ball rolling. Their reluctance to clean up their own backyards shows a serious failure of self-regulation.

The phone call from the National Association of Securities Dealers really infuriated me. It was late December 2000, and I was expecting good news from Mary Schapiro, president of the regulatory arm of the NASD. Fourteen months had passed since I had asked the association, the group best known for creating the Nasdaq Stock Market but also responsible for writing and enforcing the rules of fair play for Wall Street professionals, to come up with a new code of conduct for analysts. But the NASD hemmed and hawed, and in the meantime, one of my worst nightmares had come true. The bottom was falling out of the stock market. Many investors blamed analysts' rosy forecasts for their losses, totaling $3 trillion between March and December of 2000 alone. More than ever, I felt the NASD must act, but now an aide to Schapiro was delivering the bad news: the NASD board would not be voting on new rules after all. "We can't get our members to agree on this," the aide said. "We don't have a consensus on what to do."

I was fit to be tied, and got Schapiro on the phone. I said that she and NASD chairman Frank Zarb were letting their group revert to the old NASD—one that Wall Street's entrenched interests led around by the nose, to the detriment of the investing public—and that they had to regulate. "If you don't do it, we will," I threatened. I was probably too harsh; after all, she and Zarb had done a great job in cleaning up the NASD after a major price-fixing scandal. And I had one foot out the door, having recently announced that I would be leaving the SEC in a few months.

But I had so little time left to accomplish the rest of my agenda, and I was impatient. I had to convince Zarb and Schapiro because I had already asked the New York Stock Exchange to tighten its analyst regulations, and Chairman Dick Grasso was unwilling to take the lead because he didn't want to give Nasdaq, the NYSE's rival, any competitive advantage.

As far back as 1998, when the bull market was in full swing, I became convinced that analysts had lost their way and that it was the job of the stock exchanges to get them back on track. Too many analysts had given up all semblance of objectivity about the companies they covered and had become outright cheerleaders for an unsustainable technology stock boom.

Analysts have always had to wrestle with conflicts of interest. Naturally, they all want to be considered experts in their field, and so over time they get to know intimately the companies they are assessing. Their interests become intertwined. But the good ones— and there are many—recognize this occupational hazard and work hard not to let their relationship with corporate management blind them.

Rose-colored Glasses

What happened? In the bull market stampede of the 1990s, many analysts had become lazy. They no longer went through the laborious, but necessary, task of deciphering company earnings reports, or probing suppliers, customers, and competitors for the truth about a company's current performance and future prospects. Instead, they were addicted to handouts of inside information from companies. To protect their access, analysts were no longer asking the hard questions that might challenge a company's positive spin. It's no wonder that by the middle of 2000 few analysts could see the tech bubble bursting through their rose-colored glasses.

Even after share prices crumpled, few analysts warned investors to sell. Investors lost a lot of money, but Wall Street firms also lost something—their credibility.

If analysts do their job well, investors can prosper by buying shares in the companies analysts recommend and shunning the ones they say to avoid. When consumers buy a car or a refrigerator, they check *Consumer Reports*. When they buy a house, they have it inspected. But when they buy stock, to whom do they turn if analysts are shills for corporations?

Analysts usually specialize in a sector of the economy, such as telecommunications or autos, and write reports on the companies in that sector. Like peeling an onion, they uncover layer upon layer of information about where a company has been, and where it's likely to go. They review financial performance, the management team, product strength, and market-share position. They also assess the economic climate in which the company operates, and its ability to sell more products or services and increase profits. Some analysts kick the tires by visiting the companies they cover to size up new management or understand a new manufacturing process, though this is increasingly rare. Analysts use all this information to try to predict the company's future—and its share price—so that investors know when to buy, hold, or sell.

There are two types of analysts. "Sell-side" analysts work for investment banks, which arrange financing for corporate clients by helping them issue stocks and bonds. "Buy-side" analysts work for institutional buyers of stocks and bonds, such as mutual funds, pension funds, and insurance companies. The sell side has been the focus of much scrutiny over the past year. Because buy-side recommendations are made for portfolio managers and are rarely made public, the buy side has largely been exempt from this scrutiny. But it is not faultless, as we shall see.

The Myth of the Chinese Wall

The evolution of the analyst from detached observer to purveyor of puffery didn't happen overnight. The problem was apparent as far back as the 1960s. Even then, Wall Street firms viewed analysts as marketing tools. I recall how we boasted to investors about the "special relationship" our analysts had with the companies they followed. Some CEOs played along by leaking their quarterly earnings numbers or other valuable information to us. The SEC certainly did not condone this behavior, but when the agency did nothing to squelch it, we assumed it was legal even though we knew it was wrong. When our analysts' guidance proved correct, investors were convinced we had special access—and would send us their stock orders.

At the time, analysts were seen as intellectuals protected by a Chinese Wall that kept corporate finance separate from research. Not every Wall Street firm scrupulously honored the Chinese Wall, but they all at least accepted that an analyst's job was to help investors find promising stocks to buy, or dogs to sell. Until 1975, brokerage commissions were Wall Street's biggest revenue source. Since analysts were paid out of the commission pot, the better their advice, the more brokerage business they attracted, and the more they got paid.

When the SEC deregulated commissions in 1975, Wall Street's center of gravity shifted. The big money no longer came from commissions but from institutions such as mutual and pension funds and from investment banking. Under the new Wall Street model, analyst loyalties also shifted. Individual investors fell to the bottom of the food chain, and powerful institutions and corporate clients rose to the top.

Analysts produced no income, but they quickly learned to carry their load by grafting themselves onto the investment banking team. They went out on sales pitches to corporate clients and participated in "road shows" in which investment bankers touted companies about to issue shares to institutional investors. They began to refrain from writing anything negative about current or potential clients. And corporate managers began picking underwriters on the basis of how well the banks' analysts treated them. A sell recommendation on a company was seen as the kiss of death when competing for that company's business.

A Web of Dysfunctional Relationships

In the 1990s, the ties between analysts and corporate clients deepened, leading to what I call a web of dysfunctional relationships. Company executives figured out how to keep analysts on a tight leash by occasionally leaking important information, such as a sales figure or "guidance" on quarterly earnings. Companies also massaged their earnings to come as close as possible to the consensus numbers that analysts were peddling, preferably beating them by a penny. To ordinary investors, analysts seemed prescient. Some became cult figures. With a brief appearance on a financial news show or in a financial column, they could push a company's shares into the stratosphere. Reluctant to bite the hand feeding them by putting out a downbeat report, analysts all but stopped making sell recommendations.

As the stock market went higher and higher, investors relied more and more on financial news. Every day, Wall Street analysts would take to the airwaves to wax poetic about one company or another. It seemed that just about every time I turned on the TV, an analyst was being asked to name his top five picks. But viewers were never told that the analyst's employer likely was the investment banker for most, if not all, of the companies on his list of hot stocks.

In the fall of 1999, I asked my staff to talk to some of the executives of these financial shows. Two of my aides met with the general counsel of CNBC and the executive producer of *Wall Street Week*. Other media outlets, such as Fox News and CNNfn, refused to meet with them. While we made it clear that we did not have the authority to regulate the media, we asked for their advice on what type of disclosure would be meaningful for viewers, but not too onerous for the shows. It was like pulling teeth. Neither official would even admit that investors were harmed by not knowing about the relationship between the companies the analysts were selling and the business those companies had given the analysts' firms. The typical response was: "Our viewers know that analysts work for investment banks." The executive producer of *Wall Street Week* told my aides that his viewers didn't buy and sell stocks frequently. "Our viewers are a lot more sophisticated," he insisted. "They know how Wall Street works."

The reaction of the media executives disappointed me. In the midst of the market euphoria, they were thinking only about their own ratings and not what might be best for the long-term interest of their viewers. And while it's the regulators' and firms' responsibility to ensure that conflicts are adequately disclosed, financial news shows disavowed any obligations of their own. With the reve-

lations of just how much conflicts have distorted analyst recommendations, financial news shows are now warning viewers to do
their homework. They also are refusing to give analysts a forum
unless they reveal which companies on their buy list are firm clients.
It would have been nice to have heard that message all along.

While the meltdown of energy trading giant Enron Corp. would
not occur for another year, the demise of this once-thriving company is a perfect example of what I feared might happen. Enron's
financial statements were so byzantine that top Wall Street analysts
admitted they could not make heads or tails of them. But they recommended the stock anyway, since Enron's sales and earnings
seemed to be increasing, and, equally important, Enron meant millions of dollars in business for Wall Street banks. They blithely
accepted Enron as the model of a new, postderegulation, virtual
corporation, even if they couldn't understand who was at risk in
the multitude of partnerships Enron had created to unload debt
from its balance sheet. As it turns out, Enron's shareholders and
pensioners were all at risk because they believed the analysts. In
early December 2001, when Enron's shares were below $1, fifteen
of the seventeen analysts tracking Enron called it a "buy" or a
"hold."

Some commentators downplay this issue. Enron was an anomaly, they say. And no one really believes analysts' pronouncements
anyway. Besides, the market eventually corrects the problem by
shunning analysts who are often wrong. All of this may be true in
the case of institutional investors, but not for individuals, many of
whom are unaware of analyst conflicts. Other experts say that
investors who own shares for the long term are not affected by the
ups and downs of analysts' choices. But that, too, is a canard, now
that many individual investors trade shares daily or weekly, and are
especially vulnerable to analyst conflicts. Besides, even long-term
investors are hurt when they follow an analyst's recommendation
and buy shares in a company whose long-haul prospects are poor,
like the many dot-coms that disappeared quickly after they arrived.

Let's review briefly what insiders know about how Wall Street
really works, versus what most individual investors don't know.

Until recently, analysts used such euphemisms as "market perform" or "neutral" to signal to sophisticated investors and mutual funds that it's time to unload a stock. Those in the know understood the code; most individual investors did not.

In March 2000, at the height of market mania, analysts' hyper-optimism resulted in ninety-two buy recommendations for every sell recommendation. By the end of July 2001, when the S&P 500 had declined 12 percent and the technology-heavy Nasdaq fell by 59 percent, analysts were still issuing 65 percent buy recommendations. What most individual investors don't understand is that, statistically, only half of all stocks can perform better than the median, unless you live in Lake Wobegon, where all companies are above average. Not since the late 1980s have at least half of all analyst recommendations been a sell.

Analysts can't serve two masters, so they joke that they work 75 percent of their time for investors and 75 percent of their time for corporate clients. But unbeknown to most small investors, the corporate client has won out. Today, it's common for analysts to offer to "provide coverage"—code for positive coverage—in exchange for a corporate financing deal. Naturally, clients want their stock offering to succeed, and an analyst's favorable report can only help. How? A positive rating leads to a higher share price, which pleases shareholders, increases the value of management's stock options, makes a company less vulnerable to a takeover, and lets management use the company's shares as currency for acquisitions.

A rhapsodic analyst report also helps to boost the price of the shares the investment bank gets for underwriting, or managing, the initial public offering (IPO). A glowing report can also increase the value of the investment bank's private equity stake in the company, a sideline business that many Wall Street firms got into during the IPO craze. And if a favorable rating induces retail investors to buy more shares, the brokerage side of the business profits from increased commissions.

Institutional investors know the rules. They discourage analysts from putting sell recommendations on stocks in their portfolios—until they have disposed of the shares. Fund managers can easily punish analysts who fail to heed this unwritten rule by refusing to use the analyst's brokerage firm to execute trades. Buy-side analysts play the game, too. They often take to the airwaves to talk up the stocks in their funds' portfolios. This way, they can boost share prices either to dress up quarterly returns or to unload shares they don't want on an unsuspecting public.

Everybody Knew—Except You

As you can see, everyone's back gets scratched, except the individual investors'. Nobody explained the rules to them. And analysts have learned to play this game very well. In 1980, the best analysts pulled down $100,000 a year. Today, top analysts can get $10 million to $15 million a year in compensation, including bonus. Many are paid according to their share of the investment banking deals they help attract.

This unhealthy situation came to a head in the late 1990s. In the thirty-six months between January 1998 and December 2000, some 1,250 companies went public, raising $161 billion, according to Thomson Financial Securities Data. Celebrity analysts were indispensable adjuncts to the investment banking team. Companies looking to issue shares often selected their investment bank on the basis of which one employed the most powerful analyst in the sector. No Wall Street firm wanted to be left behind, so the pressure grew on analysts to praise companies that had no revenues, no earnings—in fact, nothing more than nonpaying visitors to a Web site—in order to get investment banking deals. Some firms required analysts to submit their reports to the bank's deal makers before publication. Credit Suisse Group's Credit Suisse First Boston unit breached the Chinese Wall altogether and had some of its tech analysts report to Frank Quattrone, its high-profile investment banker to Silicon Valley.

Morgan Stanley's corporate finance director summed up the prevailing view as far back as 1990, when he wrote in a memo to the research department: "Our objective is . . . to adopt a policy, fully understood by the entire Firm, including the Research Department, that we do not make negative or controversial comments about our clients as a matter of sound business practice. . . ." Morgan Stanley has since disavowed the memo, saying it does not reflect company policy. But consider the case of Morgan's star Internet analyst, Mary Meeker, dubbed "Queen of the Net" by one financial magazine. Meeker wrote long, detailed reports on high-flying Internet companies such as eBay, Yahoo!, and Amazon.com, and was highly sought after by tech companies because she had the stature to make their IPOs successful.

According to NASD rules, analysts must have a sound basis for their recommendations. In other words, they can't just recommend a stock on whimsy. But most Internet companies went public without showing a penny of profit—and no hope of doing so. For Meeker, that was not a problem. She relied on such measurements as "discounted terminal valuation," which purports to calculate margins and growth rates five years ahead. But she also used such unproven measurements as "eyeballs" and "page counts" to predict an Internet company's survivability.

In 1999, Meeker used these dubious tools to bring to market Priceline.com, an online service that lets consumers name their own price for everything from airfares and hotel rooms to mortgages and cars. Morgan earned the lion's share of $9.3 million in underwriting fees by managing Priceline's IPO, which raised $133 million. Meeker recommended that investors buy Priceline stock when it hit a stratospheric $134 a share in May 1999, even though losses came to $25 million on revenues of just $49 million. When the shares fell to $80, Meeker continued her buy recommendation. Even as Priceline plummeted to the single digits, Meeker said "buy."

The Securities Industry Association (SIA), which represents such prominent investment banks as Merrill Lynch, Morgan Stanley, and Goldman Sachs, scoffs at the notion that analysts are biased. Their predictions from 1988 through 1999, when the S&P 500 gained an average of 16 percent a year, were on the mark, the SIA asserts. The SIA dismisses the shabby record of 2000 and 2001 as an anomaly, and says that just about everyone working in, reporting on, and commenting about the stock market got a bloody nose in those years, too. Besides, failing to predict correctly the performance of a company is not the same as succumbing to pressure to tilt your conclusions one way or the other, says the SIA. To support its view, the SIA cites a study in the April 2001 *Journal of Finance*. The study looks at analyst recommendations over fifteen years, from 1986 to 2000, and concludes that investors following the consensus analysts' recommendations would have done as well as the stock indexes every year but for one—2000.

But too many other studies have concluded that bias exists. For example, a 1999 study by Roni Michaely, a Cornell University finance professor, and Kent Womack, a Dartmouth College finance professor, found that analysts were more optimistic about the stocks their firms underwrote than they were about stocks brought to market by competitors. Looking at 391 IPOs in 1990 and 1991, the authors concluded that in the month after the SEC-imposed quiet period (twenty-five days after an IPO), analysts who worked for the principal underwriter gave 50 percent more buy recommendations than did analysts from competitor firms. But in the two years after the IPO, the return on stocks that the underwriters' analysts touted was 15.5 percent below the return on stocks recommended by analysts whose firms didn't do business with that company.

Some analysts, such as Ronald Glantz, have provided powerful anecdotal evidence of client pressure to issue biased reports. Now retired, Glantz spent thirty-two years as an analyst with such firms as Dean Witter and Paine Webber, where he was director of research. He was on *Institutional Investor*'s All-American Research Team for seventeen years, including seven as top auto analyst. He said he once downgraded a company's stock, only to have the chief financial officer threaten to cease doing business with his firm. And if Glantz didn't change his recommendation, the CFO warned, he would order the bank that managed his company's pension fund to also stop doing business with Glantz's firm. Luckily, his bosses paid no heed to such threats. Glantz says he has seen analysts removed from company mailing lists and physically barred from company presentations. Once when Glantz was doing a reference check on an analyst he was considering hiring, a CFO told Glantz that the analyst was so uncooperative, the CFO was deliberately feeding him misleading information.

Less-than-honest analysis has one other negative effect. It distorts the markets by shifting capital away from worthy companies to those able to purchase positive research reports with their investment banking dollars. This distortion, over time, could undermine the efficient allocation of capital, which is the reason we have stock markets in the first place.

The Street Resists

To protect individual investors, it was essential that we break the cozy ties between companies and analysts. The SEC could have issued new rules, but as with the broker compensation issue, that would have stirred up a hornet's nest of opposition from Capitol Hill and the industry. It would have meant tossing aside decades of tradition in which the stock exchanges act as self-regulatory organizations, or SROs, watching over brokers, analysts, investment bankers, and the thousands of firms employing them. Instead, I hoped to convince Wall Street that it was in its own interest to clean itself up voluntarily. I also pressured the SROs to tighten rules already on the books. I met resistance at every turn.

I can recall vividly the cold reception I received at the Economic Club of New York in October 1999, when I discussed the web of dysfunctional relationships in a speech to Wall Street luminaries. I decried how analysts relied more on a company's guidance than on the models they developed to gauge earnings, and how analysts protected the investment banking relationship at the cost of fair analysis. I joked that a sell recommendation was about as common as a Barbra Streisand concert. No one laughed. I lamented that companies massaged results to fit analysts' estimates, and that auditors let slide discrepancies in company reports. Afterward, I got a scolding from Muriel Siebert, owner of the discount brokerage firm Muriel Siebert & Co. and the first woman to own a seat on the New York Stock Exchange. Until that speech, she had been supportive of my reform efforts. But this time, she said, I was mis-guided, and suggested that I refrain from tearing down Wall Street.

Nowhere was the resistance more palpable than at the NASD. Relations between the SEC and the NASD, which are tense in the best of times, had become a cat-and-mouse game. I tried to refrain from dictating to them in order to preserve the tradition of self-regulation. But the SEC ultimately is responsible for investor protection, and so it must make sure that the NASD zealously carries out that part of its function.

Still, by the time I left the SEC in February 2001, the NASD had not yet made good on its pledge to enhance analyst disclosures. But it could no longer avoid the subject. For one thing, Congress was turning up the heat. Numerous journalists had begun to link the absence of objectivity in analyst reports with investor losses. Key members of Congress took note. Representative Richard Baker, a Louisiana Republican who chairs the Subcommittee on Capital Markets of the Committee on Financial Services, read one such story and was outraged. It was a May 14, 2001, *Fortune* magazine article about Morgan Stanley's Meeker, whose recommended stocks, including Yahoo!, Priceline, and Amazon, had by then declined an average of 91 percent. Meeker expressed no sympathy for the losses suffered by small investors because of her recommendations. She said her "real" constituency is not the individual but the professional money manager and other institutional investors. "Every individual has got to be accountable for how they're allocating their investments," the article quotes Meeker saying.

When he read that, Baker went ballistic. "Her tone and lack of regret for the consequences of her actions were unprofessional, in my judgment," says Baker. "Her attitude was: if anyone invested based on anything I wrote, that's their problem." The son of a Methodist preacher, with a fiery populist streak, Baker knew a meaty issue when he saw one, and promptly launched a series of hearings called "Analyzing the Analysts." He hinted that legislation to require analysts to submit to strict SEC oversight might be in the offing.

Baker's annoyance grew when top officials of Morgan Stanley

and other large investment banks came in to "educate" him on how analysts were honest players doing their best to help investors sift the good from the bad. They hoped to persuade him to drop the matter. It didn't work, says Baker, who felt the Street's emissaries were patronizing him. Weeks later, he received disturbing evidence that some analysts were participating in practices that might be illegal—and could result in SEC enforcement actions—and his anger flared.

The SEC had quietly examined the conduct of fifty-seven analysts at eight of the top Wall Street firms. Among the findings: three of the fifty-seven were telling investors to buy shares in companies whose stock they were simultaneously selling. One analyst made $3.5 million in profit. Another analyst with a buy recommendation on a stock was selling the same stock short—a bet that the share price will fall. In sixteen cases, analysts had bought IPO shares at a fraction of the price other investors had to pay for the same stock issue. The analysts then put out buy recommendations as soon as the companies went public, boosting the value of their personal holdings.

Most disturbing about the SEC inspection was the fact that only one firm could correctly say which of its analysts were investing in companies that their investment bankers had helped finance. If they can't even track their own analysts' holdings, how can Wall Street firms claim to be patrolling conflicts?

Codes Full of Loopholes

Representative Baker's resolve to help clean up the industry increased when the SIA unveiled a code of best practices two days before his first hearing in June 2001. But the SIA's effort was a tactical and strategic blunder. By releasing a code of conduct just before his hearing, Baker felt that the SIA was trying to undercut him. As for the code itself, he viewed it as loophole-ridden.

To its credit, the SIA at least acknowledged that Wall Street had an image problem. The code calls on analysts to disclose ownership positions in companies they follow, and prohibits analysts from trading against their own recommendations, as by selling the shares they are urging investors to buy. But the code isn't mandatory, and there is no way of enforcing it or monitoring the firms pledging to abide by it. Because the SIA effort did not pass muster with Congress, the NASD had to act.

Finally, in February 2002, it did. Along with the New York Stock Exchange, the NASD proposed new rules that require firms to replace the meaningless boilerplate language that appears in fine print on the back page of most reports. The new rules, made final once the SEC adopted them in May 2002, ban analysts from reporting directly to investment bankers. Analysts cannot be paid for their help with specific investment banking deals, nor can their research reports be vetted by the firm's investment bankers. They must prominently disclose in written reports or when they appear on TV if they own shares in any company they cover. If their firm owns 1 percent or more of a company, that must be disclosed, too. Analysts must also reveal whether their firm performed any investment banking services over the past twelve months, or expects to in the coming three months, for any company its analysts write about. To prevent analysts from profiteering from their own research, they are barred from trading in the stock of companies they cover for thirty days before and five days after issuing a recommendation, and they can never make trades contrary to their most recent recommendation. Finally, research reports must include a clear explanation of the firm's ratings system and a price chart that plots the analysts' recommendation against the stock's movements. Unlike the SIA's voluntary best practices, the NASD/NYSE rules are mandatory as of November 2002. Analysts or firms found in violation risk fines and censure.

While they are an improvement, even these rules are full of holes. Although firms may not be able to tie analysts' compensation to specific deals, they can consider analysts' overall helpfulness to their investment bankers in determining bonuses. And nothing in the rules prohibits analysts from going on sales calls. I know of one company that recently invited five investment banking firms to bid for the right to handle a stock issue. The one chosen had sent its analyst, not an investment banker, to make the pitch. What kind of research report would he write following the IPO? Certainly not a negative one.

As long as Wall Street firms have a financial interest in using analysts to win underwriting deals, not much will change. The biggest obstacle to objective research is that firms are seeking lucrative corporate finance deals from companies that their analysts are following. Such deals pay analysts far more than they could earn from research alone.

Some unhappy investors are daring to make this very point in legal complaints about analysts' unbridled optimism. In one well-known case, pediatrician Debases Kanjilal filed an arbitration case against Merrill Lynch's Henry Blodget. Like Mary Meeker, Blodget epitomized the Internet frenzy. He was a frequent commentator on the CNBC and CNN cable news shows, appearing on TV at least seventy-seven times in 1999. Kanjilal claimed that Blodget misled him by maintaining bullish recommendations on InfoSpace Inc., a provider of information services over the Internet, throughout 2000, despite the stock's rapidly eroding price. Kanjilal alleged that Blodget kept a buy recommendation on the stock because Merrill, at the time, was bidding to advise an Internet company that InfoSpace hoped to acquire, and needed to keep InfoSpace's shares high enough to make the acquisition work. Merrill denied the charges, but rather than fight the case, settled for an undisclosed amount that press reports put at $400,000.

One e-mail turned up by the Spitzer investigation shows that Blodget privately did not rate InfoSpace as highly as he did in his research reports; he referred to the company as a "piece of junk." One communication to Blodget from a Merrill analyst who reported to him says: "We are losing people money, and I don't like it. John and Mary smith [*sic*] are losing their retirement because we don't want [the chief financial officer of the Internet company GoTo.com] to be mad at us." GoTo.com was one of the companies Merrill was wooing as an investment banking client, and which Blodget was recommending to investors despite the Internet search engine outfit's lack of profits the previous two years.

A Market Solution

The only way to fix this problem is for investment banks to separate their brokerage and research operations. But I'm no Pollyanna. I know that kind of divestiture will never happen unless the firms are forced to do it. One reason is that brokerage commissions don't produce enough revenue to support the research function. Individual investors, who rely most on analysts, don't want to pay much more than rock-bottom commissions for their stock trades, depriving analysts of a revenue source. But it's important to understand that research isn't free, and that individuals will pay, one way or another. You may never have to write a check for research, but there is a hidden cost. The loyalty that analysts show toward corporate clients, and the resulting lack of objectivity in their recommendations, is one such cost.

Is there a better way? It may not be possible to design a foolproof system that walls off stock research from investment banking as long as analysts depend on the banking side for revenues. But here's something else the stock exchanges and the issuers of stock can do. As in the bond market, the stock exchanges could require an independent analyst's rating prior to any stock issue. The bond market is far less transparent than the equity market in many respects, but the requirement of a rating from independent companies such as Standard & Poor's or Moody's Investor Services on every debt offering gives the bond market a leg up on the equity markets. Equity ratings would not have to be done just by S&P and Moody's, both of which disappointed investors when they failed to downgrade Enron's debt until four days before its bankruptcy. I would hope that other companies, such as Value Line, would also offer ratings on equity issues as a new service. To avoid a system in which every rating is a "buy," analysts could jointly develop a common ranking method, such as a score between 1 and 5, with a 5 being a strong buy. Mutual funds, which own 20 percent of all equities, could reinforce a ratings system by refusing to invest in a company unless it has received at least a grade of 3 from an independent analyst.

The SEC could require the audit committees of corporate boards to make sure that such ratings are truly independent, just as they are now asked to ensure that a company's auditors are truly independent. Why would a corporate board go out of its way to hire a possibly unfriendly analyst to obtain a rating? Because the imprimatur of a neutral rating service would go a long way toward restoring the faith of investors at a time when many are wary of the stock market and the dubious behavior of analysts, brokers, auditors, and corporate managers alike. Of course, this would not preclude other Wall Street firms from offering recommendations on any company's stock, but it would require that the issuing company get a grade from a neutral source before selling shares.

Or perhaps Wall Street firms could form an independent research cooperative. The cooperative would hire or contract with analysts to produce specific reports in their area of expertise. Analysts' compensation would come out of the payments that the cooperative's member firms would make to the cooperative each year. If Goldman Sachs, for example, had Ford Motor Co. as an investment banking client, Goldman would not issue research reports on Ford, but instead would rely on the cooperative to rank Ford's shares.

Put Analysts in Their Place

What can investors do? The first rule of thumb is that an analyst's recommendation should never be the deciding factor in whether you buy or sell a stock. Sure, you should read analysts' reports. They are a good way to start your own research, but consider them just one more piece of information.

Never buy a stock based solely on an analyst's recommendation. Instead, ask yourself: Is the stock right for me because it helps diversify my portfolio, or because it helps me meet an asset allocation goal? Am I expecting to hold the stock for the long term? Do I understand the company, and why I'd like to own it? Do I understand it well enough to know why I might want to sell the stock, beyond a short-term failure to meet analysts' expectations? Answering these questions in the affirmative is enough to justify owning a stock—far more than any analyst's say-so.

Ask lots of questions. You should not be influenced by an analyst's stock recommendation unless you understand why the analyst favors it; whether the analyst's firm has any business ties to the company in the form of investment banking fees; and whether the firm or the analyst owns any of the shares being recommended. If the analyst's firm does own shares in the company, you should ask whether the firm is following its own analyst's recommendations. And if an analyst recommends that you buy shares in a company whose stock offering was managed by his firm, consider that "buy" the same way you would an advertisement—with a heavy dose of skepticism.

Investors should also give greater weight to the recommendations of independent research analysts, who sell their reports to institutional clients and earn commissions when those clients trade. Prudential Securities, for example, no longer offers investment banking services, and so its analysts have far fewer conflicts right off the bat. Precursor Group, a Washington, D.C.–based research boutique, also does no investment banking and instead lives and dies on the quality of its telecom and technology research. Because Precursor's reports are written only for pension and mutual fund clients, they are not available to retail investors. But the company is leading an effort, along with Argus Research, which caters to both retail and institutional investors, to set up the first trade group for independent outfits. Called Investorside Research Association, the trade group plans to offer an Internet clearinghouse to help investors find independent stock-pickers. Once the group is up and running, you can access its Web site at *www.investorsideresearch. org.*

You should supplement what you learn from Wall Street analysts with information that is readily available from other reliable sources. Two of my favorites are owned by Value Line Inc. and Standard & Poor's Corp.

The *Value Line Investment Survey,* a weekly publication, rates 1,700 stocks between 1 (the highest) and 5 (the lowest) in its unique

Timeliness Ranking System. Stocks with a 1 usually beat the overall market, while stocks with a 5 generally are underperformers. A Value Line computer model, not judgmental humans, determines company rankings, which are based on earnings performance, safety, and volatility, or a stock's day-to-day gyrations. Value Line also employs analysts to write pithy quarterly commentaries. Trial subscriptions are available (*www.valueline.com*), but most libraries have copies.

Standard & Poor's *Outlook,* a weekly newsletter published by McGraw-Hill Cos., which also produces the S&P 500 stock index, offers a wealth of information, including investment tips and strategies. The *Outlook* ranks the stocks of more than a thousand companies on a scale of 1 to 5 (with a 5 being the highest, the opposite of the Value Line system). The *Outlook* is also available in many libraries. The Web site *www.spoutlookonline.com* offers a free thirty-day trial of the *Outlook*.

Numerous other investment advice newsletters—too many to mention here—can help you with stock-picking and market trends. One is *Dow Theory Forecasts* (*www.dowtheory.com*), published since 1946 and offering consistently good advice in both bull and bear markets, a true test of a newsletter's worth. Another respected newsletter is the *Dick Davis Digest*. Its analysts sift through hundreds of other financial newsletters and pick out what they consider the best of the best. Each biweekly issue contains advice on the market's direction and investment approaches, plus what the editors consider the single most promising stock idea. Subscriptions are available at *www.dickdavis.com*.

Another excellent source is Zacks Investment Research (*my. zacks.com*), which is chock-full of goodies for investors, and much of it is free or available on a trial basis. The Web site has market news and analysis to give you the big picture. It can tell you which analysts consistently beat the market, and offers research reports from the top-rated analysts. The site also has links to advisory newsletters on stocks, mutual funds, bonds, options, and futures.

Years ago, I came to the conclusion that conflicts of interest will exist as long as the analysts' meal ticket comes from the very companies they are reviewing. No matter how strictly the NASD and NYSE end up enforcing their new rules, analysts who are paid according to the deals they bring their investment banker colleagues will find it hard to say negative things about companies that are, or someday could be, clients. It's another case of compensation determining behavior.

CHAPTER FOUR

REG FD: STOPPING THE FLOW
OF INSIDE INFORMATION

In the summer of 2000, the time had come to give final approval to a controversial new rule, Regulation Fair Disclosure, or Reg FD. As I walked to the SEC's public meeting room on August 10, an aide rushed to hand me a pink message slip. "Hank Paulson is trying to reach you from China. He strongly urges you to vote no." While the timing of the call from Paulson, the chairman and CEO of the investment bank Goldman Sachs Group, was a surprise, the message wasn't. He and the rest of the securities industry thought I was about to apply the executioner's noose to Wall Street's way of life.

Reg FD would require companies to release important information to all investors at the same time, and not just to a favored few. Such "selective disclosure" had gotten out of hand in the 1990s, and put small investors at a disadvantage to the analysts, brokers, and institutional investors who were routinely getting advance information on corporate earnings ahead of the rest of the market. That was wrong, plain and simple.

Individual investors I spoke to were incredulous that the SEC didn't already have such a rule. Nor could they understand why anyone who professed to believe in fair and open markets would oppose it. Reg FD was meant to shut down the flow of leaks and force analysts to become analysts again. Still, it was an audacious move. Never before had so many lined up against me. For the past year, much of Wall Street and the corporate establishment fought to kill Reg FD. Some of my staunchest supporters, such as Larry Tisch, chairman and CEO of Loews Corp., the insurance-hotels-tobacco holding company, who had applauded many of my earlier actions, said I was going too far. Even at the SEC the rule did not sit well with two of my fellow commissioners and some of my most senior staff.

In the end, it was a cliffhanger. Of the four commissioners at the time, I knew I could count on only one—the late Paul Carey, whose loyalty to investor interests was unflagging. I also knew Laura Unger believed that FD would do more harm than good, and that she would vote no. It was one of the few times, in my nearly eight years as chairman, that the commission would not vote unanimously on a major matter. That left Isaac Hunt as the tiebreaker. Hunt had doubts about Reg FD and was still undecided two days before the meeting. On the night before the vote, he hinted that numerous changes we made to the proposed rule had placated him. But he was under a great deal of pressure from all sides, and when he called in sick the day of the big vote, I wondered whether to go forward without him. I could have declared victory on a two-to-one decision, but as a matter of principle I thought every commissioner should cast a vote. Besides, I wanted the credibility that a three-to-one vote would provide. I decided to get Ike Hunt on the phone and patch him through to the meeting. This was a gamble on my part, not knowing for sure how Ike would vote. But thank goodness he said yes. Reg FD was made official by a vote of three to one.

The intent of Reg FD is really quite simple. If a company wishes to pass on market-moving information, it must share the news with everyone at the same time. In practice, it means that if senior management or other top officials—those who are authorized to speak on a company's behalf—intentionally release material, nonpublic information to market professionals, they must simultaneously release it publicly to all. If management unintentionally releases market-moving information to someone who is likely to take advantage of it, such as by trading on it or giving it to a client to trade on, the rule requires the company to disclose the information publicly within twenty-four hours. If an inadvertent disclosure happens on a weekend, the correction must take place before the opening of the next day's trading.

The rule applies to material information. But what qualifies as material? Well, anything a reasonable shareholder would consider important in making an investment decision. A probable merger, a major setback on a new product, or a change in top management are all widely accepted as material events. Although materiality decisions can be easy, sometimes they are tough to pin down, and we purposely did not set bright-line boundaries. What is material depends on the unique facts and circumstances of each company.

The rule took effect on October 23, 2000, and within weeks we began to see results. The tipped playing field between Wall Street's privileged elite and millions of ordinary investors started to level off as more and more companies opened up their private analyst meetings and conference calls to all shareholders and the press. In the fourth quarter of 2000, 1,474 companies publicly announced whether they would hit their earnings target, up an astounding 96 percent over the previous quarter's public preannouncements.

There have been some hiccups in adjusting to this new openness, which is to be expected. In some cases companies have resisted the new openness regime, and the SEC has had to bring actions to make it clear that Reg FD is not voluntary. On Nov. 25, 2002, for example, the agency issued three enforcement decisions, one of which involved software company Siebel Systems Inc. CEO Tom Siebel a year earlier had revealed nonpublic details about his company's prospects to investors at an invitation-only conference held by Goldman Sachs. That day, Siebel's shares jumped 20 percent. Without admitting guilt, Siebel paid $250,000 to settle the case. Despite these and other violations, I now believe Reg FD has done more to restore investor confidence in the stock market than any other rule the SEC adopted during my tenure. And I'm encouraged that new SEC Chairman William Donaldson, who once said that Reg FD was "crazy," showed a change of heart in his Senate confirmation hearing, during which he pledged not to try to alter the rule.

I think it's important that investors know how the rule came about, and why the securities industry bitterly opposed it. Even today, Wall Street firms would like nothing better than to turn back the clock and either erase Reg FD or water it down. I knew first-hand as a former broker and investment banker that corporations sometimes leaked big news to analysts. I recall one chief executive in particular who, in the 1970s, used our firm's analyst to leak his company's earnings-per-share. He hoped the indebted analyst would write a favorable report—and push the stock to our brokers. Sometimes he hoped to enlist our analyst's help in softening the blow to the share price if the news was bad. At the time, there were no court rulings that said leaks of this sort were illegal.

For the next two decades, companies would increasingly leak to analysts what they thought their earnings would be. They did this to help shape, and thus avoid missing, the analysts' consensus forecast, since the stock market severely punished companies that missed earnings estimates by even a penny a share. A 1998 survey by the National Investor Relations Institute (NIRI), a Vienna, Va.–based trade association of 2,750 companies, found that 86 percent of its members reviewed drafts of analyst reports, and 79 percent went so far as to check analysts' earnings projections before they were released.

Every time analysts received material earnings information, their brokerage firms had inside information on which to trade. And trade they did. Week after week, I read news stories about a company's shares rising mysteriously prior to the release of a quarterly report. To expose such incidents, Bloomberg News began compiling a "hush list" of selective disclosures, sparking a campaign against the unseemly practice (full disclosure: I serve on the board of Bloomberg LP). Sometimes unexplained leaps in share prices would occur during a gathering of analysts at an exclusive golf resort, where companies courted analysts with lavish hospitality.

For example, in December 1998 disk-drive manufacturer Western Digital Corp.'s stock mysteriously jumped 37 percent in one day. The company had received no new contracts, nor had it issued any upbeat press release to justify a $427 million rise in market value. Instead, the CEO had met with analysts, and then granted an interview to a Dow Jones wire service reporter later that day at the Phoenician Resort in Scottsdale, Ariz., where he painted a glowing picture of the company's future. A spokesman says the company did nothing wrong but concedes that Reg FD would not allow such selective briefings today.

In October 1999 investors filed class-action lawsuits against Abercrombie & Fitch Co., the teen fashion retailer, for allegedly telling an analyst with Lazard Freres & Co. that sales growth would not meet earlier estimates. Such crucial intelligence, the lawsuits claimed, allowed the analyst's clients to bail out of Abercrombie's stock when it was trading at $39. A week later, when Abercrombie formally announced that sales growth was slowing down, the shares plunged 33 percent to $26. As of the end of June 2002 Abercrombie & Fitch was still fighting the lawsuit.

Similarly, in September 1998, shares of Nortel Networks Corp. mysteriously fell 12 percent despite no extraordinary event that would explain such a steep decline. What happened? Turns out the company had warned selected analysts that revenue growth from overseas operations would be disappointing. Four hours later, after Nortel's market value had declined by $3 billion, the company made the news public.

The list goes on. Each case is slightly different, but they all have this in common: individual investors never knew what was going on. And they were left holding the bag. By the time small investors found out what favored analysts, brokers, and portfolio managers already knew, because they were part of Wall Street's grapevine, it was too late.

Insider Trading?

The SEC considered bringing insider trading charges against companies that engaged in this practice. Altogether, the SEC's Enforcement Division had more than a dozen meaty allegations of selective disclosure on which to base a case. But even as the lawyers worked up their evidence, we realized our hands were tied. The Supreme Court had ruled, in a 1983 case called *Dirks v. SEC,* that to bring insider trading charges, the SEC must prove that the company insider providing the information acted in breach of a fiduciary duty by receiving a personal benefit. Examples of such a benefit might include cash payments or reputational gain. This was a high hurdle.

If a CEO tips friends and family to a pending merger and they trade on that information, that's insider trading. But in the years since *Dirks,* many securities lawyers concluded that the High Court had given companies a green light to disclose important matters to analysts, since it was in a company's interest to want analyst reports to be accurate. The beneficiary of such disclosures was the company, not the insider releasing the information. The justices, in effect, said that an analyst's job is to ferret out as much information as possible, through whatever means possible, in order to get information to the market. Most experts even accepted that it was legal for analysts to trade on that information.

To me, this was not right. In mid-1998, Harvey Goldschmid, a Columbia University law professor who had agreed to take a leave and be my general counsel for eighteen months (Goldschmid is now an SEC commissioner), set up a task force to study our options. At first, Goldschmid's group debated internally whether to pursue enforcement cases on the theory that the market was defrauded by selective releases of material information. To bring a case, we would have to expand the Supreme Court's definition of personal benefit to cover cases in which company officials making the release personally benefited by currying favor with analysts, who in turn benefited financially by trading on the information. Goldschmid thought it would be possible, but difficult, to do. David Becker, then a deputy to Goldschmid who later became SEC general counsel, thought it would be easy, "like shooting fish in a barrel," he said at one meeting. But outside securities law experts, such as Goldschmid's Columbia colleague John Coffee, thought we were dead wrong to assume that the federal courts would allow us to extend the reach of *Dirks* and other cases that far.

In the end, we held our "insider trading" fire, and not just because of the legal uncertainties. All of us agreed that any new set of test cases would create enormous fear among companies and analysts, and could seriously chill the flow of information. Nervous corporate lawyers would almost certainly warn their bosses, in order to avoid liability, to cut off communication with analysts altogether. Otherwise, they could face severe insider trading sanctions, including possible prison sentences, civil penalties in actions brought by the SEC that would recover three times the illicit gain, and the stigma of a fraud conviction.

We were back where we started. We needed a different hook, and Goldschmid found one. Instead of focusing on insider trading, he turned to the part of the securities laws that allows the SEC to regulate communications between public companies and the marketplace. If the SEC can require companies to reveal material information in SEC filings or a prospectus prior to a stock offering, or to observe a "quiet period" for twenty-five days after an offering, then why not require them to disclose important information to all shareholders simultaneously? It was a novel and bold idea, but it seemed workable. We quietly began writing the details of how such a rule would work.

Toward the middle of 1999, the Securities Industry Association, which represents some seven hundred brokerage and investment banking firms in Washington, got wind of what we were doing, and set off alarm bells. But it was difficult for the SIA to stop us, especially since it couldn't be sure what we were doing. Then, on December 15, 1999, the commission proposed a rule, dubbed Regulation Fair Disclosure. We purposely chose that name to make our opponents think twice about fighting it. The hullabaloo triggered by the proposal was bigger than any I had so far experienced at the SEC.

The agency was inundated with comments—more than six thousand in all, the highest in SEC history. It made a deep impression on me when I saw that the industry comments were almost uniformly negative while the public comments were almost uniformly positive.

Lobbying Blitz

The SIA put on a lobbying blitz. Stuart Kaswell, the SIA's general counsel, led the charge, along with Merrill Lynch general counsel George Schieren and Prudential Securities general counsel Lee Spencer. They met numerous times with the other commissioners, especially Hunt, whose vote was in play once he publicly revealed that he was on the fence. The SIA rounded up four of its past chairmen—all close friends of mine—to urge me to back down. The industry also sent a posse to Capitol Hill, but failed to arouse much interest. One reason: I preempted them by going to Senator Phil Gramm, the Texas Republican who chaired the Senate Banking Committee.

Ordinarily, the conservative lawmaker and former economics professor opposes financial regulation; his position is that it stifles free markets. I appealed to his sensibilities by explaining that rather than just adding to existing layers of securities rules, Reg FD would make the markets more efficient by making sure that all players had the opportunity to get the same information at the same time. Gramm believes in fair and efficient markets, which to him means that all players should have access to the same information. He never interfered.

The SIA kept the heat on for months. I recall a particularly tense showdown in my office in late May 2000 with Kaswell, SIA president Marc Lackritz, and Prudential's Spencer. They couldn't very well argue against the principle of fair disclosure. Instead, they insisted that the rule would stifle the free flow of information just as companies were flocking to the Internet to broadcast analyst meetings and press conferences. They said companies were voluntarily ending such old-boy practices as the closed conference call, in which only hand-selected, friendly analysts were allowed to ask questions. They claimed Reg FD would turn back the clock by giving companies an excuse not to open up, citing potential liability. Lee Spencer pointed to Marc Lackritz and said that if Lackritz were the CEO of his company, "no way would I let him speak to analysts. The risk of talking would be too great, and the benefits too small."

I listened, but in the end discounted the idea that the flow of information to investors would dry up, saying that I just plain didn't believe it would happen. The truth is, I honestly couldn't say for sure that companies wouldn't react by clamming up. But the SIA had no factual basis for concluding that they would; I asked them if they had a better argument.

They were nonplussed, but carried on. Next they complained that the SEC had failed to prove that any heinous practices were actually taking place. They conceded knowing of a few isolated cases of selective disclosure, but those were the exception, not the rule, they insisted. Surprisingly, Kaswell and company then suggested that if the SEC believed that abuses were widespread, the agency should go after them with enforcement actions. I say surprisingly because the SIA normally grouses when the SEC defines the boundaries of the securities laws through enforcement cases. Usually the industry prefers to know what the rules of play are, then tries to abide by them. We knew—and we knew that they knew—that such a route was difficult because of the *Dirks* case. We were not about to fall into the trap of pursuing an enforcement case against a company or an analyst that we might not win and, even if we did, could seriously chill the flow of information.

At the end of the meeting, I announced that we would be moving full steam ahead and that they could either work with us to refine the proposal or get out of the way. And I invited the group to provide us with an alternative, if they had one.

Kaswell later recalled that he left with a sinking feeling. He was taken aback by our dismissal of the idea of a chill factor, which he considered the most compelling argument against FD. The SIA team never responded to my invitation to come up with an alternative, except to suggest that the SEC convene a panel to study the matter. Instead, the SIA continued its flat-out opposition. But the trade group did point out a number of flaws in the proposal, and we worked to fix those. For example, we exempted foreign companies whose shares are traded in the United States. We did this to avoid interfering with other countries' rules and customs on when and how corporations can communicate with shareholders. We also limited the rule to disclosures by senior management and investor-relations professionals. Unauthorized disclosures by mid-level management would not trigger the rule. Nor would it extend to communications with suppliers, customers, the press, and rating agencies such as Standard & Poor's.

We also agreed with the SIA that we needed to clarify that the rule would not create liability for fraud. We made it clear that if a company was thought to be in violation, the SEC would not bring fraud charges. It could, however, start an administrative proceeding or a civil case on nonfraud grounds. Finally, we exempted information released by companies during road shows—pre-IPO sales meetings that investment banks conduct to drum up interest among potential investors—which have a separate disclosure regime to follow.

Still, the SIA was unhappy. Why? Because Reg FD upset Wall Street's applecart. Over the past few decades, as it became clear that the SEC had uncertain legal authority to stop selective disclosure, the conduct of analysts and the companies they followed became more and more brazen. It was common for analysts to get regular tips from chief financial officers on everything from sales and profit margins to earnings forecasts and management changes.

Analysts often passed on these tips to their firms' institutional customers and their brokers, who then forwarded them to their favorite clients. The pecking order for such valuable tips depended on how much business the recipient generated for the analyst's firm. The practice of tipping also enabled companies to withhold information from analysts who were uncooperative.

The result was an unhealthy form of barter, in which some companies gave away information in return for favorable ratings. Barter had become a way of life on the Street, and many resented the SEC for interfering with it. Even among the most scrupulous of my Wall Street friends, this imperfect system was the price of capitalism. To them, selective disclosure of information was the grease that made the wheels of the market run smoothly, even if such disclosures gave analysts crucial details ahead of most everyone else—and even if they traded on them.

Ending the Barter System

The barter system left some corporate officials uneasy. While many companies, especially those in the high-tech sector, were dead set against FD, some CEOs privately let us know that they welcomed the rule. Small-cap companies were especially positive. Only a few analysts follow small-cap companies, and sometimes analysts make unreasonable demands on chief financial officers (CFOs) for inside information, occasionally threatening to drop coverage if they don't get what they want.

Among large companies, drug maker Pfizer Inc. worked with us the most to improve the rule and get it adopted. William Steere, the now-retired chairman and CEO of Pfizer, was especially helpful. At the time, Steere chaired the Committee on Corporate Governance for the Business Roundtable, an association of chairmen and CEOs of large corporations. We met for lunch at a New York club in March 2000, and he advised me on the best way to approach this august group. His advice was solid: keep it low-key, let them ask all their questions, don't act like an overeager regulator or a cop looking to skin corporate hides, and be prepared to make changes. He was right on every level. In two subsequent conference calls between Roundtable members and my senior staff, they asked a lot of questions, and we showed our willingness to compromise in several areas. But most of all, we made sure they knew we weren't looking to play gotcha.

A survey of Roundtable members turned out to be very helpful, especially since it was conducted as Wall Street executives who were also Roundtable members were lobbying the group to denounce the proposed rule. The survey showed that only 18 percent of members said their companies would behave differently under Reg FD, and only 10 percent thought the rules would have a chilling effect. The consensus was that we weren't imposing anything that wasn't good business practice.

As a voice for moderation, Steere persuaded other Roundtable members not to fight, but to help improve the rule. That attitude led to several changes, such as clarifying that the rule does not apply to everyday conversations between companies and their suppliers, or between management and employees, and that helped us avoid unintended consequences. The lack of resistance from the Business Roundtable was an important signal to the rest of corporate America. I considered this a huge victory.

Today, analysts can no longer rely on the gravy train of free, market-moving information from companies. And CFOs can no longer steer analysts to a preferred earnings figure, then massage the numbers to come in just above that to pleasantly surprise the market—and get a boost in the share price as a reward.

Just one year after Reg FD, the salutary effects were obvious. Most companies were not using FD to clam up, as the SIA predicted. In a September 2001 survey of 201 companies by Pricewaterhouse-Coopers, the auditing and consulting firm, 37 percent said they were disclosing even more information and another 52 percent said the quantity of their disclosures was about the same. Should FD be repealed? No, said 88 percent of the responding companies, although 68 percent said more SEC clarification on what is "material" would be helpful. Only 10 percent wanted to repeal it.

The SIA continues to claim that Reg FD is living up to its billing by contributing to the stock market's volatility, which is a measurement of price gyrations. A high level of volatility can be an indicator that the market isn't getting the information it needs to agree on a company's "correct" share price, or one that reflects a company's true value, and thus its price bounces around a lot more. But FD's effect on volatility has been minimal, according to the PricewaterhouseCoopers survey. Of the 201 respondents, 74 percent said Reg FD had no impact on the volatility of their company's stock price.

Throughout 2001 there was great volatility in the financial markets. But FD had little, if anything, to do with that. The Federal Reserve Board cut interest rates eleven times; the tech sector remained in a deep slump, while corporate profits overall deteriorated; and the September 11 terrorist attacks sent the economy, already heading toward recession, into a tailspin. All of this tells me that, in such a tumultuous period, Reg FD's timing could not have been better. As stocks steadily declined throughout the bear market of 2001, the rule gave individual investors bad news straight from the horse's mouth. This provided investors with a sense of fair play, and protected them from analysts' disingenuous buy ratings.

Charles Hill, director of financial research at Thomson Financial/First Call, which keeps track of analysts' recommendations, agrees. Hill spent twenty-two years as an analyst, and today is a vice-president and director of the Boston Society of Security Analysts. Some of the huge increase in earnings preannouncements midway through the quarter may have happened anyway, says Hill, "but I would maintain you're getting much more because of Reg FD. And it's a good thing it's happening now, what with the economy coming apart. Without FD, there would have been all kinds of attempts by analysts to get special treatment from the companies they cover."

Information Bonanza

Thanks to a combination of Reg FD and technology, investors are benefiting from an information bonanza. The Internet makes it easy for companies to offer live broadcasts of analyst conference calls and quarterly earnings announcements. The beauty of such Webcasting is that it's convenient and inexpensive. A basic Webcast of an analyst conference call starts at about $650, which often includes archiving the call so that investors can access it several days later.

The rule does not require companies to open up their analyst briefings, most of which take place midway through a quarter and again just before quarterly earnings are released, to all shareholders. But thousands of companies have done so, to avoid running afoul of FD. In 1999 most companies excluded shareholders from analyst conference calls. By late 2001, 90 percent of National Investor Relations Institute members allowed shareholders to listen in as executives parried questions on sales, profits, expenses, and strategy. A mere 1 percent of NIRI members were restricting conference calls to analysts alone.

Now, use of the Internet to Webcast quarterly earnings announcements is de rigueur. When investors listen in, they are often rewarded for their effort. They hear for themselves how well managers field tough questions—even the tone of a CEO's voice can tell you something. And about 20 percent of companies that offer a near-term forecast do so only in the conference call, not in the news release announcing the call. Access to such vital information in a down market has given ordinary investors a second opinion—their own—and has helped to erase the notion that the deck is stacked against them. "You don't have to be a sophisticated investor to understand what it means when a CEO says we're not going to make our numbers," says Charles Hill.

True, most analysts are not as sanguine. They are especially unhappy that some companies no longer allow one-on-one meetings with top officials, depriving them of the nitty-gritty detail necessary to paint a more vivid picture of a company's future prospects. I was chagrined to learn that some companies abruptly canceled one-on-one meetings with analysts in the first few months after FD took effect (such meetings are allowed under FD). But that was a knee-jerk reaction, and most companies have now resumed one-on-ones. In a July 2001 survey of NIRI companies, 74 percent said they were conducting the same number of one-on-one meetings, with 5 percent conducting even more.

Analysts also say they no longer get valuable "guidance" to make sure their financial models, and thus their forecasts, are correct. Many companies have curtailed the use of such private hand-holding out of fear that they'll violate Reg FD. Earnings guidance is not verboten, but it is now a tricky business. If a CFO confirms previously disclosed earnings guidance by saying, for example, that she is comfortable with yesterday's projections, she may not be giving anything away. But if such a confirmation comes near the end of a quarter, she could be revealing how the company actually performed, and that may well be material information.

That's why companies that continue to give guidance should give it to everyone. I expect more companies will do so in the future because it's in a company's best interest to be open. Harvard Business School Professor Amy Hutton has studied company policies on guidance. She found that companies offering guidance experience a more positive impact from good news than those providing no guidance. Her research also shows that when the news is bad, companies that provide no guidance take a more negative hit in the market.

Piecing Together the Mosaic

Nothing in Reg FD precludes analysts from doing their jobs properly. A CFO can't whisper important numbers in their ears anymore, but that doesn't mean analysts can't draw conclusions on the quality of senior management and their ability to execute a strategy. Nor does FD prevent the smart analyst from seeking, or a company from providing, nonmaterial information that helps the analyst piece together a mosaic that, when completed, is material.

A drug company analyst, for example, might attend a hearing on a new drug application at the Food and Drug Administration. From the hearing, he might get a strong sense that the FDA harbors doubts about research results submitted by the company seeking to market the new drug. The analyst then might speak to competitors of the company, who also express doubts. Then the analyst might ask the company CEO if the new drug is critical to the company's future. If the CEO says yes, then the analyst may have pieced together a mosaic that, all told, yields material information. By itself, the CEO's statement that the new drug is critical to his company's future does not reveal much of anything to other people. But to the analyst who has done his homework, it can be highly revealing. This is the kind of spadework Reg FD hopes to encourage.

The truth is, materiality is not as hard to grasp as some lawyers and analysts would have you believe. No doubt, companies must think twice before blithely responding to the inquisitive analyst. For example, in most cases where a company's market share is stable, confirming a week-old forecast—or steering an analyst to statements made a week earlier—reveals little that is newsworthy. But if a company just suffered the cancellation of a major contract, confirming a week-old forecast is likely to reveal material information. If a company chooses to answer that question, then it should make it available to all interested parties via a news release or an SEC filing.

Still, analysts remain unhappy. The quality of information they now get is much lower, they assert. They complain that conference calls are stilted, and the ability to ask follow-up questions is limited when a gang of thousands is on the line. They gripe that responses to questions seem scripted, even dumbed down to accommodate the wide range of listeners. Their hope is that the SEC, under a new chairman, will make it easier on companies by clearly defining materiality with yes-or-no bright lines. That way, anything not on the SEC list automatically becomes okay to release to a select few, and probably will be. If this happens, I believe it will gut Reg FD.

For example, the SEC could decide to put something as mundane as inventory levels on the nonmaterial list. For banks and insurers, inventories may not be important indicators of financial health. But for technology companies caught with huge equipment backlogs in 2000 and 2001, inventory levels were crucial factors in determining whether they would meet their earnings forecasts.

While the hue and cry for clarification of what is material, and thus must be disclosed widely, has some validity (some additional guidance from the SEC may be useful), it reflects mostly transitional problems. In some cases, overly anxious corporate lawyers have muzzled management by advising them to err egregiously on the side of caution. I believe what's really going on is that analysts are feeling withdrawal pains. For a decade, they were spoon-fed important numbers and other material information from CFOs, and now it's painful for them to live without.

In some ways, Reg FD has reduced the quarterly earnings number to a commodity, something that is easy to obtain and available to all. Financial experts are even starting to question what a quarterly number really tells us about a company's value. Because of this, many analysts are asking themselves: Am I relevant? How can I add value when the numbers and management's discussion are on full public display for everyone? My answer: It's time to return to good old-fashioned analysis. Distinguish yourself from the crowd by not simply regurgitating what you get from companies. Focus on the nonfinancial measures that add value to a company, such as the ability of senior management, the quality of the overall strategy, how well the business plan is being executed, the condition of competitors, and customer satisfaction.

Senior analysts remember fondly—and privately say they welcome a return to—the days when analysts did more than schmooze corporate management to get them to reveal the next quarter's earnings number. Louis Thompson, who as president and CEO of NIRI spent years cajoling his members to end the practice of selective disclosure, sees the move away from a single-minded focus on quarterly earnings as an unintended but positive consequence of Reg FD. I agree, especially if the obsession with short-term performance also brings an end to the accounting games companies employ to manage earnings. It's my hope that, in time, Reg FD will be seen as relatively unimportant as companies pump out monthly, weekly, maybe even real-time updates of sales, costs, margins, new products, new markets, and changes in strategy.

Reg FD has unlocked a treasure trove of information that previously was off limits to ordinary investors. You should take advantage of the new era of openness by listening to the Webcasts of companies whose shares you own or are considering buying. Reg FD requires companies that plan to reveal material information in their Webcasts to give you ample notice in a press release when a conference call is scheduled. On the day of the conference call, you don't have to interrupt your work to listen in now that most companies archive Webcasts of conference calls and quarterly earnings announcements for several days. Two Web sites, *www.ccbn.com* (full disclosure: I chair the advisory board of Corporate Communications Broadcast Network, which owns this service) and *www. bestcalls.com,* maintain lists of companies conducting Webcasting. They also provide instructions to help you tune in. Or, if you are keenly interested in one company, send an e-mail to the investor relations officer of that company, asking if she will automatically notify you by e-mail of any Webcasts.

Reg FD has also reinvigorated many company Web sites. Partly because of FD, companies have become acutely aware that individual investors crave information. They want the company's history, access to historical and real-time financial figures, and copies of analysts' research. They want to see calendars showing when briefings and other key events will take place, biographies of top personnel and how to reach them, and instructions on how to buy stock in the company.

As an investor, keep in mind that the most forthcoming companies are generally the ones that care the most about their shareholders. If a company's communications are frank and open, then it probably values you as an investor, and is likely to be more vigilant about improving shareholder returns. As you research which stocks to buy, a good proxy for shareholder value is the company's willingness to open itself up. You can view some model Web sites on your own to see what I mean. Some of my favorites are *www.Target. com*, *www.Intel.com*, and *www.IBM.com*.

Keep this onslaught of new information in perspective. Just because you can trade like the pros on the basis of what you hear in a Webcast or conference call, it doesn't mean you should. Impulsive trading on the basis of a single quarter's results is the mark of a day trader, and not a long-term investor.

You should also know your rights under Reg FD. Companies cannot put material information on their Web sites and expect to be in compliance with the rule. For now, the SEC has said that Website dissemination is not enough, since many investors still do not have Internet access or, if they do, aren't in the habit of using the Net every day. Until Internet access is more universal, companies must use a widely circulated press release or a prescheduled Webcast or conference call. They can also send the information to the SEC as part of a Form 8-K, which can be viewed at *www.sec.gov.* Once at the Web site, click on "EDGAR," the database of SEC filings, and follow the instructions to access a company's 8-K filings. A press release can be used to direct investors to a Webcast, where the actual information is revealed, but the Webcast must be open to all. This does not necessarily mean that you will be allowed to ask questions, as most companies continue to give only analysts that privilege.

In many ways, Regulation FD is an experiment in democracy. Its goal is to give all investors an equal opportunity at getting information at the same time. Of course the SEC can't guarantee that everyone will actually read or hear every important piece of news simultaneously. After all, most individual investors can't interrupt their workday to watch cable TV for long periods, nor can they afford to take the time to browse through hundreds of forms filed with the SEC each day. But it's now possible for individual investors to keep up with a short list of companies whose stocks they are following closely, or for their advisers to keep a more watchful eye on their portfolio. The point is, investors who do want their information on a par with Wall Street can now have it. And that helps disabuse many small investors of the widely held belief that the Wall Street deck is stacked against them.

As the fight over Reg FD drew to a close in the summer of 2000, the battle lines were already being drawn for the next showdown: restoring the credibility of company financial statements. Now that we were making it possible for all investors to get important financial data on an equal footing with the pros, it was time to improve the quality of the numbers themselves. Too many companies were using aggressive accounting practices, with the approval of their auditors, to meet their earnings forecasts. They were using all kinds of accounting tricks to hide problems, and investors were being misled. The worst offenders were technology companies. They didn't take kindly to my efforts to crack down on them, nor did the auditors like being told that they had failed in their professional duty. As tough as it was, the battle over Reg FD would be a mere skirmish compared to the war of the numbers game, the manipulation of financial statements.

CHAPTER FIVE

THE NUMBERS GAME

Two things, I've learned, defy the political process: closing military bases and setting accounting standards. Constituent pressure has made it next to impossible for Congress to decide which military installations to shut down, so instead Congress has punted the hard decisions to independent base-closing commissions, two of which I sat on. But setting accounting standards is even more politically fraught than that. The debate over accounting for stock options is a perfect example. When I arrived at the SEC in mid-1993, I inherited a controversy over whether companies should have to treat stock options as an expense on their income statement. Stock options give the recipient the right to purchase shares in the future at today's price. If the share price rises above the grant price, the holder can cash in by using the options to buy actual shares, then immediately selling the stock at the higher price. The difference can be substantial. For the CEO holding one million stock options—not an unusual amount for a top executive—an increase in the company's share price of just $10 produces a $10 million windfall.

But the debate was not really about the outlandish sums that some corporate managers were getting from stock options. Instead, it was over whether options, like salaries, bonuses, and other forms of compensation, should count against earnings. Corporations insisted they should not, since no money actually flowed from company coffers. The private-sector body that sets accounting standards for all public companies said they should, since options have real value to their owners, and involve real costs to shareholders.

Mention accounting standards and most people want to change the subject. But how those standards are developed can influence the health of your investments. If companies set the standards, they would be less likely to put investors' need for greater disclosure above their own impulse to hide important details that make earnings seem less stellar. Standards produce more transparent numbers and consistency, which together help steer capital to the companies that deserve it the most. In turn, this leads to greater confidence in the markets, which makes investors even more willing to participate. Once the standard-setters ruled that companies had to deduct the value of stock options from their earnings, it came down to this for me: would the SEC guard the process by which accounting standards are developed, or would it allow companies to take over the process, thereby allowing weaker rules and undermining the capital-raising process?

The Gnomes of Norwalk

There is an organization few Americans have heard of, the Financial Accounting Standards Board (FASB, pronounced *faz-bee*), an independent, industry-funded group in Norwalk, Conn. Even if you don't understand or care to know about accounting rules, you should know what the FASB does. Its job is to help investors decide where to put their money. They do this by issuing standards to make sure that company financial reports clearly reflect the underlying financial position and the results of operations. The FASB does not favor one type or size of company over another, nor does it take public policy stands. Its aim is neutrality and transparency. If every company follows the same set of basic accounting rules, investors should be able to make apples-to-apples comparisons, and better understand what might otherwise be a jumble of numbers.

When Congress created the SEC, it mandated that publicly traded companies must submit annual financial statements that follow generally accepted accounting principles (GAAP) and are audited by a certified public accountant, or CPA. Though paid by the corporation being audited, the CPA is supposed to protect the public interest. Congress authorized the SEC to define GAAP, and for decades the agency has depended on the private sector to arrive at its own consensus on reasonable standards, which the SEC then enforces. That's where the FASB comes in.

The integrity of the markets depends on how high the FASB sets the bar and on how seriously auditors take their gatekeeper role. Over the years, however, the standard-setting process had failed to keep up with the games companies play to make their numbers appear better than they actually are. And auditing firms had grown reliant on the money they received by selling consulting services to their audit clients. Whenever the FASB tried to crack down by tightening accounting standards, it ran into a phalanx of corporate, Congressional, and auditor opposition.

Let's go back to stock options. Under GAAP, companies did not have to deduct the value of stock options from their earnings, even though options are a type of compensation, and all other forms of compensation must be deducted. For years, companies had successfully argued that subtracting options from earnings was unnecessary because no checks were actually written when options were awarded or exercised. Besides, the business lobby argued, it's too difficult to value stock options, a process that requires estimating future share prices and predicting when holders will decide to cash in. Moreover, companies warned, subtracting the cost of options from profits would have dire economic consequences. Share prices would certainly suffer. And many companies, unable to afford the earnings hit, would curtail the use of options, thus giving up a valuable recruitment and retention tool. Rank-and-file employees would no longer have a stake in their company's success, which might hurt productivity. The high-tech industry, which made generous use of options as an alternative to salaries, would especially be hurt.

None of these arguments holds up under close inspection. Money may not flow out of company coffers when options are granted, but real costs are incurred. One is the cost to existing shareholders when their equity stake is diluted, or watered down, as options are exercised. Dilution is not a minor issue. If a company has one thousand shares outstanding, and you own one hundred of them, your stake is 10 percent. But if the company grants its CEO two hundred options, it must issue two hundred new shares when the CEO exercises his options. When that happens, your stake suddenly shrinks to 8 percent. And once companies issue options, they also give up the right to sell those shares on the open market, thus forfeiting whatever cash they would have received.

And while valuing options is not simple, it's not impossible. Accounting is often imprecise, especially when it comes to estimating the future value of a corporate jet, or the losses a bank will suffer on its loans. In both cases, companies and their accountants have figured out ways to make reliable estimates. Most companies today use the Black-Scholes model, developed by economists Fischer Black and Myron Scholes, who won a Nobel Prize in economics for his work on the model, to explain to employees what their stock options are worth. Once they run that calculation, which considers such variables as the stock price when granted, the exercise price, the options' expected life, stock price fluctuations, and interest rates over the life of the option, companies can figure the long-term cost of options to shareholders.

The argument that expensing stock options might hurt share prices was akin to complaining that investors would pay less for shares if they knew that profits were inflated. Of course they would, and that was the whole point. The business lobby essentially wanted to withhold information the market needed to fully determine a company's value. No one was telling companies they could not use options as an incentive, only that they would have to fully disclose it if they did. By not subtracting options from earnings, the market and shareholders were being kept in the dark.

The FASB considered this deceptive accounting. In June 1993 it voted unanimously to put out a rule for comment that would require companies to put a fair value on their stock option grants and to record that number as an expense on the SEC-reported income statement. By the time I arrived that summer, nearly all of corporate America was vehemently fighting the FASB proposal.

The standard-setters, called the gnomes of Norwalk by some in the corporate community, were under siege. Corporate lobbyists persuaded Congress to hold hearings to condemn the FASB proposal. The pressure from Silicon Valley's high-tech industry, whose lack of revenues and weak profits made cash compensation difficult, was particularly intense. Hundreds of tech executives flew to Washington to lobby. At one point, tech workers held a noisy "rally in the valley," complete with "Stop FASB" signs and T-shirts, to show off their anger. The industry passed around alarming studies predicting that profits would decline, along with economic growth. Even the Clinton administration pressured the FASB to withdraw its rule.

Congressional Interference

Senator Joe Lieberman, the Connecticut Democrat who would become Al Gore's running mate in 2000, led the charge against the FASB rule. He introduced legislation that would bar the SEC from enforcing the FASB stock-option rule. In addition, Lieberman's measure would strip the FASB of authority by requiring the SEC to ratify every FASB decision, in effect relegating the private sector's standards to mere recommendations. Lieberman didn't stop there. He also sponsored a Senate resolution that declared the FASB proposal a cockamamy idea that would have "grave consequences for America's entrepreneurs." Joining Lieberman were numerous Republicans and a smaller group of so-called New Democrats who prided themselves for their probusiness positions, especially toward Silicon Valley, a fount of large campaign contributions. By saying that stock options were essential to growth, especially for one particular segment of the economy, these legislators essentially were arguing that transparent reporting should be secondary to other political and economic goals.

While Lieberman's bill did not pass, his resolution did—by an overwhelming 88–9. Though it was nonbinding, it was an unmistakable signal that Lieberman had the votes to stop the FASB if it pushed ahead.

I, too, was lobbied hard to oppose the FASB proposal. During my first few months in Washington I spent about one-third of my time being threatened and cajoled by legions of businesspeople who wanted to kill the proposal. I met with numerous CEOs, each of whom wanted to impress upon me the importance of stock options as a human resources tool. I recall one such discussion with Home Depot chairman Bernard Marcus, who became increasingly animated throughout our meeting, at the end of which he warned me: "This will be a terrible blow to the free enterprise system. It will make it impossible to start up new businesses." I chuckled at the notion that an accounting standard developed by an industry-backed panel might snuff out entrepreneurialism. It's not that I was unsympathetic to the arguments that stock options helped motivate employees. But I believed that options had real value and that the FASB was correct to insist that companies properly account for them as an expense. Arguments otherwise did not sway me.

Politics did, however. The controversy dragged on through the November 1994 elections, which put the Republicans in charge of the House of Representatives and vaulted Newt Gingrich, the conservative lawmaker from Georgia, into the Speaker's chair. It appeared the country had taken a sharp turn to the right, and regulation of any sort, even accounting rules proposed by a private-sector body, would come under close scrutiny. I came to the conclusion that the FASB rule would not survive in this atmosphere. I worried that, if the group continued to push for the stock-option rule, disgruntled companies would press Congress to end the FASB's role as a standard-setter. To me, that would have been worse than going without the stock-option rule.

At a private meeting with the FASB in Norwalk, I urged them to retreat. I warned them that, if they adopted the new standard, the SEC would not enforce it. Shortly thereafter, the FASB backed down in favor of a weaker rule that requires companies to disclose stock option grants in the footnotes to income statements.

In retrospect, I was wrong. I know the FASB would have stuck to its guns had I not pushed it to surrender. Out of a misguided belief that I was acting in the FASB's best interests, I failed to support this courageous and beleaguered organization in its time of need, and may have opened the door to more meddling by powerful corporations and Congress. The last thing I wanted was to politicize the FASB, which can't function if it must please every last CEO and deal with the whims of Washington lawmakers. I may also have been wrong about the political scene. By mid-1995, the country began to swing back to the center because of what many voters viewed as extreme positions taken by Gingrich and his House Republicans. The FASB might have been on solid ground, after all.

The use of stock options soon mushroomed, in large part because lax accounting encouraged them. By 2001, some 80 percent of management compensation was in the form of stock options. But instead of aligning employees' interests with shareholders', the options craze created an environment that rewarded executives for managing the share price, not for managing the business. Options gave executives strong incentives to use accounting tricks to boost the share price on which their compensation depended. And as many feared, stock options made corporate earnings look a lot better than they really were. Because of this, Federal Reserve Chairman Alan Greenspan joined the chorus of stock option critics. Fed researchers found that, between 1995 and 2000, the average earnings growth of the companies in the Standard & Poor's 500 index would have been 9.4 percent, not the 12 percent they reported, had they expensed stock options. If Cisco Systems Inc. had expensed options for its 2001 fiscal year, for example, it would have had to reduce earnings by $1.7 billion, turning a $1 billion loss into a $2.7 billion deficit. Moreover, when employees exercise their options, companies get a hefty tax break on the difference between the grant price and the exercise price. Cisco's tax deduction in 2000 came to $1.4 billion, on top of a $2.5 billion tax break in 1999.

In 2001 Oracle Corp. CEO Larry Ellison showed how options had failed as a tool to motivate managers to boost shareholder return, and instead had become a license to print money. Ellison reaped a record $706 million by cashing in his Oracle options in the same year that the software company missed earnings projections and its share price declined 57 percent.

The Takeover Attempt

Emboldened by their stock options victory, companies next tried to pull off a hostile takeover of the standard-setting process. Their target: the Financial Accounting Foundation (FAF), which is the FASB's governing board. It appoints FASB members and the board's all-important chairman, a position that would soon be vacant. High-level financial executives hoped to influence the FAF's choice of chairman. Their ultimate goal was to gain a louder voice on the board and to be able to set the FASB's agenda.

The FAF attack came from a trade group called Financial Executives Institute, now called Financial Executives International (FEI), which at the time was led by the controllers or chief financial officers of such blue-chip giants as Motorola, Procter & Gamble, General Electric, General Motors, and Citicorp (now Citigroup). Through the FEI, they fired the first volley in a November 1995 letter to the FASB's governing board, alleging that "the credibility of the FASB has significantly declined, and . . . unless major revisions are made to the process, quickly, private sector standards-setting may be jeopardized." One of the biggest complaints was what the executives considered to be the FASB's antibusiness bias and lack of "concern" for the realities of business. To fix these shortcomings, they proposed to reduce the FAF's size, impose strict time limits on projects to establish new rules, close some of the FASB's meetings to the public, establish a separate organization to set the FASB's agenda, and subject existing standards to a time limit.

I smelled a rat. Rather than speed up and improve the standard-setting process, I believed this cabal was looking to place it in the corporate equivalent of leg irons. Waiting in the wings in Norwalk was consideration of a new accounting standard that, if adopted, would require companies to reveal the current market value of derivatives on their balance sheets. Derivatives are options, interest rate swaps, and other financial products whose values are determined by other securities. A currency swap is an example of a derivative. These swaps help companies protect profits against the risk that the value of a foreign currency they hold in large quantities will move against them. In 1994, several prominent companies suffered large losses because of derivative blowups. In some cases, shareholders did not know that the companies were major users of derivatives because no rules required disclosure.

Many of the same companies behind the FAF putsch were either the biggest holders of or dealers in derivatives. The last thing they wanted was a rule that dampened the use of derivatives by forcing companies to reveal the extent to which derivatives helped them not just manage risk but also smooth the ups and downs of quarterly earnings. Putting a fair market value on their derivatives contracts also might make their balance sheets look less healthy.

At the SEC, we went on the offensive and demanded that the FAF remake itself. We wanted to increase the number of independent trustees, in the belief that only then would the FAF properly exercise its crucial role as a protector of the public interest. Of the then fourteen FAF trustees, only two could be considered truly disinterested public representatives. Four were auditors; three were corporate officials; three represented state and local governments; and one was an investment manager. Of the fourteen, ten were chosen by, and beholden to, special interest groups. The accounting profession had the right to name four FAF trustees; the FEI had two seats; the Securities Industry Association had one, and so on. Not only did we want to end the special interests' grip on the FAF, we also wanted a majority of public members, and we wanted the SEC to have veto power over who those members were. To gain some leverage over the negotiations, we played a dangerous trump card by threatening to end FASB's role as the SEC's standard-setter if our demands were not met.

The FAF's constituent groups fought back—hard. I mistakenly gave them ammunition when I insisted that Kathy Wriston, the wife of former Citicorp CEO Walter Wriston, vacate her at-large seat. I knew that Kathy Wriston was one of the FAF's most active and respected participants. She also understood complex accounting issues and she rarely missed a meeting. But I believed her seat should go to a more neutral person without her ties to the banking industry and Wall Street. It was a mistake to try to oust her, since that allowed my opponents to make her a victim and blur the larger point—that the FAF lacked members who spoke for the public interest.

The FAF just didn't see it my way. We were at loggerheads, and I was extremely frustrated. So I called General Electric CEO Jack Welch and asked him to get involved. I knew he would have the respect of the business community if he spoke in favor of a strong FASB overseen by a governing board whose members represented the investing public. I explained what was at stake: if the FAF and the FASB were weakened, they would lose credibility. The outside world would view the FASB's standards as flimsy. The private sector's ability independently to produce standards eventually would crumble. The SEC and, heaven forbid, Congress would have to fill the vacuum, and that would politicize the process for good. Welch grasped my point immediately. He suggested we bring in two other corporate *éminences grises,* Chase Manhattan CEO Walter Shipley and J.P. Morgan CEO Sandy Warner. At a dinner in Welch's corporate dining room, the three agreed to help me work out a deal that would strengthen, not weaken, the FAF.

I recall one tense meeting in the summer of 1996 in the New York office of Deloitte & Touche, whose then CEO Michael Cook was the FAF chairman. I explained why I believed the group should have a majority of independent trustees, and said that some of the current group would have to resign. I left the meeting, but my top aides—general counsel Dick Walker, counsel Michael Schlein, and chief accountant Michael Sutton—stayed behind to continue the negotiations. After several hours and little progress, the three of them trooped over to Sandy Warner's Manhattan office. With Warner conducting telephone shuttle diplomacy, the logjam broke at seven o'clock that night. The American Institute of Certified Public Accountants (AICPA) and the FEI each agreed to give up a seat. We agreed to let Kathy Wriston stay. The FAF promised to fill two at-large vacancies, bringing to 50 percent the portion of trustees who represented the public interest. We would have preferred more than that, but settled for a fifty-fifty split as a show of good faith. We also backed down on veto power, but we had the FAF's assurance that it would consult the SEC before making appointments. To prove that I wasn't trying to put a bunch of Arthur Levitt cronies on the board, I recruited three well-respected people to fill the vacant slots. They were former Federal Reserve vice-chairman Manuel Johnson; former SEC chairman David Ruder; and John Biggs, chairman and CEO of the pension fund TIAA-CREF.

The FAF showdown ended on a higher note than the one over stock options. The FASB went on to approve a new accounting standard that forced companies to reveal the value of derivatives contracts they held or were exposed to. But I came away from these back-channel brawls with one overriding impression: accounting firms were passive when it came to standing up for investor interests. It wasn't surprising that chief financial officers would fight for standards that let them understate expenses and exaggerate profits. But I was shocked when I saw how the auditors behaved in these dustups. They failed to rally to the cause of investors, and instead supported the demands of their corporate clients. They had become advocates. I would forever look upon the accounting profession differently after this episode.

How the Numbers Game Was Played

Over the next several years, a succession of SEC chief accountants—Walter Schuetze, Mike Sutton, and Lynn Turner—would warn me that they were seeing a marked increase in corporate numbers games. For example, so-called one-time restructuring charges were increasingly used to exaggerate operating performance, and hidden "cookie-jar" reserves were being used to smooth earnings from period to period. They were seeing more companies push ordinary expenses into the category of unusual, one-time, or nonrecurring costs. Then they would add these expenses back into their earnings and call the result "pro forma" earnings. To be GAAP-compliant for SEC filings, these so-called one-time expenses were properly subtracted from earnings. But many analysts and investors didn't bother to read filings made four to six weeks after a company had issued its quarterly earnings release. It was old news by then. Analysts who did read the SEC disclosures often waved them off as irrelevant historical reports that revealed little about a company's future.

More than any other accounting trick, "pooling of interests" was responsible for the 1990s merger spree, especially among high-tech companies with soaring stock prices but little in the way of profits. Pooling occurred when two companies merged their assets at book value, ignoring the much higher purchase price one paid for the other. This practice made it seem as if both had always been one entity, and allowed CEOs to hide from shareholders the huge premiums they were paying for acquisitions. Say a technology company bought a smaller one for billions of dollars. No cash changed hands. Instead, one company simply issued stock to the shareholders of the acquired company. The purchase price more often than not would be far above the value of the start-up's physical assets. This difference was called "goodwill."

Goodwill is an accounting term for the amount of the purchase price over and above the fair market value of the acquired assets. Companies wanted to use pooling for a good reason. Goodwill had to be depreciated, or included as an expense, over as many as forty years, depressing earnings over that period. (This rule has since been changed.) But with pooling, companies could pretend no goodwill was acquired, thus artificially inflating their earnings.

Through creative use of these and other accounting conventions, we began to see a pattern in company earnings announcements. Corporations were playing with the earnings calculation until they arrived at the best possible number. Earnings press releases revealed only the good news—or those details that helped boost the share price. Auditors, increasingly captives of their clients, would give them the clean audits they wanted, despite lots of chicanery. Consulting fees—for everything from information technology design and installation to management compensation advice and merger analysis—were pouring in. Audit fees made up 70 percent of accounting firm revenues in 1976 but only 31 percent in 1998. More and more, it became clear that the auditors didn't want to do anything to rock the boat with clients, potentially jeopardizing their chief source of income. Consulting contracts were turning accounting firms into extensions of management—even cheerleaders at times. Some firms even paid their auditors on how many nonaudit services they sold to their clients.

The accountants were also doing internal audits for companies. That meant that auditors were part of the very control systems producing the financial statements that they later audited. By conducting internal audits as well as external audits for SEC reports, some auditors were passing judgment on their own work.

Within the auditing profession itself, there was no watchdog willing to discipline unethical conduct. In case after case we saw auditors who failed to probe behind the numbers CFOs gave them. We saw improper applications of GAAP. And we saw auditors who were more than willing to overlook major accounting infractions by company officials on the rationale that they were "immaterial," or too small to matter.

Analysts, themselves reliant on investment banking deals for their compensation, were equally reluctant to blow the whistle. Many analysts had also grown dependent on company leaks of upcoming earnings figures. Companies that refused to leak, or that failed to meet analysts' earnings expectations, swiftly found their shares being dumped in retribution. That induced CFOs to play the numbers game even more.

Boards of directors, and especially the audit committees that are supposed to oversee the auditing process, were either asleep at the wheel or lacked the expertise to challenge the CFO. Adding to the problem was the out-of-control stock market, the frenzy of initial public offerings of dot-coms, and the unsupportable market valuations of technology and telecommunication companies. The rise of momentum investing, in which day traders and other investors buy shares on the basis of one all-important measure—whether a company's earnings per share grew in the latest quarter—pushed the market to new heights. It seemed the entire country had succumbed to a get-rich-quick mentality. Standards were for dummies.

It wasn't just a case of a few bad apples, either. Blue-chip companies with sterling reputations were manipulating their numbers in ways that were downright misleading. We quickly learned that if we let one company get away with stretching the boundaries of acceptable accounting, other companies flocked there—and beyond. It became hard to discern exactly what a company earned and what its stock was worth.

Over the next four years, from 1997 through 2000, 700 companies would belatedly find flaws in past financial statements and restate their earnings. By comparison, only three companies restated earnings in 1981. The restatements came at a tremendous cost to investors, whose shares would lose tens of billions of dollars in market value. I'm fairly certain that many investors never knew what happened to them.

The Solution: Independent Auditors

Honest numbers, and investor confidence, depend on auditor independence. Without independent audits, investors have no basis to believe that a company's reported numbers are correct. Audited financial statements are the means by which we decide where to put our capital. Naturally, we want our money to go to the companies that we believe will give us the highest return on our dollar. In turn, our investment helps create jobs and boost overall economic growth. An investor's analysis starts off with a review of the financial statements. These offer a snapshot of how well the company performed in the past quarter or year, and whether management achieved what it promised. Lenders, bondholders, credit rating agencies, suppliers, customers, and shareholders all rely on unbiased financial reports. And that's why auditors must be like the umpire in a baseball game and call 'em like they see 'em.

Independence means that auditors should not be in bed with the corporate managers whose numbers they audit. They cannot review their own work or that of their partners. If an accountant keeps the books for a client, he can't turn around and vouch for the accuracy and completeness of those books. After all, what accountants would want to draw attention to their own mistakes?

These aren't just my own high-minded ideals. The U.S. Supreme Court, in a 1984 decision in *U.S. v. Arthur Young,* confirmed the auditor's watchdog function when it wrote that the auditor's "ultimate allegiance" is to "a corporation's creditors and stockholders, as well as to the investing public." The High Court further stated that the watchdog function "demands that the accountant maintain total independence from the audit client at all times and requires complete fidelity to the public trust." To maintain such checks and balances, auditors are not allowed to own stock, for example, in a client company.

The solution rested on three pillars. Regulators at the SEC and standard-setters at the FASB had to improve the transparency of financial statements and insist, through SEC enforcement actions if necessary, that companies adhere to the letter and spirit of GAAP. The auditing profession had to renew its commitment to independence and discipline the auditors behind the growing number of failed audits. And corporate managers had to change their culture, from one of massaging earnings to meet Wall Street's expectations at any cost, to letting the unvarnished numbers tell the story. In a speech given at New York University on September 28, 1998, called "The Numbers Game," I laid out the SEC's agenda to tackle all three areas. Starting that day and continuing to the end of my tenure, there was no turning back. The SEC aggressively pursued this agenda. But the accounting industry and its allies in the business community and on Capitol Hill also pursued theirs. Every time we made a move, they fought back.

Even before the speech, we had proposed that the SEC and the AICPA together establish a new body to set independence standards for auditors of public companies. It took a year of frustrating negotiations, but the AICPA and the Big Five accounting firms begrudgingly went along with the formation of a new group called the Independence Standards Board (ISB). Harvey Pitt, my successor as SEC chairman, represented the accounting industry in these talks. At the time, Pitt was a partner in the law firm of Fried, Frank, Harris, Shriver & Jacobson, where he represented the AICPA and each of the Big Five, along with numerous other securities industry clients. The ISB's charter called on it to come up with rules that hopefully would renew the accounting profession's commitment to auditor independence. At the top of my list: new rules that would keep the growth of consulting from compromising audits. The ISB came into being in May 1997, with half its members representing the accounting industry and the other half representing the public (either side had veto power).

I was to learn that every positive step forward by the accounting industry was always accompanied by a giant step backward. The AICPA commissioned a lengthy white paper, presented at the ISB's first meeting, to question the need for national standards at all. Instead, it suggested that the ISB outline broad principles. From those, each firm would customize its specific standards, and each auditor would determine whether he was in compliance. The paper also took the SEC to task for its overreaching "command and control" regulations. Finally, the paper argued that firms should be able to perform almost any service provided certain safeguards were in place. Indeed, the document advocated the expansion of nonaudit services as a means of improving the quality of audits.

The white paper's lead author was the very same Harvey Pitt who helped us create the ISB. Even after becoming the agency's chairman in August 2001 (he would resign in November 2002), Pitt continued to hold the view that the growth of consulting does not interfere with auditor independence. To him, the solution to the industry's problems are new rules that require companies to disclose more information, and more frequently than once a quarter, about their operations and strategic plans. More disclosures would be an important step. But I believe that the first priority and critical need is to get companies and their accountants to comply with existing rules.

The AICPA deftly maneuvered itself into position with the ISB. It supplied the ISB's agenda, staff, and funding. It soon became clear to me that the AICPA had gone along with the ISB's creation because it believed it could control the group. This was typical for the AICPA, which for decades had managed to co-opt numerous other commissions, study panels, and disciplinary bodies set up to rein in the industry. In protest, I boycotted the ISB's first meeting. The ISB's stormy first few months of existence did not bode well for its future effectiveness. Over the next two years, it would get bogged down in endless discussions over where to draw the line of independence. The SEC would have to take matters into its own hands.

The SEC Cracks Down, But FASB Relents

SEC chief accountant Turner and his staff, meanwhile, were busy pumping out accounting bulletins to clarify existing accounting rules. These bulletins closed off some of the most popular methods companies were using to cook their books. One such missive, called *Staff Accounting Bulletin 101,* was issued to clarify when companies could record revenue on their books.

The target of *SAB 101* was the growing tendency by companies to book revenues prematurely. Errors in revenue recognition were a major factor in recent earnings restatements. A common ploy involved recognizing all at once the total value of a multiyear contract, when only portions of the contract's revenues were earned each year. Once again, the main culprit was the high-tech industry, which was under pressure to boost revenues quarter after quarter, in line with analysts' expectations. We knew of technology equipment companies that were booking revenues when they received up-front payments on multiyear service contracts, not when they satisfied contractual milestones, as accounting rules dictate. We also knew of cases in which companies were booking revenue before they shipped computer or networking gear, contravening rules that say revenue cannot be recognized until equipment is received by the customer and the customer has agreed to pay for it.

The outcry from Silicon Valley was deafening. Numerous members of Congress and tech industry lobbyists called or wrote to request a delay in the date by which company reports had to comply with the bulletin (even though it was only a clarification of existing rules). They pressed their case with Senator Phil Gramm, who chaired the Senate Banking Committee, which oversees the SEC. The Texas Republican was a tough customer, and we never took lightly a Phil Gramm request to delay a rule. Concerned that we were making policy through staff bulletins, Gramm called several times and wrote letters seeking a postponement, even though we had already twice delayed the effective date.

If Gramm and the many other lawmakers pushing for postponement had had their way, *SAB 101* would not have taken effect until after the November 2000 elections. At that point a Republican administration might have decided not to issue the bulletin at all. We rejected these entreaties. In the end, we were proven right: some two hundred companies had to change their future accounting practices to comply with *SAB 101*.

Two of Silicon Valley's leading lights came to lobby me personally around this time. Cisco Systems CEO John Chambers and venture capitalist John Doerr, a partner in the venture capital firm of Kleiner Perkins Caufield & Byers, showed up in my office in the fall of 1999. They were irritated by a recent FASB proposal to end pooling of interests for mergers. An end to pooling would especially hurt Cisco, which was in the middle of a five-year acquisition spree. Pooling allowed Cisco to inflate earnings by avoiding deductions for billions of dollars' worth of goodwill.

I told them that I supported the FASB's efforts to get rid of pooling because it had become subject to much abuse and was highly misleading to investors. When I refused to back down, Chambers three times reminded me that he had "lots of friends in this city." In his not-so-subtle way, Chambers was implying that he had leverage at the White House and on Capitol Hill, and could use it to force me to retreat. I had to restrain my temper before showing him the door.

Chambers and Doerr easily found sympathetic listeners on Capitol Hill, and I heard from dozens of them over the next few months. Interestingly, I never heard a peep from the White House, the Treasury Department, or any other branch of the Clinton administration on accounting matters or other issues. Maybe the captains of the tech industry didn't have as many committed friends in the capital as they thought.

Chambers and Doerr, along with an army of other technology executives, worked their magic on Congress and the FASB, however. Gramm's Senate Banking Committee held hearings. Technology company CEOs swarmed all over Capitol Hill to press their case. It was déjà vu all over again. The standard-setters, in the end, got rid of pooling of interests for mergers. But at the same time they made it easier for companies such as Cisco to cope with the goodwill burden that would show up on their books from future acquisitions. They did this by not requiring companies to count as an expense a portion of the goodwill they were carrying. Today, goodwill no longer cuts into earnings. Instead, companies must examine their acquisitions to see if the goodwill they acquired is "impaired," or still worth the price they paid. If not, they must reduce the value of the asset on the balance sheet. Interestingly, this was exactly the outcome that Gramm advocated to me months earlier during a meeting in his office. I guess the politicians were setting accounting standards after all, despite my efforts to shield the FASB from political interference.

In 2002, companies began writing down billions of dollars worth of 1990s-era acquisitions. Instead of getting punished in the market for making bad decisions and vastly overpaying for their purchases, corporate execs were waving a magic wand over their mistakes and attributing these massive write-downs to a "change in accounting principle." The FASB had succumbed to corporate pressure. By allowing subjective inputs, it enabled companies to massage away goodwill and recast their earnings. The costly legacy of this compromise is likely to be years of financial reports that fail to reflect the true economics of many business combinations.

As I hosted a steady stream of unhappy corporate lobbyists, the SEC's Enforcement Division wrestled with numerous, high-profile probes of accounting fraud. These investigations, against such companies as Waste Management Inc. and Sunbeam Corp., involved allegations of aggressive accounting to disguise poor earnings growth. They also involved earnings restatements going as far back as five years. In Waste Management's restatement, for example, the company admitted that it had exaggerated earnings by $1.4 billion from 1992 to 1997—at the time, the largest restatement in history—causing its share price to plummet and investors to lose $26 billion.

But it would take three years to piece together the evidence needed to bring a case that would hold up in court. The SEC eventually would allege—four months after my February 2001 departure—that Waste Management, with the help of its auditor, Arthur Andersen, had manipulated its financial statements to hide $1.7 billion in expenses. One way the company did so was by arbitrarily increasing the useful life of its garbage trucks, thus failing to properly depreciate the trucks (depreciation is an expense and thus it reduces earnings). At the same time, the waste hauler declared an increase in the salvage value of its trucks. In other words, the more the trucks were used, and the older they became, the more the company said they were worth.

The SEC alleged that Andersen had known about this and numerous other instances of improper accounting by Waste Management. Not only had Andersen allowed them to go uncorrected, but it had knowingly put its stamp of approval on four years of false and misleading financial statements, the SEC charged. It's no wonder. Andersen had audited Waste Management since it became a public company in 1971. Until 1997, every CFO and chief accounting officer in Waste Management's history had previously worked as an auditor at Andersen. In the 1990s, some fourteen ex-Andersen employees worked at Waste Management in key financial positions.

Without admitting or denying guilt, Andersen paid a $7 million fine and agreed to an injunction that prohibited it from future misdeeds. The settlement would serve as the accounting firm's undoing: After the Enron meltdown, the Justice Department would use Andersen's violation of its pledge not to break accounting rules again as one of the main reasons for indicting the entire firm, instead of just the individual Andersen partners involved in the Enron audits.

It would take another nine months, until March 2002, before the SEC would bring charges against six former Waste Management executives for manipulating the company's books, allegations that the former officials deny. Another landmark case, this one against Sunbeam, would take just as long to complete. Even though Sunbeam CEO Albert Dunlap was ousted by his board in 1998 because of a major accounting scandal, it would be May 2001 before the SEC would bring charges of accounting fraud against him, other officers, a partner at Sunbeam's auditor—once again, Arthur Andersen—and the company itself. The company settled the charges without admitting fault, as did the auditor's lead partner, whom the SEC barred from practice for three years. Dunlap and his chief financial officer were barred permanently from serving as officers or directors of any public company. Dunlap also paid $15 million out of his own pocket to settle a separate civil suit brought by shareholders.

While we suspected serious irregularities at Waste Management and Sunbeam, we could not use these investigative bombshells to bolster our contention in the summer of 2000 that something was dreadfully wrong with the state of accounting. We had to find other ways to correct the problems we were seeing but could not yet publicize.

We did get help from the stock exchanges. At the SEC's urging, the New York Stock Exchange and the National Association of Securities Dealers, the parent of the Nasdaq Stock Market, set up a blue-ribbon panel to study ways to improve the vigilance of board audit committees. These committees are supposed to oversee the audit process, but for many reasons they were outgunned by management, and especially crafty CFOs who could not meet Wall Street's earnings expectations without massaging their numbers. At the end of 1999, the stock exchanges agreed that companies, as a condition for listing their stock, had to have audit committees whose members were independent of management. The audit committees also had to be made up of board members who were financially literate, and at least one had to be an expert in finance and accounting.

But the accounting industry itself continued to stonewall, arguing that independence was no issue at all. On the contrary, it seemed to us at the SEC that the surge in consulting revenues at the Big Five firms raised serious questions about whether the independence of the audit, the most valuable public service provided by the profession, was being compromised. The time had come to regulate.

The Anonymous Letter

In the winter of 1997, an anonymous letter arrived at the SEC's Southeast Regional Office in Miami. It would greatly improve the hand we were holding. The letter alleged that certain audit staff in the Tampa, Fla., office of Coopers & Lybrand owned stock in the companies they were auditing. If true, this was a violation of independence rules if ever there was one.

We didn't take the letter seriously at first because the writer, we learned, had recently been fired. We had to be sure she wasn't making wild charges to harass her former bosses and coworkers. Once we investigated, though, we found that the violations in the Tampa office were even more widespread than our whistle-blower realized.

While we were investigating, Coopers merged with Price Waterhouse to form PricewaterhouseCoopers (PwC), reducing the Big Six accounting firms to the Big Five. But the merger also exacerbated the stock ownership problem. After the merger, Coopers partners and staff had to divest shares they owned in companies audited by Price Waterhouse, and vice versa. Some of the required divestitures, however, never took place. At the SEC's insistence, PwC hired a special counsel to conduct a nationwide internal investigation. The results shocked us.

PwC partners, it seemed, viewed compliance with the stock ownership rules as merely optional. The investigation uncovered an incredible 8,000 violations, involving half the firm's partners. A random check also showed that three-fourths of PwC partners had failed to disclose violations of independence rules when they were asked to do so voluntarily. Admittedly, some were minor infractions, such as when the shares in question were held in trust for the children of a partner. Some, however, were more serious. The heads of major PwC divisions and top managers in charge of enforcing the conflict-of-interest rules owned stock in audit clients.

Even PwC chief executive James Schiro owned forbidden stock. He and eight other partners owned shares in Emcore, a New Jersey semiconductor manufacturer whose auditor had been Coopers & Lybrand, and then PwC after the merger. Schiro was obligated to sell his shares by the end of July 1998, but instead he transferred them to a family member who sold them at the end of the year—five months after the merger and two months after PwC had completed Emcore's audit. The SEC did not charge him with an independence violation.

Because of the massive number of stock-ownership infractions, we now had irrefutable evidence of independence violations by PwC, the largest of the Big Five. When an auditor violates independence rules, the SEC has the right to reject audit clients' filings. Had the SEC taken that step, PwC almost certainly would have been fired by hundreds of companies. With that possibility hanging like a sword over PwC, the firm agreed to conduct an internal investigation.

Once again, we entered into protracted negotiations, this time to get the remaining four firms to examine their own past compliance with stock ownership rules. It was during these talks that the AICPA made one of its biggest blunders. The Big Five firms, using the AICPA as a conduit, provided most of the funds for a panel called the Public Oversight Board (POB). This five-person panel, which went out of business in May 2002, was even more obscure than the FASB, but its intended role in helping to maintain the credibility of the capital markets was just as important. The AICPA created the POB to carry out certain self-regulatory functions to forestall tougher regulation after a wave of 1970s audit failures.

Since 1977, the POB had reviewed the quality of audits and overseen the peer review process, in which accounting firms scrutinize one another's quality controls and audit procedures. At our request, in the spring of 2000 the POB began preparing to conduct the stock ownership probes for the rest of the Big Five. But when the POB hired a law firm and a consultant to help with the reviews, the AICPA balked. In a May 2000 letter to the POB, the AICPA said that it "will not approve nor authorize payment for invoices submitted by the Public Oversight Board or its representatives that contain charges for the special reviews. . . ." This was a declaration of war by the accountants.

After months of grueling back-and-forth, we were able to strike a deal that June 2000. Each of the firms agreed to hire an independent counsel to look for any financial interests in audit clients by auditors or their firms during the nine-month period ending March 31, 2000. In exchange, the SEC agreed not to prosecute firms for voluntarily reporting minor violations. In addition, the firms agreed to let the POB review the adequacy of the firms' efforts to ensure that stock ownership problems did not crop up again. This would involve reviews of training programs, random checks of partners' investments, and testing of computer systems set up to alert auditors if they bought stock in a client company. While the independent counsel "lookbacks" have been completed, the POB's investigation never got off the ground because of industry foot-dragging in turning over internal records that the POB needed, says Chuck Bowsher, the POB chairman at the time. Because of this, and because the POB felt that SEC chairman Pitt's proposal for a new accounting oversight board, post-Enron, did not include any role for the POB, it voted itself out of existence. The lesson of this episode is crystal clear: self-regulation by the accounting profession is a bad joke. They wanted the POB to remain a gentlemen's debating society and planned to keep it on a tight leash. The firms would never subject themselves to scrutiny unless forced to do so.

Each of the items on our agenda—protecting the FASB from outside interference, investigating stock ownership by auditors in client corporations, changing the composition of audit committees, issuing SEC staff accounting bulletins—helped us in part to achieve our goal of more accurate numbers and greater investor confidence. But much work remained.

The big sticking point was still auditor independence. The stock market had reached dizzying heights, and the corporate numbers game had grown more and more brazen. It began to appear as if the towering market rested on fictitious numbers. The ISB was proving to be a dead end as a solution to this mess, and the accounting industry was using all its political, legal, and financial clout to fight us, so we invited the three most recalcitrant accounting firm CEOs to discuss our plans to issue new rules. But the three—KPMG chairman Stephen Butler, Arthur Andersen CEO Robert Grafton, and Deloitte & Touche CEO James Copeland—refused to see us anywhere but on their own premises. We agreed to convene at Deloitte & Touche's midtown Manhattan office on June 20.

Two of the Big Five weren't present, for separate reasons. Price-waterhouseCoopers, because of its massive stock ownership violations, had little choice but to be uncommonly cooperative. And Ernst & Young was in the process of seeking SEC approval to complete the sale of its consulting business to French computer consulting giant Cap Gemini Group, and didn't want to jinx those talks. They pledged neutrality, but they didn't always remain so as the accounting industry waged guerrilla warfare against the SEC over the next five months.

The atmosphere at Deloitte & Touche was frigid. The firm leaders sat across the conference table from chief accountant Turner, former general counsel and now legal adviser Harvey Goldschmid, and me like combatants, cross-armed and stony-faced. They said that our planned rules would severely limit the kinds of consulting services they could perform for their audit clients, and they would never abide by that. As we explained our reasons for regulating, they said little and yielded nothing. I asked them to help us arrive at a solution, but they wanted nothing to do with rules that would force them to give up their profitable consulting businesses for audit clients. At one point, Arthur Andersen CEO Bob Grafton said, "Arthur, if you go ahead with this, it will be war." After ninety minutes, we left. They had drawn a clear line in the sand.

Independence Defined

The rules proposed a week later did not ban auditors from doing all consulting work for their audit clients, but they did severely limit such activities. For example, if an accounting firm designed and installed a financial information system, it could not audit the numbers that such customized software produced. After all, what auditor would alienate both his own firm and his client by pointing out flaws in a multimillion-dollar software program designed by his firm?

The proposal also said that any accountant who acted as a company's internal auditor could not also be the public auditor. Other verboten areas included designing compensation systems, acting in an advocacy role, as by giving legal advice or engaging in lobbying activities, providing bookkeeping services, conducting appraisals, recruiting or evaluating employees, and giving investment advice.

We believed that by providing any of these services, auditors were jeopardizing their objectivity by acting as a management adjunct or by reviewing their own work. That would be like a student grading her own term paper.

The firms mounted a no-holds-barred public relations and lobbying campaign to stop us. They accused us of pushing a last-gasp attempt to regulate in the dying days of the Clinton administration. This baffled me. From October 1999 through June 2000, we held dozens of meetings with the accounting firms to try to find a solution to the independence dilemma. For the previous six years, I barely had a conversation or meeting with accounting industry leaders in which I did not press them to act on independence.

More substantively, they argued that the rules were unnecessary. The SEC, they said, had not proven that any auditor had compromised himself in order to win or keep a consulting contract. And the SEC, they argued, could not point to a single case in which a lack of auditor independence caused an audit failure. This "no smoking gun" argument was harder to fight. No auditor would ever admit that he allowed bad numbers because he wanted to bring more consulting business to the firm. But the ascendancy of consulting and the coincidence of accounting misdeeds, company restatements, and billions in shareholder losses were too striking to dismiss as happenstance.

The no-smoking-gun argument worked wonders on Capitol Hill. Members of Congress parroted it back to us in letters, phone calls, and personal visits, as they sought to persuade us to withdraw the rule. Post-Enron, the argument has come back to haunt many lawmakers, who now look shortsighted for arguing that a regulator shouldn't take preventive action to stop disasters like Enron from happening. Of course, I could not have known that Enron would melt down a year later. But why wait for a corporate train wreck to justify a separation of auditing from consulting, when we could prevent one now?

Then there was the New Economy angle—that the SEC needed to forget about "command and control" regulation and instead focus on new standards for technology and service companies whose value GAAP failed to capture. For example, the argument went, human assets, market share, quality of customer service, Web-site traffic, and other "intangibles" never appear on company balance sheets, and yet investors view them as valuable assets. Moreover, GAAP is backward-looking, the argument went. Today's investors want real-time updates of information, not the out-of-date snapshot that an annual report provides. And by restricting auditors from consulting for the same company, they won't be able to develop the techniques to measure these assets and give investors a clearer picture.

The "we can't measure the New Economy" argument was a canard. Nothing in our rule prevented companies from hiring accounting firms to develop these measures. They just can't hire the same firm that audits their books. Furthermore, nothing in our rule stopped companies from providing investors more real-time information. In fact, I favor more disclosure on a real-time basis. But that shouldn't excuse companies from putting out GAAP-compliant statements once a quarter. The numbers must be reliable and comparable. Indeed, the historical statements are a report card on management. Can you imagine capital markets functioning efficiently with no periodic reckoning of the numbers?

Accounting firms had one other major argument. They insisted that they would not be able to recruit and retain the best audit talent if 25 percent to 40 percent of the market—the range of business that they estimated would be affected at any one firm—is off limits. The best and brightest college grads, the argument went, would not be interested in working at a company with limited career opportunities. This argument's hidden message was that the universe of consulting business would shrink and audit quality would decline if auditors could not consult.

This was hogwash. If an Ernst & Young audit client required expert help with information technology, it could go to four of the other Big Five. Corporations wouldn't necessarily go outside the Big Five, which had built up considerable expertise in designing large computer systems, just because they couldn't use their own auditors.

The argument also papered over the fact that accounting firms were already having trouble recruiting college grads. The average annual growth rate in revenues for management advisory services was 26 percent from 1993 to 1999. But over the same period, the number of candidates sitting for the CPA exam dropped from 53,763 to 38,573. The percentage of students majoring in accounting fell from 4 percent in 1990 to 2 percent in 2000. Clearly, the firms were having trouble interesting college grads in accounting careers despite the lure of their consulting sidelines. They could hardly blame accounting's lack of magnetism on a rule that hadn't yet taken effect. Besides, if young people were uninterested in auditing, the profession bore much of the responsibility for downgrading the importance of audits. The salaries the firms were offering to auditor recruits, we discovered, had fallen way behind the offers they were making to new consultants.

The Lobbying Begins

Soon, I was spending almost all my time deflecting a barrage of phone calls, visits, and letters from House and Senate members. Within a month of issuing the proposed rule, I received negative letters from forty-six members of Congress, including two-thirds of the Senate Banking Committee's Securities Subcommittee. Even normally pro-consumer Democratic senators, such as Evan Bayh of Indiana and Oregon's Ron Wyden, opposed the rule. Some, such as Pennsylvania Republican Rick Santorum, asked me to postpone a final vote on the rule until 2001. The aim, of course, was to wait for a possible George W. Bush administration, which would almost certainly nix the proposal. Others simply demanded that I back down. They questioned the SEC's authority to regulate accounting firms, and some threatened to cut the agency's funding. I heard from dozens more lawmakers over the coming months.

The accountants fired back by opening the campaign contribution spigot. The Big Five firms, their partners, and the AICPA pumped gobs of money into the election coffers of hundreds of Congressional candidates and the Bush campaign. Altogether, they gave $14.5 million in the 2000 election cycle, according to the Center for Responsive Politics, a nonpartisan research group. The center lists the industry as number 27 in total contributions, out of 122 sectors it ranks. That puts accountants above the defense industry but below telecoms. Each of the Big Five also appears on the list of President Bush's top twenty contributors.

And boy did those donations get results. Not only could the AICPA get lawmakers to contact me on demand, they also persuaded the Senate Banking Committee's Securities Subcommittee to hold a hearing; its chairman, Minnesota Republican Rod Grams, had received $60,000 from the industry. (He would lose his reelection bid that November.)

We sought to neutralize the Senate Banking Committee, which could especially wreak havoc as the agency's oversight committee. We decided to do something unique in SEC history: to let Enforcement Division director Dick Walker give the panel a confidential briefing, without company names, about several serious cases of alleged audit failure that his staff was investigating. The cases all involved allegations of auditors compromising their audits out of fear of jeopardizing a consulting relationship with the client. In one case, the auditors agreed to overlook numerous infractions after obtaining promises from the client that it would correct the problems the following year. In another case, the auditor willingly went along with the client company's claim that an egregious error did not involve enough money to be material. The chief financial officer of one of the companies had previously worked for the outside audit firm, and was able to influence the compensation of the accountants on the audit team. By the end of the briefing, a number of senators were shaking their heads in disbelief. The saber-rattling by the committee, especially the charge that the SEC had no smoking gun, decreased. Meanwhile, chief accountant Lynn Turner and I over a four-week period briefed two dozen other House and Senate members on the reasons for the auditor independence rules.

If the accountants failed to get their way by lobbying Congress or by using the influence of campaign contributions, they were ready to sue us. Arthur Andersen hired David Boies, the lawyer who fashioned the government's antitrust case against Microsoft

Corp.; the AICPA retained the Gibson, Dunn & Crutcher law firm. Their legal strategy was to challenge the SEC's authority to dictate to accounting firms whom they can and cannot do business with.

As I was trying to cope with this frenzy, I received an ominous phone call from Phil Gramm, who opposed the rule but who had a finely tuned sense of fair play. The senator warned me that his colleague, Alabama Republican Richard Shelby, was preparing an "appropriations rider," or an amendment to our funding bill that would bar the agency from spending any of its funds to implement and enforce the rule. A similar amendment, to be sponsored by Texas Republican Henry Bonilla, was in the works on the House side. Appropriations riders are difficult to fight because they are almost always offered in closed-door, members-only meetings. When spending bills go to the floor, lawmakers often vote on the figures they contain without seeing the accompanying riders until after the vote. Gramm advised me to cut a deal with the accountants, or else the riders would pass.

Alarmed, I called Senator Trent Lott, then majority leader, at home. I pleaded with the Mississippi Republican not to let this important issue be resolved by dead-of-night appropriations riders. "No matter what you think about the issue," I said, "the process should be aboveboard." I told him that numerous publications, including the *New York Times, Los Angeles Times, Washington Post,* and *Business Week,* had all endorsed the rule. "Well, Arthur," Lott said, "I'm not familiar with what you're proposing to do, but if those liberal publications are in favor of it, then I'm against it."

With that, it was clear that I would be heading into rough waters if I moved ahead with the proposal. Most of all, I feared retribution in the form of a funding cut for the agency. Never before had the SEC faced such a threat to its independence. What's more, I was simultaneously pleading with Congress to raise the salaries of SEC lawyers and other professionals to prevent a brain drain to the private sector. Not only would Congress almost certainly reject this request, but vindictive lawmakers could decimate the SEC's budget and tie its hands for years to come. Such an outcome would hurt not just the auditor independence rules. It would also impair the

SEC's ability to take on any new projects or carry out its day-to-day responsibilities to police the stock and bond markets, oversee the mutual fund industry, and monitor thousands of public company filings. The possibility of a drawn-out legal challenge also gave me pause. For one thing, the industry would almost certainly get the matter delayed into the next administration, the result it was so fervently lobbying for. And there was always the risk that the federal courts would tie our hands in some way.

The Compromise

We had no choice but to compromise. But even that wasn't easy, since three of the Big Five and the AICPA weren't even on speaking terms with the SEC. For several weeks, I sought an invitation to speak to this group because I believed that its management team was misrepresenting our proposed rule, especially when it came to the effect that it would have on the vast majority of the AICPA's membership—the small audit firms. The AICPA was trying to scare these firms by telling them that our proposal would put them out of business. The truth was quite different: Small firms rarely audit public companies, and so our rule would hardly affect them.

But AICPA president Barry Melancon resisted my many requests to speak to his group. At one point, he said he would extend me an offer but only if I secretly agreed in advance to turn it down. Two weeks before his group's annual meeting in Las Vegas in September 2000, Melancon finally relented. He granted me time to deliver a short speech but made no room for a question-and-answer session afterward. The group listened politely to my pitch, but I knew I didn't win them over.

Just as the situation seemed hopeless, Joseph Berardino, a managing partner of Arthur Andersen, played a crucial role. Berardino, who later briefly served as Arthur Andersen's CEO until he resigned because of the Enron disaster, broke ranks with KPMG and Deloitte & Touche, unbeknown to both firms. For weeks he worked with SEC general counsel David Becker to craft an acceptable compromise. At the same time, Becker, chief accountant

Turner, and I began an intense game of three-dimensional chess as we tried to shape what that compromise would look like. We knew, for example, that what might be acceptable to one firm could be rejected by the others. Or that what might be acceptable to the Big Five would be abhorrent to the AICPA.

The proposed ban on computer-systems consulting was far and away the most threatening part of the rule. Information technology (IT) services were the largest and the fastest-growing services accountants were offering. Ernst & Young and PwC already had told us they would accept a ban on IT consulting. This was not a huge concession on their part: Ernst & Young had sold its computer services consulting arm and PwC had announced plans to sell its consulting business to Hewlett-Packard Co. The rest of the Big Five, however, would not accept such a ban.

We scrambled to come up with an alternative. This involved requiring companies to disclose in their proxy statements the amount they paid their audit firms for consulting services, with IT broken out separately. This way, investors could judge for themselves if an auditor was truly independent. Berardino said he thought he could sell this compromise to his colleagues. But once Ernst & Young and PwC got wind of our climb-down on an IT consulting ban, they accused us of stabbing them in the back.

We also had to wrestle with whether auditors could perform internal audits, that is, help produce the very financial statements the independent auditor is supposed to review. The proposal called for an outright ban, but we were willing to accept that no company could rely on its independent auditor for more than 40 percent of internal audit services. Once again, Berardino got KPMG, Arthur Andersen, and Deloitte to agree.

There was one more sticky issue. The Big Five objected to the part of the proposal that said an auditor must be independent in fact and appearance. This reflected the strong belief by many of us at the SEC that auditors had to address the popular perception that they were turning a blind eye to accounting improprieties. To restore their credibility, auditors had to show that they were independent in both fact and appearance. They should avoid doing anything that leads investors to doubt their independence. We insisted, therefore, that an auditor could violate independence rules if a "reasonable investor" looked at a set of circumstances and concluded that the auditor was incapable of acting without bias. This meant that an auditor couldn't hide behind the absence of direct evidence—a remark to a colleague or a diary notation, for example—to escape punishment. This test also meant that while the SEC rule named specific acts—providing actuarial or appraisal services, giving investment advice, owning stock in a client company, and the like—there could be times when other, unnamed services might cause a conflict. As you can imagine, the Big Five balked over an appearance standard, but on this one, we held our ground.

Berardino was a calming influence. He lowered the rhetoric at a time of high tension. But by November 5, 2000—the Monday before the presidential election—we still had no final agreement, despite tremendous Congressional pressure. We needed another week to forge a compromise. In the meantime, we did not want anyone to conclude that our final decision was based on which party won the election. So that day we announced that the SEC would adopt final rules the following week.

At the end of the week, Deloitte & Touche CEO James Copeland called to propose a meeting. We met in my conference room. Copeland, Arthur Andersen CEO Bob Grafton, KPMG chairman Steve Butler, and AICPA president Melancon participated. Berardino was traveling in Europe. I described the major points in our package and said, "Take it or leave it." In hindsight, hubris was probably not the best approach. But we had already given up much ground on IT consulting and internal audits and could not retreat any further. Our terms included disclosure of IT services and a 40 percent cap on the amount of internal audit work the auditor could perform. We also wanted audit committees to state publicly whether they had considered the effect of consulting services on auditor independence. There would be no change in the appearance standard. Finally, we wanted AICPA president Melancon's pledge to boost to one-half the ratio of public representatives on an AICPA disciplinary board.

The firms and Melancon caucused among themselves for forty-five minutes and came back saying they couldn't accept our terms. A key point of disagreement: whether auditors had to be independent in fact as well as appearance. The meeting ended with everyone walking away in a huff.

The next morning, Berardino called Becker from Europe and asked, "What the hell happened? I thought we had everything worked out?" Luckily, Berardino was committed to getting the talks going again, and spent the next forty-eight hours playing diplomat. He was willing to split with KPMG over the appearance issue, as was Deloitte & Touche. With those two firms joining Ernst & Young and PwC on the appearance standard we had four out of five firms on board. Melancon, however, held his ground. This was no surprise. For the past few years, Melancon had followed a stubborn "no how, no way" strategy that I believe cost the profession dearly. Whenever compromise seemed possible, Melancon would hold out.

Ernst & Young and PwC had a different problem. They felt we had hung them out to dry because we were no longer going to ban the firms from providing IT consulting services to audit clients. But that weekend, by some miracle, the proposed $18 billion acquisition of PwC's technology consulting arm by Hewlett-Packard fell apart. With no other buyer in sight, CEO James Schiro suddenly reversed his commitment to a ban on consulting. If he were eventually to sell his IT consulting business, he had to make sure it didn't atrophy, as would certainly happen under a total SEC ban. Now it was in Schiro's interest to accept our latest offer.

Schiro called me later that day, right after Berardino, and said he was willing to talk compromise. Schiro promised to help us persuade Ernst & Young chairman Philip Laskawy to go along. For the rest of the day, I was on the phone nonstop. At one point I had three of the Big Five CEOs on three separate phone lines. I shuttled between my office, a conference room, and an aide's office listening to offers, making counteroffers, and simultaneously cajoling and threatening. In between, I returned phone calls from members of Congress checking on our progress.

By the end of the day we had everyone on board except Laskawy.

This was ironic, since Laskawy had been the most moderate and enlightened of the Big Five leaders. He had smartly spun off his IT consulting services to Cap Gemini, and had less to lose than the other firms under our rules. While Schiro had cooperated largely because PwC's independence violations required the firm to prove to clients that it was rehabilitating itself, Laskawy's motivation was his belief that the profession had gone astray and needed to get back to basics. But now, in a phone call with Laskawy and his top management, his general counsel argued strongly against the proposal. I found this extremely frustrating. I yelled at his counsel to be quiet, and demanded an answer from Laskawy: "Do I have your support or not?" He was silent for a few nerve-wracking seconds, then overruled his lawyer and said he felt it was in the best interest of the profession to get a deal done. Finally, we had everyone's vote.

Fortunately, the SEC staff had worked around the clock over the weekend finalizing two different versions of the rules. No matter how the negotiations ended, we had papers the entire commission could review the next morning.

We ended up accepting new independence rules that, quite frankly, did not go far enough but were important nonetheless. The final rules, adopted on November 15, 2000, forbid auditors from performing many of the same services named in the proposal, such as keeping the books, providing appraisals, acting as a broker, and managing human resources for an audit client. But we gave up considerable ground on the two biggest issues. The final rules allow an unlimited amount of IT consulting to audit clients, though there are some restrictions. Auditors cannot, for example, make management decisions on the types of financial information a client's computer system will capture and cannot actually operate a client's IT system. The final rule also allows auditors to perform up to 40 percent of a company's internal audit work, and it exempts companies altogether if they have less than $200 million in assets.

I was particularly pleased with the final rule's requirement that client companies disclose in their annual proxy statement the amount of nonaudit services their auditors provide. Companies must reveal how much they pay their auditors each year for nonaudit work, and they must break out how much of those fees are for the design and implementation of financial information systems.

Once these disclosures began to appear in company proxy statements in 2001, shareholders could see for themselves how much consulting fees dwarfed audit fees. A study by Dow Jones Newswires found that the companies making up the S&P 500 paid their auditors $3.7 billion for nonaudit services in 2000 alone. That's more than three times the $1.2 billion in audit fees that these same companies paid. Motorola Inc., for example, paid KPMG just $4 million for audit services but $35 million for computer consulting and another $27 million for other consulting services. General Motors Corp. paid Deloitte & Touche $17 million for auditing and another $79 million for other services. And Sprint Corp. paid Ernst & Young only $2.5 million to conduct its audit but $64 million for consulting and other services.

I'm not suggesting that each of these audit firms has compromised its independence. But I have to wonder if any individual auditor, working on a $2.5 million audit contract, would have the guts to stand up to a CFO and question a dubious number in the books, thus possibly jeopardizing $64 million in business for the firm's consultants. The chances of that happening seem even smaller when you consider that many auditors are compensated partly on the basis of how much nonaudit business they sell.

The accounting industry likes to boast that it forced the SEC to back down. I think we won a major victory for shareholders by pressing the case for independence and exposing the industry's underbelly. And by fighting back, the profession made a colossal public relations mistake. The accountants gave themselves a black eye in the summer of 2000 when we held a series of hearings to shed light on audit failures and conflicts of interest. I knew our message had gotten through to ordinary investors when, sitting in the dentist's chair one day that summer, I heard my own dentist declare, "You sure can't trust those accountants anymore."

The industry's "no smoking gun" claim now seems ludicrous. Accountants are in the embarrassing position of having to explain Enron's bankruptcy, Arthur Andersen's disintegration, and the record $10 million fine that Xerox agreed to pay in April 2002, without admitting or denying guilt, for overstating revenues by more than $2 billion from 1997 through 2000. That's just for starters. By mid-2002, the SEC had opened investigations into alleged accounting shenanigans or insider trading at conglomerate Tyco International, drugmaker ImClone Systems, cable company Adelphia Communications, and long-distance provider WorldCom, among dozens of others.

In the end, the SEC got the best possible outcome, considering the dicey politics of the situation. I hoped that by giving the independence issue a higher profile than ever before, I had helped to make it difficult for the profession to continue sweeping its problems under the rug. I knew the era of big accounting scandals, company restatements, and shareholder losses was not over, but I never imagined a failure on the scale of Enron.

The Enron Train Wreck

I left the SEC three months later. Eight months after my departure, Enron, the seventh-largest company in the country with $108 billion in revenues, collapsed. Its auditor, Arthur Andersen, had approved the use of accounting tricks that resulted in financial statements that were misleading and incomplete at best, and possibly fraudulent at worst.

Enron started out in 1985 as a plain-vanilla natural gas pipeline company, but tried to transform itself into a global trading company. It borrowed heavily to finance an aggressive expansion, but didn't want a mountain of debt to reduce its credit rating or depress the share price. So instead of listing debt on the balance sheet, Enron formed hundreds of off-the-books partnerships. Enron's chief financial officer ran some of the partnerships in a blatant conflict of interest, but one that Enron's board approved anyway.

The partnerships, called "special purpose entities" (SPEs) in accounting lingo, allowed the company to take in capital from outside investors or lenders, such as pension funds and insurance companies, to finance its many ventures. Accounting rules allowed Enron to keep a partnership off its books as long as the equity of the SPE was 3 percent of its total capital (in other words, the SPE couldn't borrow more than 97 percent of its capital), and Enron as the sponsoring company did not contribute any of that equity. The FASB had been dealing with the question of how to account for SPEs for nearly twenty years. Because of fierce business lobbying, the FASB was unable to reach a consensus on a new standard. If one had been in place, Enron might not have occurred.

The SPEs let Enron manipulate its accounts by inflating earnings and hiding losses, especially on overseas acquisitions and investments in technology companies. The SPEs also helped Enron keep investors in the dark on total debt levels, artificially improve its credit rating, and enrich several top managers who participated in the partnerships.

Only one problem. The dubious structure and backroom dealings of the partnerships led to Enron's demise. In four such partnerships called the Raptors, Enron borrowed heavily to obtain the capital needed to fund the ventures, and then backed up those loans by promising to issue Enron stock to cover any shortfall. So when the partnerships' asset values fell, or they were unable to make a loan payment, Enron had to fork over its own shares. At the same time, the value of Enron's stock was sliding, along with the rest of the stock market, because of the overall market decline and the global recession. That put Enron even deeper in the hole as it scurried to make up for partnership losses by issuing more and more of its own sinking stock.

Unbeknown to shareholders, Enron's partnerships substantially raised the level of risk the company had assumed. Not only were Enron shareholders on the hook if any of the partnerships went sour, but the value of their own shares would be diluted if Enron had to make good on pledges to issue stock to cover any partnership losses.

Of course, that is exactly how the story ends. Enron's house of cards collapsed with the stock market's decline. For the 2001 third quarter, Enron had to report a $618 million loss because of the partnership losses. That was only the first shoe to drop. Three weeks later, Enron restated net income back to 1997—trimming it by $586 million. And two weeks after that, it announced that it had to repay $690 million in partnership debt. All these revelations undermined investor confidence and caused Enron's stock to plummet from a high of $90 in the fall of 2000 to under $1 in December 2001. The company filed for bankruptcy on December 2.

It's worth dissecting how Enron skirted existing accounting rules. One egregious example involves Enron's issuance of $1 billion of its own stock to the Raptor SPEs. In return, Enron accepted IOUs worth $1 billion, but never received any cash for them. According to a report by a special committee of the Enron board, Enron pulled off an accounting sleight-of-hand that would have made Houdini proud. It called those $1 billion in notes "receivables" and used them to artificially inflate its balance sheet. Simply put, Enron shareholders thought they were $1 billion richer than they really were. Arthur Andersen belatedly forced Enron to comply with SEC rules that prohibit a company from counting as equity on its balance sheet any issues of stock that have not been paid for. That forced Enron to reduce shareholder equity, a measure of net worth, by $1 billion.

Other accounting violations seemed minor at the time, but if auditors hadn't let them go, Enron might have been able to avert disaster. In 1997, Andersen found that Enron avoided $51 million in additional losses that it should have booked. Andersen then rationalized that $51 million was "immaterial"—a drop in the bucket of Enron's $20 billion in total revenue. But Enron's net income, or profit, that year was only $105 million. Put in this light, the $51 million that auditors labeled immaterial was almost half Enron's profit that year. If Andersen had not let Enron use the immateriality ploy, maybe Enron would not have tried to get away with much more serious accounting flimflam in later years.

A Failure of Independence?

Aside from admitting to a few small errors in judgment, Andersen CEO Berardino claimed in Congressional testimony that his firm did nothing wrong (although Andersen fired the lead partner overseeing Enron's audits because, Andersen alleged, he approved the shredding of documents. The audit partner eventually pleaded guilty). Berardino pointed an accusing finger at his client, however, and said that Enron hid the fact that it had illegally contributed more than half the equity to one of the partnerships, called LJM Swap Sub. Berardino hinted that if Andersen had known this from the outset, it would have forced Enron to consolidate that partnership onto the balance sheet.

Perhaps Andersen would have done so. But it had many, many other opportunities to prevent this tragedy. It did not force Enron to clearly explain to investors any of the partnerships, which exposed shareholders to huge financial liabilities. Subpoenaed documents and the internal investigation by a special committee of Enron's board show that Andersen played a major role in setting up some of the partnerships, and then blessed their accounting treatment. This is a conflict of interest for any auditor.

In addition, internal documents show that Andersen officials held discussions as early as December 2000 about the risks entailed in allowing Enron's aggressive and creative accounting. Documents also show that Andersen knew as early as August 2001 about accounting irregularities at Enron, and while it consulted with its own legal counsel on what to do, it failed to let shareholders know. In fact, it stood by its client for another three months before forcing it to restate five years' worth of earnings.

I think it's fair to say that Andersen's independence was compromised. Andersen had been acting as Enron's internal auditor, as well as its independent, outside auditor. This meant that Arthur Andersen was, at times, reviewing its own work rather than acting as an impartial check on the accuracy of the client's figures. And whereas Andersen was paid $25 million for its audit work, it received even more than that—$27 million—for nonaudit services. According to internal memos, Andersen expected total Enron fees eventually to grow to $100 million, making Enron its largest client, by far. Finally, many Andersen employees over the years became Enron employees, working in the auditing and finance departments. Andersen auditors, then, were reviewing the work of former bosses and friends.

When you add it all up, the Enron/Andersen audit failure is a perfect example of what I was trying to prevent. Investors lost more than $60 billion. Some five thousand Enron employees lost their jobs, and many also lost their retirement savings because their 401(k) plans held mostly worthless Enron stock. Enron executives, meanwhile, made $1.2 billion by cashing in stock options in the two years prior to the company's collapse.

As bad as this is, the loss of investor confidence in audited numbers is much worse. The lack of trust in the numbers cast a pall over the stock market for much of the next year and into 2003. Investors were beating down the shares of companies ranging from IBM to General Electric and Disney because their financial statements were viewed as less than transparent or their board of directors was perceived as weak.

Sometimes it takes a crisis to convince the world that the status quo has to change. If there's a silver lining in the Enron disaster, it's that important public policy issues that consumed us at the SEC—the composition of oversight boards, how to make sure that CPAs serve the public interest, and how to make company financial statements more transparent—have finally caught the public's imagination. It certainly made Congress see the light. Spurred on by scandal after scandal, Congress adopted the Sarbanes-Oxley corporate reform law in 2002. In doing so, it prohibited nearly all forms of consulting by auditors for corporate clients. The SEC rules we fought for are now the law of the land. Moreover, Congress forbade nearly all forms of IT consulting. Today, only tax consulting is allowed, but even that requires preapproval by the board's audit committee, all of whose members must now be independent of company management. And I'm encouraged by the new Public Company Accounting Oversight Board's promise to review whether tax consulting of any kind should be allowed when it involves an audit client.

CHAPTER SIX

BEWARE FALSE PROFITS: HOW TO READ FINANCIAL STATEMENTS

In the prolonged market meltdown that began in March 2000, no sector lost more money for investors than telecommunications. Some $2 trillion in shareholder wealth and 400,000 jobs were wiped out as fifteen high-flying telecom companies failed over an eighteen-month stretch. The Securities and Exchange Commission in early 2002 began investigating several of the companies for allegedly swapping network capacity with one another in deals that had no economic value but that helped them inflate revenues artificially. One of these, Global Crossing Ltd., a fiber-optic cable company, was pointing to strong annual growth in revenues as late as November 2001. The CEO was telling shareholders that he expected the company to improve its operating results as it cut expenses and benefited from "strong growth" in certain business lines. Three months later, Global Crossing was the fourth-largest bankrupt company in U.S. history.

Where were the danger signs? They were staring investors right in the face. Global Crossing's SEC filings showed that the company had lost money eight straight quarters going back to 1999. Total debt as a percentage of its capital grew from 24 percent in September 2000 to 41 percent the next year; experts consider anything higher than 15 percent to be a warning sign.

The fact is, too many investors don't pay enough attention to the fundamentals of a company's business. By learning how to read financial statements and looking for common accounting tricks, you can be your own watchdog. This isn't as daunting as you think.

The best way to do this is by ignoring the glossy annual report that comes in the mail. Instead, go right to the dry, but far more informative, Form 10-K, or annual report, on file at the SEC. Unlike the quarterly Form 10-Q, the 10-K must be audited by an independent auditor. To find the 10-K you want to read, just go to *www.sec.gov,* then click on "EDGAR" (EDGAR stands for Electronic Data Gathering, Analysis & Retrieval), then fill in the blanks for the company name plus the type of report and year you want to examine.

The 10-K is where the company must disclose everything that might affect its future performance, whether that's a lawsuit, a shrinking market share, or the pending expiration of a key patent. The 10-K is also where you will find the company's financial statements. This chapter will give you tools to pick apart each of the components of these statements. It will also explain some of the more popular devices companies have used to make their accounts seem rosier than they are.

Such blue chips as Lucent, Motorola, AOL Time Warner, Cisco, and WorldCom have all played the numbers game. Unfortunately, you can't take the attitude that investing in high-quality companies protects you from accounting trickery. No company is completely immune from the pressure to cut corners. But many on Wall Street and in corporate America would have you believe that you need an accounting degree to understand financial statements. Don't believe it. As you'll see, with a little bit of work, you'll be able to determine by yourself how well a company is really doing and even make some educated guesses about its future performance.

The Balance Sheet

When a company files an annual report with the SEC, it must contain three documents that the accountants produce: the balance sheet, the income statement, and the cash-flow statement.

First, the balance sheet. This statement is a snapshot of the company's overall financial health, similar to the annual checkup you get when you visit the family doctor. It tells you which companies are growing internally and which are using debt to pump up results. The balance sheet lists assets, which are resources such as cash and equipment, and liabilities, which are obligations such as debt and accounts payable (payments the company owes to others), at a specific point in time—the last day of the reporting period. The difference between assets and liabilities is called shareholders' equity. Shareholders' equity includes any investments by the company's owners (such as you, if you own shares) plus any profits that have been reinvested in the business rather than paid out as dividends to the owners.

The first items in the balance sheet are current assets, or assets that are cash or will be converted into cash in the short term (generally within one year). This includes short-term investments, accounts receivable (payments due for services already delivered or products already sold), and inventories (raw materials or finished product available for sale but not yet sold).

Listed after current assets are noncurrent assets, or those that are not as liquid as current assets. This includes medium- and long-term investments, real estate, physical plant, and equipment. To comply with generally accepted accounting principles, or GAAP, many of these assets must be either depreciated (tangible assets such as buildings, furniture, and equipment) or amortized (intangible assets such as patents, trademarks, and copyrights). Depreciating an asset means allocating its cost as an expense over the period the company uses the asset to generate revenue. On the balance sheet, depreciable assets are shown at their original price, offset by depreciation that has accumulated over the years. Because depreciation is also an expense, it has the effect of reducing earnings in the income statement each year, which I'll explain below.

Amortization similarly recognizes that an intangible asset has a limited useful life, and therefore a portion of the asset's cost is recorded as an expense each year. On the balance sheet, intangibles are recorded at their historical cost less amortization. GAAP used to require companies to amortize all intangible assets over a maximum of forty years. In 2001, the Financial Accounting Standards Board, which determines GAAP, eliminated any maximum life over which intangible assets must be amortized and instead required companies to write down the assets when they lose value.

Listed after the assets on the balance sheet are the company's liabilities and the stockholders' equity. Total assets must equal the total liabilities and stockholders' equity.

Liabilities are also classified as current and noncurrent. Current liabilities, which generally must be paid within a year, include such items as outstanding supplier invoices, short-term notes (or IOUs), the current portion of any long-term debt, and income taxes not yet paid. Noncurrent liabilities are those that are not due in the next year, such as the long-term portion of notes and mortgages (any interest payments due on these will appear as interest payable under current liabilities) and capital leases. Liabilities and equity are listed in the general order in which they are expected to be paid in case of bankruptcy or liquidation. Money owed to suppliers is first in line, while common stockholders are last in line.

One more feature of the balance sheet you will want to pay attention to is the line item called retained earnings. This is the dollar amount of a company's earnings that was not distributed to shareholders as dividends. This does not mean that the money is in the bank or available for distribution to shareholders. Instead, earnings most likely were reinvested in the business, for example to expand a company's product lines or to build a new manufacturing facility.

That's the balance sheet in a nutshell. So what clues should investors look for? An easy way to get a feel for a company's health is by checking inventories and receivables (remember, these appear as current assets on the balance sheet). If either one is growing a lot faster than sales (or revenues) on the income statement, then trouble may be brewing. If inventories are rising, the company could be having trouble selling as much product as it forecasted. If demand is weakening, have the company's products lost customer acceptance in the marketplace? Has technology changed? Has a new competitor entered the marketplace? Is a general economic softness hurting the company?

If accounts receivable are growing faster than sales, has the company induced customers, using discounts and easy cancellation terms, to buy more goods than they really need? One dangerous by-product of such a trend is called channel stuffing. When a company shoves its products out to retailers and distributors, these buyers often delay payment for shipments, pushing up the accounts receivable number. Rising receivables can also signal a change in a company's credit policy. Some companies will lower their credit standards by accepting, for example, payment in ninety days versus sixty days, in order to boost anemic sales.

When inventories are written down in value, investors should ask: What was the root cause? Did the company overestimate what it could sell? Is this a sign of poor sales forecasting, order management, or production quality controls? Normally, temporary reductions in revenues and profits do not result in assets being written down in value, under GAAP. Rather, write-downs typically are caused by longer-term or permanent reductions in sales value. A write-down means that the company does not expect to recover the money it invested in inventory. Companies are required to explain these changes in trends, and their expected effect on the future operations of the company, in an important section of their financial reports called "management's discussion and analysis."

It's vital to understand that a write-down is not just the onetime, historical event that analysts and corporate executives would have you believe. Instead, a write-down could indicate problems with the business strategy, product development, or marketing channels. Most importantly, it could be a distress signal about the company's future stock value.

Some companies write off inventory as worthless, but don't dispose of it. Why would a company incur the cost of maintaining and warehousing what it has declared as worthless inventory? One reason is that the company may intend to use the inventory, either by selling it or by using it in a production process. In the future, only the lower, written-down cost gets expensed under "cost of sales," and future earnings look rosier than they really are. This dubious practice has allowed companies, such as Cisco Systems Inc., to gussy up earnings and boost gross margins, as we'll soon see.

When analysts refer to a company's "strong balance sheet," they are usually referring to the level of debt. By itself, debt isn't a bad thing. But if a company can't produce sufficient revenues to pay its debts, then it's asking for trouble. The reason so many telecom companies failed in recent years is that they took on huge amounts of debt in the late '90s to finance the building of fiber-optic networks. When the technology bubble burst and demand for network capacity withered, the telecoms had miles and miles of networks but too few paying customers. Their equipment suppliers also found that the inventory piling up in warehouses was worthless. Bankruptcies quickly followed, as the telecoms and equipment vendors were unable to make the interest payments on their debts. On the other hand, companies that took on less debt in the high-flying '90s were able to weather the downturn.

One way to measure debt is to look at the ratio of long-term debt to the company's total invested capital. Here's how: In the balance sheet, find the amount of long-term debt (remember, that's debt that does not come due for more than one year). Divide that figure by the total amount of capital—all equity invested in the company plus all debt. A ratio above 20 percent is considered high.

If the debt-to-capital ratio seems complicated, here's a simpler way to size up the balance sheet. Just compare the amount of cash (listed under assets) to the amount of debt (listed under liabilities). Enron's balance sheet is instructive. At the end of 2000, it had $1.4 billion in cash, but debt of $10.2 billion. Such a huge gap between the two is a strong indicator that something is amiss.

The Income Statement

The income statement, sometimes called the profit-and-loss statement or the statement of operations, is a report on the company's business activities for one quarter or one year. While the balance sheet measures a company's overall health, the income statement measures its performance. It has two main components: revenues (money or promises of money flowing in) and expenses (money or promises of money flowing out).

When a product or service is sold, the money received is called revenue. This is the first item on most income statements, and one many analysts consider the most important. Revenue growth, more than earnings, was a key determinant of stock market value during the Internet boom because investors believed revenues showed whether or not a company was steadily gaining a customer base and a larger piece of the overall market. Revenues are important, but it's a mistake to focus just on this top-line number. You need to look at the quality of the revenues and the company's entire income statement to gauge its true financial performance.

There are strict rules for when revenue can be recognized under GAAP. For example, revenue cannot be counted if the seller must provide a significant amount of services in the future to the buyer. Many companies abused the revenue recognition rules during the 1990s bull market, but more on that later.

The next item on the income statement is the cost of goods sold, or the amount paid for the items sold out of inventory. Naturally, a service company will not have this kind of expense. The income statement also lists operating expenses, such as "selling, general and administrative costs." This important category of expense measures how good management is at controlling the overhead costs associated with running its operations. Selling expenses include the salaries of the sales staff, travel and entertainment costs, advertising, and distribution.

Administrative expenses include officers' salaries, legal services, utilities, insurance, office equipment depreciation, and the like. Another important expense to watch is the cost of research and development. When viewed as a percentage of revenues, R&D expenses can be compared across similar types of companies. If the percentage is unusually high or low, the company may not be managing or investing its R&D dollars wisely. If the percentage is falling, the company may be trying to cut R&D to prop up earnings. It is also important to watch how much of a company's revenue is generated by new products coming out of the R&D pipeline. This provides a good measure of how well the R&D process is being managed as well as whether management has a good understanding of what new products customers want.

Also appearing on the income statement are gains or losses from discontinued operations and extraordinary gains or losses. Extraordinary items must be unrelated to the business's normal activities and they must be onetime and highly unusual events. The damage from a fire or, for companies in California, an earthquake, is not considered extraordinary. By segregating extraordinary items, one year's income statement can be compared with another's. Another line item that sometimes appears on the income statement is "restructuring costs" or a similar label. Be careful: in the last dozen or so years, companies have made liberal use of this description for items that are not, in fact, unusual or onetime events.

If a company has determined that one of its operating divisions has experienced lower sales and reduced profitability, it could decide to restructure that division by laying off employees, reducing inventories, and closing plants. Many of the costs associated with this downsizing are called restructuring charges, and they also appear on the income statement. The expense will be equal to what management thinks it will cost to pay severance to workers, the amount of decline in the value of the manufacturing plant, and other costs, such as ending leases on equipment no longer needed. A restructuring is a signal that the underlying economics of the business have changed—R&D has not been successful in reinvigorating the product line, or revenues are suffering because competitors have gained market share—and can be a red flag that the company has long-term problems.

The income statement also lists taxes due on the revenues and expenses listed on the statement. Keep in mind that this figure is for accounting purposes only and may differ from the actual taxes paid, which may cover a different time period and include revenues or expenses not on the income statement. A company determines actual taxes owed to the government using arcane rules put out by the Internal Revenue Service. Any difference between taxes based on earnings reported in the income statement and what the company currently owes the IRS is called deferred taxes.

At the end of the income statement are two important numbers. The first is net income, also called the bottom line. This is the profit the company is showing after subtracting out all expenses. This is a GAAP number, and differs from so-called pro forma or operating earnings, which are numbers that exclude a lot of noncash charges (such as amortization and depreciation) and large expenses (such as restructuring costs). Companies will go to ridiculous lengths to pump up their pro forma earnings number; some as far as excluding marketing expenses from the calculation.

While GAAP may not be perfect, at least it forces companies to follow consistent rules for the sake of comparison. Until the FASB can come up with a better definition for core operating or recurring earnings, net income is more trustworthy than pro forma figures. If each company decides what to include or exclude from its pro forma earnings, the result is what former SEC chief accountant Lynn Turner calls EBBS numbers, or "everything but the bad stuff."

At the end of the income statement is the earnings per share (EPS). This figure tells investors how much money the company earned for each share of stock outstanding. Again, be careful. The truer measure of how successful a company has been is the fully diluted EPS number, rather than the basic EPS number, which is the first one you see. The fully diluted figure takes into account stock options issued to managers but not yet exercised. It also figures in bonds, preferred shares, and stock warrants that can be converted to common stock, thus causing basic EPS to drop significantly.

One useful measurement is return on assets (ROA), which also connects the balance sheet to the income statement. Find the net income number on the income statement and divide that figure by the total assets number on the balance sheet. The higher the ROA, the better management is at using your capital to increase returns. A healthy company will have an ROA of at least 5 percent.

The Statement of Cash Flows

To really understand the quality of a company's earnings, you need to analyze the cash-flow statement, the last document in a company's financial reports. As its name implies, this statement shows the actual cash that came into the company and the actual cash that flowed out. Remember that the balance sheet reveals a company's assets, liabilities, and shareholders' equity at the close of the fiscal year or the most recent quarter. The income statement reflects the changes that have occurred in the balance sheet items, including promises of money that the company has made or received. The cash-flow statement differs in that it reveals the changes in actual cash that the business has generated and the actual cash raised from creditors and investors. It also shows how the company invested that cash between the start of one fiscal year to the end of another. In short, cash flow shows where the money is coming from and how the money is being spent.

The cash-flow statement has three parts. First, you'll see "cash from operating activities," which is the money that comes in from sales of the company's products and services and the money going out to produce those sales. It also includes interest and tax payments. Recall that accounting rules allow companies to list revenues on the income statement before they receive actual payment. Not so on the cash-flow statement, which lists only revenues actually collected.

You may see negative cash flow from operations. While on its face that may seem like a bad sign, it isn't always a signal to sell. Fast-growing start-ups, which consume more cash than they can generate in the first few years of the business, will especially show negative cash flow. They cover the shortfall by borrowing money or issuing stock. But sometimes negative operating cash flow indicates that a company is in serious trouble, especially if the company is disposing of assets, as by selling off pieces of the company, because it can't persuade investors to buy its stock or bankers to lend it money.

The second item on the cash-flow statement is "cash from investing activities." This is where the company reveals how it's using its excess cash, either by investing in other companies or by expanding its own business. If the company, like thousands of others, invested in the stock market in the go-go '90s, this is where you'll see how much cash it received from stock sales, or how much it spent to buy shares. Any gains or losses on such stock, however, are reported in the operating activities section of the cash flow statement. The investing part of the cash flow statement also reveals any investments in long-term assets, such as an acquisition (or a sale) of a manufacturing plant or equipment, or the opening of new retail stores. Finally, if the company lent money to its executives to allow them to buy stock, that loan will be listed here.

The third part, "cash from financing activities," includes money that comes in or goes out when a company sells or buys shares of its own stock. Issuing new debt or bank borrowings also will show up here as an increase in cash. Paying dividends or paying down debt will show up as a decrease in cash. A start-up company with little or no sales is more likely than a mature company to show lots of financing activity, since the cash to run the business has to come from somewhere.

So there's the cash-flow statement in a nutshell. If you look back at the balance sheet for the amount of cash the company has—listed under current assets—that figure comes from the final cash balance on the cash-flow statement.

When sifting for clues in the cash-flow statement, it's sometimes necessary to examine cash flow side by side with the income statement, and also to examine both statements over multiple reporting periods. For example, if net earnings on the income statement have rocketed, but actual cash received from operations is much lower, that could be a sign that bad debts or obsolete inventories are piling up and next period's earnings could be lower.

To see if a company is playing the numbers game, compare the rate of growth in net income with the rate of growth in operating cash. If net income is growing at 10 percent but operating cash is growing at only 1 percent, while in years past the two numbers moved at a fairly even pace, that could signal that net income isn't as muscular as it appears. Or you can divide the net income on the income statement into the total cash from operating activities. The closer the answer is to one, the higher the quality of the earnings.

It's far more difficult to manipulate the cash-flow statement than the income statement. Still, cash flow can be artificially inflated. Adding the tax benefits of stock options is one way companies improve cash flow. When employees exercise certain kinds of stock options, the difference between the grant price and the exercise price is counted as a deduction on the tax return, reducing the company's tax bill. With stock compensation, companies are giving employees something of value—the right to participate in the appreciation of the stock without having to pay a cent. But 99 percent of companies elect not to report an expense for that item on the income statement. That doesn't matter to the IRS. Companies can still deduct the "expense" for tax purposes when employees exercise their stock options. The refund from the U.S. Treasury boosts operating cash flows without ever having the fair value of the stock options recorded on the income statement. Sounds deceptive, but it's perfectly legal. But if you want a truer picture of operating cash flow, subtract the stock option tax benefit.

Enron's cash-flow statement is worth examining. In 2000, Enron showed that cash provided by operating activities came to $4.8 billion. But investors who looked carefully at the balance sheet and its footnote 3C would have seen that the cash-flow total includes $5.5 billion in customer deposits that Enron required of its California customers to make sure they didn't skip out on their bills during the state's energy crisis. So Enron's true operating cash flow was a negative $700 million. Enron also reported onetime asset sales of $1.8 billion on its cash-flow statement. Without that, Enron's cash flow would have been a minus $2.5 billion. Considering that Enron was showing total sales of $101 billion, a negative $2.5 billion cash flow is a sign that something is fundamentally wrong.

Don't Ignore the Footnotes

After plowing through the balance sheet, income statement, and cash-flow statement, you'll still need to parse the footnotes. The footnotes are important; they give you vital additional information, and they sometimes leave an entirely different impression from the rosy portrait the company may have painted in the financial statements. So don't be intimidated. Too many companies would prefer that you not read the footnotes. That should be incentive enough to delve into them. The footnotes tell the story behind the numbers, and they may contain valuable information about risks and uncertainties that could affect future performance.

What little Enron told the world about its off-balance-sheet shenanigans, for example, appeared in the footnotes. To maintain a high credit rating, Enron pushed loads of debt off its balance sheet and into so-called special purpose entities. Enron did not report the financial details of these SPEs by consolidating them into its own statements, but instead revealed their existence in footnotes.

One such footnote on "preferred stock" in the Form 10-K for 2000, for example, says that the company might be obligated to issue stock to a related party, Whitewing Associates. A related party is often one that the company's own executives manage. The mere fact that a company has engaged in related-party transactions could be a warning. The footnote further revealed that the triggering event for the stock issue would be a decline in Enron's share price to $48.55. While the footnote was not very forthcoming, it should have raised eyebrows. Why was Enron obligated to issue stock in the first place? What, exactly, was Whitewing's purpose? How much liability was Enron taking on? If Enron shareholders were shouldering this risk, why was the partnership off-balance-sheet? What other partnerships did Enron have like this? The answers to these questions would have revealed a multitude of problems.

Footnotes typically start out with an explanation of the company's accounting policies, such as how and when it recognizes revenue. Footnotes fill you in on the number of stock options granted to executives and other employees, and how those options would affect earnings per share if they were included as an expense on the income statement. Those are important numbers, since many companies have showered their managers and employees with stock options. In doing so, companies are giving up the income they would receive if they sold those shares on the open market. And when those options are exercised, existing shareholders' stakes decline in value.

The footnotes also give you vital details on operating leases, the kind where a company makes monthly payments for the buildings it occupies but doesn't have a buyout option at the end of the contract. Accounting rules say that operating leases are not assets to the company, so they can't go on the balance sheet. Still, leases are often a major liability that investors should know about, especially if the company operates a chain of retail stores and has hundreds of operating leases for its outlets.

Airlines use operating leases all the time to acquire rights to aircraft, but the rent payments on the leases don't show up on the balance sheet. A 1998 Morgan Stanley report showed that 42 percent of United Airlines' fleet did not appear on the balance sheet because of the heavy use of operating leases.

A company's pension assets and liabilities won't appear on the balance sheet, either, but you'll find the details in a footnote. In bad times, underfunded pensions can cause net income to decline. The opposite is true in good times, when pension plans can be a significant contributor to net income. Jane Adams, an accounting analyst at New York hedge fund Maverick Capital, and who specializes in interpreting footnotes, found that in 2000, 30 percent of the companies in the S&P 500 used overfunded pension plans to goose their net income. On average, they added a hefty 12 percent to pre-tax earnings. This is perfectly legal, but it obscures how much of the company's core operations contributes to net income.

The fine print in the footnotes is often vexingly confusing, sometimes purposely so. Some company managers use footnotes to avoid legal liability for failing to disclose important information. Some use footnotes to hide aggressive accounting maneuvers, as Enron did, and would rather not trumpet that to the stock market. Investors should be aware that footnotes sometimes are purposely obfuscatory, and avoid the stock of companies that seem to be burying gory details. If a footnote seems confusing, there's probably a reason.

The SEC could do a lot more to improve disclosures by requiring companies to use plain English in their financial statements, and especially their footnotes. Companies now need to translate only certain portions of the prospectus—the document a company must file with the SEC before it can offer its shares to the public—into plain English. By extending the plain English rule to footnotes and possibly other disclosure documents, investors of all sophistication levels will be able to decipher the meaning of corporate legalese.

This would be a time-consuming effort. It took the SEC three years to get companies to adopt plain English in prospectuses. But it would be one of the most pro-investor steps the SEC could take to avoid future Enrons.

Now comes the fun part. Here are some examples of common tricks used by real companies to distort or disguise their actual performance and how they buried the truth in their financial statements.

The Pro Forma Pretense When two companies merge, they often issue "pro forma" or "as if" financial statements so that investors have some idea of what the merged entity's financial numbers will look like, as if it had been operating as one. But in the 1990s, companies began using the pro forma concept to obscure shaky finances. To cover up the fact that they had little or no earnings as defined by GAAP, high-tech companies discovered the trick of issuing pro forma earnings announcements, which selectively exclude lots of expenses that reduce earnings. Companies in many other industries have since adopted the technique. Because the SEC, until recently, had little authority over company news releases (unless there was gross deception), it was unable to crack down on pro forma ruses. And because pro forma earnings by their very nature are not GAAP-compliant, few rules dictated what went in, or what stayed out, of a pro forma calculation. Some companies excluded restructuring costs under the excuse that they were "unusual" or not part of the company's core operations. Others left out depreciation and amortization expenses, and still others excluded interest and tax payments.

Passage of the Sarbanes-Oxley corporate reform law changed all that. The law gives the SEC the authority to clamp down by requiring pro forma earnings announcements to include a GAAP reconciliation. This means that any pro forma number, under SEC rules effective on March 28, 2003, must be accompanied by a GAAP number—in that same press release and even in speeches or statements that cite a a pro forma figure. But investors must still be on their toes for pro forma tomfoolery. From now on, if a company announces pro forma earnings, make sure you keep reading until you get to the GAAP number, which will give you all the ugly details that pro forma leaves out.

Amazon.com is one company that loves to use pro forma earnings to downplay losses. In the 2001 first quarter, for example, Amazon reported a pro forma "operating earnings" loss of just $49 million. Using GAAP, Amazon really had a loss of $234 million. Why the difference? The pro forma results excluded such items as $24 million in net interest expenses and $114 million for restructuring costs. To its credit, Amazon included GAAP figures at the end of its press releases even before the new law required it to do so.

Nortel Networks Corp.'s earnings press release for the 2001 third quarter shows how ridiculous the pro forma pretense had become. It contained three earnings numbers: a $1.08-per-share loss under GAAP; a $0.68 pro forma loss that excluded certain one-time acquisition costs and restructuring charges; and a $0.27 pro forma loss that excluded the acquisition and restructuring charges plus $1.9 billion in inventory write-downs.

In January 2002 the SEC tried to clamp down on pro forma mischief in a case it brought against Trump Hotels & Casino Resorts, the company chaired by developer Donald Trump. The Trump case illustrates just how far companies had bent the rules to get investors to focus on pro forma results. In October 1999 the company issued a press release announcing third-quarter pro forma net income of $14 million, and said that the resort group's positive operating results had beaten analysts' expectations. The release made clear that the pro forma results excluded a one-time charge of $81 million from closing down a hotel and casino in Atlantic City. But the release did not say that the pro forma figure included a $17 million, one-time gain, which was the fair market value of new light fixtures and other improvements made to a recently acquired restaurant.

What happened? Trump Hotels had simply chosen to include in its pro forma calculation a one-time event that made its earnings look rosier, while selectively excluding a much larger charge that would have made earnings look anemic.

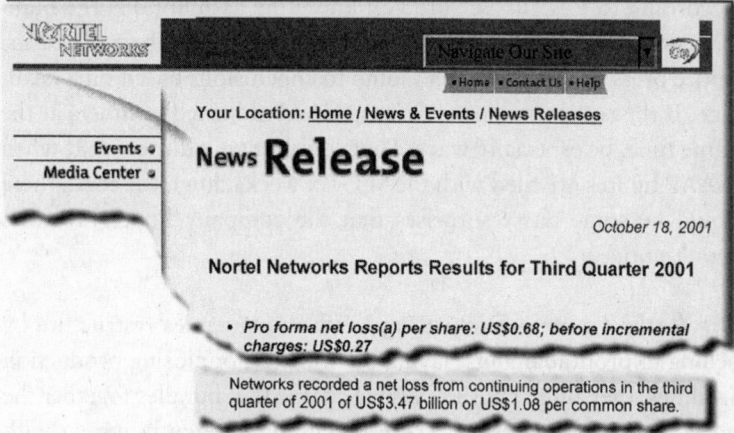

*A Nortel news release gave three different
net-loss-per-share numbers.*

Luckily, the SEC said "no dice." By picking and choosing among numbers, Trump Hotels left the false impression that the quarter was better than the year-earlier period. The misleading announcement led investors wrongly to conclude that the 1999 results came about because management had been able to control costs and boost operating performance. Indeed, Trump's stock price jumped almost 8 percent on the day of the pro forma announcement. But once analysts figured out the unvarnished truth—that net income for the quarter was just $3 million and that Trump Hotels had negative, not positive, trends in revenues and earnings—the share price dropped 6 percent.

The hotel group agreed to a cease-and-desist order, which amounts to a slap on the wrist. The company admitted to no wrongdoing, and it was not required to pay any penalties. But the message was clear: pro forma deceptions will no longer be tolerated.

Next time you see a company tout its pro forma earnings, ask yourself: What is the company hiding? Why isn't it reporting results according to GAAP? Be sure you know the assumptions the numbers are based on, and that you look behind the numbers. Read the entire press release, and don't jump to conclusions based on a headline. If the company doesn't release GAAP-adjusted numbers at the same time, be especially wary. That could be an indicator that when GAAP figures are filed with the SEC six weeks down the road, there could be some nasty surprises that the company hopes investors won't notice.

Big Baths Leave a Dirty Ring   When companies restructure by selling unprofitable units, laying off workers, or closing production facilities, they often take a one-time charge that bundles together the costs of the restructuring. There is nothing inherently wrong with that, as long as management views restructuring charges as a last resort to boost efficiency and restore profitability, and writes off only those expenses that directly relate to the restructuring. But some companies use restructuring charges like a cemetery—to bury all kinds of everyday operating expenses. By doing so, companies can pretty up otherwise desultory earnings. In 2001 alone, companies wrote off "unusual charges" of $165 billion, more than the previous five years combined.

Companies are even routinely taking restructuring charges—sometimes called nonrecurring, special, or one-time charges—that overstate costs, even though that makes losses look worse. But why would a company want to do that? Because managers and analysts have convinced investors that big one-time losses don't matter. Most analysts will tell you that a restructuring charge is all about the past, and that it says little about a company's future prospects. For companies, the beauty of such charges is that they can front-load several years of expected future expenses into one big package. This allows the company to boost future earnings by not offsetting income-producing activities with their associated expenses, such as the future revenue from the sale of computer equipment and the cost of manufacturing that equipment.

Investors should not ignore big-bath restructuring charges. Former SEC chief accountant Turner warns investors to dig out the

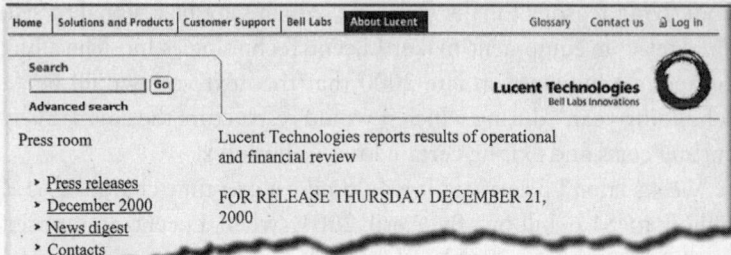

Home | Solutions and Products | Customer Support | Bell Labs | **About Lucent** | | Glossary | Contact us | Log in

Search [_____] Go
Advanced search

Lucent Technologies
Bell Labs Innovations

Press room

> Press releases
> December 2000
> News digest
> Contacts

Lucent Technologies reports results of operational and financial review

FOR RELEASE THURSDAY DECEMBER 21, 2000

and will initiate a business restructuring program to drive out in excess of $1 billion in costs as the company re-designs its internal systems and processes for long-term, sustainable growth.

```
                    FORM 10-K

    [x] ANNUAL REPORT PURSUANT TO SECTION 13 OR 15(d) OF
            THE SECURITIES EXCHANGE ACT OF 1934

        FOR THE FISCAL YEAR ENDED SEPTEMBER 30, 2001

                        OR

    [ ] TRANSITION REPORT PURSUANT TO SECTION 13 OR 15(d) OF
            THE SECURITIES EXCHANGE ACT OF 1934

    FOR THE TRANSITION PERIOD FROM _____ TO _____
                   --------------------

              COMMISSION FILE NO.: 001-11639
                   --------------------

                 LUCENT TECHNOLOGIES INC.

    (EXACT NAME OF REGISTRANT AS SPECIFIED IN ITS CHARTER)
```

```
    Phase I of our restructuring program resulted in business restructuring
charges of approximately $2.7 billion in the second fiscal quarter of 2001 and
$684 million in the third fiscal quarter of 2001.
```

```
    Our restructuring actions related to Phase II in fiscal year 2001 resulted
in a business restructuring charge of $8 billion, recorded in the fourth fiscal
quarter of 2001.
```

Lucent issued a press release on December 21, 2000,
that warned of upcoming charges of about $1 billion, but its
annual report showed $11.4 billion in "one-time" charges.

underlying reasons for the write-off, which may be a signal to sell. Take telecom equipment-maker Lucent Technologies Inc. The ailing company announced in late 2000 that the next year would be "a rebuilding year," during which it would restructure the company by cutting costs and exiting certain lines of business.

Weeks later, Lucent said it would take a one-time charge of $1.2 billion to $1.6 billion. By April 2001, when Lucent announced results for the just-completed second quarter, the write-off had climbed to $2.7 billion worth of unusual charges. The mushrooming of the charge alone should have warned investors that Lucent was putting everything but the kitchen sink into the write-down. Not to worry, said Lucent in a press release announcing its pro forma results. The company had lost $1.26 billion, a slight improvement from the previous quarter's $1.3 billion loss. But adding in the one-time charges and translating the results into GAAP, Lucent had actually lost $3.38 billion.

Even a casual reader of Lucent's quarterly SEC filing could see that the $2.7 billion charge, rather than an inconsequential event, revealed serious problems. Management had projected overly ambitious sales and profits and had hired far too many people to work in unprofitable divisions. Margins (revenues from sales minus the costs involved in generating those sales) were rapidly deteriorating. And the customer base was drying up. In short, Lucent's management team had missed the mark by a huge amount.

Sure enough, the initial charges were a signal to sell: by September 30, the end of Lucent's fiscal year, it had taken charges for another $8.7 billion worth of restructuring and other costs, for a fiscal year total of $11.4 billion. This was one big bath that portended more than a one-time cleanup of the balance sheet. Investors who failed to bail out of the company at the first sign of trouble saw the share price plummet from a high of $75 in late 1999 to just $5 in the fall of 2001.

Cookie Jars and Channel Stuffing Companies looking to make quarterly sales appear better than they really are can deceive investors with a number of accounting methods. Two of the most common practices are called "cookie-jar reserves" and "channel stuffing." Cookie-jar reserving occurs when a company purposely overestimates future liabilities for such items as loan losses (for banks), warranty costs, and sales returns. In doing so, they stash money in cookie jars during the good times and reach into them when needed in the bad times. As mentioned earlier in this chapter, channel stuffing happens when a company ships products to customers, such as retailers and distributors, loading them up with, or "stuffing," their shelves with excess inventory. Often this practice is accompanied by company offers of discounts, below-market financing, and other inducements to get customers to purchase products ahead of time. While such hurry-up sales rob from future quarters, they help cover up a bad quarter so that management can boast that it met analysts' expectations.

In May 2001 the SEC alleged that Sunbeam Corp. used both methods in a fraudulent attempt to trick the market into believing that the company was worth more than it really was. Former chairman and CEO Albert J. Dunlap—more infamously known as Chainsaw Al for his penchant for cutting costs and slashing jobs—was hired by Sunbeam's board in 1996 to restructure the ailing company, which makes Oster, Sunbeam, Mr. Coffee, and First Alert home appliances. As a so-called turnaround specialist, Dunlap set to work reorganizing the company, and promised shareholders quick results. After taking a restructuring charge and reporting huge losses for 1996—which Dunlap was able to blame on previous management—the company then reported record pre-tax income for 1997 of $186 million. But the SEC alleged that Sunbeam achieved that feat in part by reaching into the cookie jar of 1996 reserves and by inducing distributors to buy merchandise they didn't need.

Sunbeam also allegedly used a scam called "bill and hold," in which it recorded the sale of barbecue grills and other items but held them in its own warehouses because customers didn't yet need, or didn't want, the goods. Under GAAP, a bona fide sale takes place only when the customer takes possession of the goods or requests that they be stored. Of that $186 million, the SEC alleged that $60 million came from accounting fraud.

Because Sunbeam robbed from future results in 1997, it became increasingly desperate to make its numbers in 1998, and was forced to repeat its sins. This time, it also allegedly concealed company records showing that large lots of merchandise were being returned. Only the sales, and not the returns, appeared on the books. After news reports questioned the quality of Sunbeam's earnings, the board mounted an internal investigation, the result of which was the firing of Dunlap and his senior management team, restatement of six quarters of earnings, and shareholder losses of $1.2 billion the week of the restatements. An SEC lawsuit alleged securities fraud by Dunlap, four senior managers, and a partner at accounting firm Arthur Andersen, all of whom settled the charges without admitting or denying guilt.

Write-downs and Reversals   When a company stockpiles equipment or other goods that it can't sell, and the value of that inventory declines below what it will be sold for, accounting rules require that the company write down, or reduce the value of, the inventory on the balance sheet. In a well-run company write-downs should be minimal; they happen rarely if managers are paying proper attention to the supply-chain signals of customers and inventory levels and to the timing of new product introductions. But in 2001, telecom and Internet-gear companies wrote down massive amounts of equipment because they missed warning signs that their sales forecasts were overly optimistic. Cisco Systems Inc. shocked investors when it took one of the biggest such write-downs in April 2001.

Cisco embodied the Internet era. After all, it made many of the computers for corporate networks and Internet traffic routing. Its stock was worth $560 billion in mid-2000. With the pricking of the Internet bubble, however, customers quickly disappeared and equipment that had been ordered but was no longer needed piled up in warehouses. Making matters worse, Cisco had entered into "take-or-pay" supply contracts that required the company to buy specified amounts of product from its contract manufacturers. Cisco did not reveal the existence of these commitments until it filed its January 2001 quarterly report.

When demand for those products did not materialize as Cisco

had forecast, it had to pay for the product anyway. In April 2001 Cisco announced that it would take a $2.2 billion write-down on the inventory. By the end of the fiscal year (July 28, 2001), the write-down had grown to $2.8 billion.

Instead of liquidating the unnecessary inventory, Cisco kept it in warehouses and denied that it ever intended to use or sell the goods in a future quarter. In a pro forma earnings press release, Cisco buried the $2.2 billion excess inventory charge. Instead of a $2.7 billion net loss, according to GAAP, Cisco proclaimed that it had achieved a $230 million pro forma net gain. Analysts happily went along with the game by also excluding the write-downs in their earnings estimates, arguing that inventory write-downs were history, and revealed little about Cisco's future earnings prospects.

But Cisco's inventory pileup was no mere bookkeeping flub: real money was spent—unwisely, as it turns out. Treating the error as a bookkeeping exercise meant that Cisco managers weren't held accountable for a huge miscalculation in supply and demand—the crux of their job—and downplayed the loss of real shareholder wealth. In future years, Cisco would be able to report far better profits by comparison to its outsized loss in 2001. Profits can appear even healthier if a company ends up using or selling the gear it has written down, since the offsetting expenses associated with those sales will be vastly lower.

Eight months after Cisco's whale of a write-down, the company revealed in its first-quarter 2002 earnings report (for the quarter ending October 27, 2001) that it had done just that: it had sold or used in production or research $290 million in "excess inventory" that it had previously termed worthless. Cisco also admitted that it had overestimated the cost of terminating take-or-pay contracts by $187 million, for a 39 percent overestimation error. The upshot was that Cisco's 2001 net loss of $1 billion and its first-quarter 2002 net loss of $268 million would have been much worse without these inventory benefits.

Vendor Financing To boost sales, companies sometimes lend their customers the funds with which to make purchases. This practice, called vendor financing, is a favorite marketing technique of

---

CISCO SYSTEMS, INC.

NOTES TO CONSOLIDATED FINANCIAL STATEMENTS
(UNAUDITED)

Provision for Inventory

In the third quarter of fiscal 2001, the Company recorded an additional excess inventory charge of $2.2 billion. This additional excess inventory charge was subsequently reduced in the fourth quarter of fiscal 2001 by a $187 million benefit primarily related to lower settlement charges for purchase commitments. In the first quarter of fiscal 2002, this additional excess inventory charge was further reduced by a $290 million benefit primarily related to inventory used to manufacture products sold and for internal use in research and development and was credited to the provision for inventory.

A note in a Cisco Systems financial statement explained
that the company had sold or used inventory it had said
was worthless and had wrongly estimated the cost
to end certain contracts.

telecom companies. The problem is that telecoms had financed some $15 billion worth of sales by the end of 2000, producing a glut of products that would take a year to work off. For a while, vendor financing made telecom sales look spiffy, but that came back to haunt the companies when their customers could not pay their debts and certainly could not order more equipment.

Motorola offers a good illustration of how vendor financing can backfire. In February 2000 Motorola announced that it had sold $1.5 billion worth of equipment to Turkey's wireless carrier, Telsim. But investors had to wait more than a year to read in Motorola's proxy statement of March 30, 2001, that the company had lent $2.8 billion to customers to finance their purchase of Motorola wireless gear. Of that, $1.7 billion had gone to Telsim alone, a significant amount considering the risk to shareholders if a single customer fails to repay its debt.

Six weeks later, in a quarterly SEC filing, Motorola revealed that Telsim's debt was an even heftier $2 billion, out of a total $2.9 billion in so-called finance receivables, or customer loans. At that point, investors also learned that, of the $2 billion, $728 million was past due. Motorola's filing, however, left the strong impression that it had adequate collateral if Telsim failed to repay in thirty days. For example, Telsim had pledged 66 percent of its stock to Motorola in case of default.

In Motorola's next quarterly filing in July 2001, shareholders got some alarming news: the entire $2 billion Telsim loan was now in default. Under the terms of the loan, failure to repay a portion of the debt when it came due placed the entire loan in default. When Motorola notified Telsim that it was in default, the Turkish carrier issued more shares to the Turkish stock market and diluted the Telsim shares that Motorola held as collateral from 66 percent to 22 percent. That left Motorola little recourse but to write off the loan.

The following quarter, Motorola did just that when it took a $1.3 billion charge against earnings. Another $530 million in Telsim loans remained on the books, but Motorola may yet need to write that amount off as well.

A vigilant investor on the prowl for risky vendor financing would have spotted clues in Motorola's financial statements. The first hint of any exposure was buried on page 53 (of 104) in Motorola's March 2001 proxy statement. It referred to "one customer in Turkey" responsible for $1.7 billion out of $2.8 billion in long-term finance receivables. In the next three quarterly reports, or 10-Qs, Motorola parsimoniously dribbled out information about the Telsim loans. Finally, in November 2001, Motorola hit investors with the equivalent of a two-by-four when it announced the $1.3 billion charge in a press release.

A company spokesman says that because telecom companies use vendor financing as a competitive tool, it was not in Motorola's interest to reveal how much it had lent to finance its customer equipment purchases. Perhaps Motorola should ask itself: why is it in shareholders' interest to invest in a company that fails to disclose an enormous risk taken with their money?

Goodwill Games   A company measures the value of an acquisition by forecasting the cash it expects the acquired company to generate.

It also places a price on each of the assets, such as computers, physical plant, and inventory. Assets can also be intangible—that is, they have no physical presence—and include intellectual property such as patents, brand names, the quality of personnel, and market share. When one company buys another and pays a premium in excess of the value of its identifiable assets, the premium is called goodwill. Until 2001, companies could account for business acquisitions in two ways. Using the "purchase" method, they could allocate the amount paid to all the assets acquired, recognize the excess as goodwill and amortize, or charge as an expense each year, a proportionate amount of the goodwill over a period not to exceed forty years. Purchase accounting was unpopular because it caused a drag on future earnings. A far more popular alternative was called pooling-of-interests accounting, in which companies simply combined their assets and liabilities by declaring their combination a mere uniting of shareholder interests, as though no resources were used up and no goodwill was involved. Many companies, however, abused the pooling method and used it to disguise the true economic effect of mergers from shareholders.

The Financial Accounting Standards Board changed all that in 2001 when it closed the pool. It disallowed the pooling method, but at the same time it lifted the requirement for companies to amortize goodwill. This means goodwill no longer will reduce earnings for years to come. Instead, companies must determine annually the value of the goodwill acquired, and must write down that value on their books if they determine that it has been "impaired," or lost value, since the purchase took place.

AOL Time Warner Inc., the media titan created out of the merger of America Online and Time Warner, quickly showed how goodwill accounting changes can affect shareholders' interests, and laid bare the misjudgments of managers. AOL and Time Warner announced their merger in 2000, at the height of Internet frenzy. Once the merger was completed a year later, the combined company carried $127 billion in goodwill on its balance sheet. The large number reflected both the inflated stock prices of the era and the excessive prices companies paid for acquisitions.

SCHEDULE 14A INFORMATION
Proxy Statement Pursuant to Section 14(a) of the Securities
Exchange Act of 1934 (Amendment No.)

As of December 31, 2000, approximately $1.7 billion of the $2.8 billion in gross long-term finance receivables related to one customer in Turkey. At December 31, 2000, the Company had outstanding unfunded commitments of $494 million. At March 30, 2001, there are approximately $75 million of outstanding unfunded commitments.

*A Motorola proxy statement revealed for the first time
that a company in Turkey owed it $1.7 billion.*

Under the new FASB rule, the company announced that its goodwill was no longer worth $127 billion. To reflect the "impairment," it took the largest write-down in history, a $54 billion charge, in its 2002 first-quarter earnings report. Company officials and most analysts downplay the discrepancy by arguing that the write-down is nothing more than a paper correction. They also wave away the write-down because it involves no hard cash, and would have no effect on future earnings.

But such huge write-offs of goodwill aren't meaningless, mechanical events. They show that both companies hugely overvalued themselves and caused shareholders to overpay when the two companies merged. And writing off $54 billion means AOL Time Warner is admitting that nearly 25 percent of its $200 billion in assets is suddenly worthless. Says Jack Ciesielski, publisher of the *Analysts' Accounting Observer*: "How could a value impairment of that size have escaped detection?" True, the FASB's new rule is forcing AOL's hand, he concedes, but the timing is suspicious. "How can an asset be so glaringly impaired under one methodology today, but you didn't know it was impaired, under a different methodology, yesterday?"

Many other companies are following AOL's lead. In 2002, companies engaged in a massive effort to fool investors into believing that write-offs are unimportant. The truth is, goodwill write-offs let companies artificially lift their return on assets and return on equity, two key measures of a company's true value. AOL, for example, expects to generate as much as $6.8 billion in additional 2002 profit because it won't have to amortize any of the goodwill it carries on its balance sheet. Likewise, Bank of America has $12 billion of goodwill on its balance sheet that it no longer needs to amortize. By not deducting the goodwill from earnings over the next twenty years, the result could be a 2002 earnings boost of about $600 million ($12 billion divided by 20 equals $600 million).

In-Process R&D   Another purchase accounting trick occurs when the acquiring company takes an immediate, one-time write-off of research and development that is not yet ready for commercial use, and calls it "in-process R&D." Such R&D write-downs have the effect of immediately reducing the amount of goodwill on the balance sheet. What's wrong with that? First, because accounting rules allow companies a great deal of flexibility in determining which R&D costs will never result in a commercial product, some of these R&D expenses may be vastly overstated. Second, some of the R&D may, in fact, produce future revenues. But when excessive R&D write-offs are made, they aren't properly offsetting, as accounting rules require, the resulting revenues. This way, future earnings numbers are inflated. Best of all for company managers, most investors won't remember the big write-off from years earlier.

IBM Corp. first showed the usefulness of this technique in 1995 when it acquired software company Lotus Development. IBM wrote off much of the purchase price by calling it in-process R&D. The practice reached ridiculous heights in the 1998 purchase of

MCI Communications Corp. by WorldCom. Of MCI's $40 billion price tag, WorldCom sought to write off $6 billion as in-process R&D. If the SEC had not forced WorldCom to lower the R&D write-off to $3 billion, the company could have boosted earnings by $50 million for decades to come.

Even though the FASB has made it a lot easier for companies to cope with goodwill, most experts expect companies to continue to use the in-process R&D ploy to shrink the amount of goodwill on their balance sheet. The new FASB rules give company managers an incentive to load as much of the purchase price as possible onto in-process R&D, to get the earnings charge behind them. This way, companies can reduce their chances of having to write down impaired goodwill in the future. You can watch for this ploy by carefully reading what is called the "management's discussion and analysis" section of a quarterly or annual report, where most companies explain how much of an acquisition's R&D costs they're writing off.

Recognizing Revenue Before Its Time　When a company sells a product, it records the sale on the books as revenue. Companies must follow a variety of accounting rules to determine when revenue can be recorded. The sale of a $2,000 computer, for example, is recorded once it is delivered and the customer is obligated to pay for it, not when payment is actually received. Not all sales are straightforward, either. For example, a company may sell a five-year service contract along with the computer, with payment for the service contract spread equally over the five years. Under GAAP, the service contract revenue can be recorded only as it is "earned," or 20 percent each year. If the computer and the service contract are sold together for a single price, separating the components can be subject to manipulation. Likewise, a company may sell computer equipment and accompanying software, granting the customer the right to test out the software for sixty days before the sale is final. Under GAAP, the software revenue can be recorded only after the sixty-day trial period has ended and the customer is satisfied. Booking premature revenues results in inflated sales figures and false earnings numbers.

How quickly revenue is booked is especially important in high-tech industries where multiyear service contracts, follow-on equipment upgrades, and no-fault equipment returns often occur.

An SEC enforcement case involving software company Micro-Strategy Inc. illustrates the accounting games companies can play with revenue recognition. MicroStrategy sells software that helps companies manage their inventory better by analyzing customer sales patterns. Chairman and CEO Michael J. Saylor, however, had big plans to turn his company into a provider of intelligence to busy Americans—instantaneous reports of everything from stock prices to airport delays—over personal communication devices. To do that, he needed to pump up MicroStrategy's stock price and convince investors that he wasn't just another dot-commer. And goal number one was showing that MicroStrategy, almost alone among the new generation of Internet companies, could deliver profits quarter after quarter. A typical press release read like the one issued for the fourth quarter of 1999, in which MicroStrategy touted its "12th consecutive quarter of positive earnings" of $3.8 million. Over three years, the company claimed to have earned $18 million on revenues of $365 million. At its height in March 2000 the share price hit $333. But this symbol of the New Economy quickly became a prime example of Internet bubble-mania.

As it turns out, the SEC would allege MicroStrategy was cooking the books by repeatedly violating accounting rules on when to recognize revenue on its software and service contracts. At the end of a quarter, the company often did not sign or date contracts that customers had inked. This was done so that management could decide, after the fact, in which quarter to assign the revenue. In addition, the company three times applied revenue to an already completed quarter, even though the customer hadn't signed a contract by the end of the quarter. It also booked revenue on service contracts before their time. By doing so, the company was on the hook to deliver consulting and new software applications to customers for years into the future, but the revenue for those services had already been recognized, in violation of GAAP.

Altogether, MicroStrategy had wrongly recognized revenues of

$66 million on $365 million in revenue from 1997 to 1999. Instead of positive earnings, MicroStrategy should have reported net losses all three years. The miracle was a mirage. When the restated results were announced in March 2000, the stock lost $11 billion in value in one day. The shares kept dropping like a stone until they hit a rock-bottom $1.10 in 2001. Without admitting or denying guilt, Saylor and two other top company officials settled an SEC complaint, paid a total of $1 million in civil penalties, and disgorged, or gave up, a total of $10 million in ill-gotten stock sales.

As you can see, companies will use all kinds of accounting tricks to make their earnings glow more brightly. Most companies aren't committing fraud when they resort to smoke-and-mirrors accounting, though the SEC increasingly is forcing companies to adhere to the spirit of accounting rules and be more transparent. The real travesty with earnings manipulation is that much of it is perfectly legal. That's because GAAP has plenty of built-in flexibility that allows companies to take liberties.

To stop the numbers game, Warren Buffett suggests, and I agree, that corporate boards should require auditors to rate the aggressiveness of the accounting practices used by the companies they audit. Such ratings would rank, on a scale of 1 to 10, how aggressive a company's accounting policies are. The use of vendor financing, or stretching the boundaries of revenue recognition, would push a company's rating upward. In addition, audit committees should ask the accountants—and record in the minutes of the board meeting—which of the client company's accounting practices the auditor finds unsettling or most aggressive. Which practices would the auditor handle differently if it could?

In the end, investors must change their behavior, too. You should not follow the herd and grab for shares just because the headline on a press release trumpets an increase in pro forma earnings per share. Conversely, investors should not abandon ship just because a company fails to meet analysts' expectations. It's your responsibility to dig deeper to see what the company's true prospects are. It's a

SECURITIES AND EXCHANGE COMMISSION
Washington, D.C. 20549

FORM 10-K

[X]   Annual Report pursuant to Section 13 or 15(d) of the Securities Exchange
Act of 1934

For the fiscal year ended December 31, 1999

MICROSTRATEGY INCORPORATED
(Exact name of registrant as specified in its charter)

Recent Developments

Our operations and prospects have been and are significantly affected by the
recent developments described below.

Restatement of Financial Results. We are revising our 1999, 1998 and 1997
financial statements. The principal reason for these revisions to revenues and
operating results was to conform with the accounting principles articulated in

Statement of Position 97-2 "Software Revenue Recognition." These revisions
primarily addressed the recognition of revenue for certain software arrangements
which should be accounted for under the subscription method or the percentage of
completion method,

In the
course of reviewing our revenue recognition on various transactions, we became
aware that, in certain instances, we had recorded revenue on certain contracts
in one reporting period where customer signature and delivery had been
completed, but where the contract may not have been fully executed by us in that
reporting period.

With the concurrence of our auditors, we reduced our 1999 reported revenue
from $205.3 million to $151.3 million and our results of operations from diluted
net income per share of $0.15 to a diluted net loss per share of $(0.44).
Correspondingly, deferred revenue at December 31, 1999 increased from $16.8
million to $71.3 million. We also reduced our reported revenue for 1998 from
$106.4 million to $95.5 million and our results of operations from diluted net
income per share of $0.08 to diluted net loss per share of $(0.03). In addition,
we reduced our reported revenue for 1997 from $53.6 million to $52.6 million and
our results of operations from diluted net income per share of $0.00 to diluted
net loss per share of $(0.02).

*MicroStrategy's 1999 annual report contained revisions because of
revenue recognition errors. Three years of profits turned into losses.*

lot safer to own shares in a company that believes in transparency and whose earnings have not been gilded than to own shares in a company that smooths out earnings by manipulating reserves. Eventually, accounting tricks will force companies to restate earnings, and huge shareholder losses almost always follow a restatement.

Nothing will change corporate managers, auditors, and boards more than a change in investor expectations. If you demand more transparency and an end to the numbers game—and you back up those demands with your investment dollars—companies will have little choice but to change their behavior, too.

CHAPTER SEVEN

PAY ATTENTION TO
THE PLUMBING

Ever wonder what happens to your order to buy stock once you place it with your broker, or hit "send" to an online broker? If you think it goes directly to the floor of the New York Stock Exchange (NYSE) or into the computerized network run by Nasdaq, think again. What happens to your order is one of the mysteries of Wall Street that few people understand. Many orders are matched off-exchange, then centrally reported to an exchange. There is a cost to buying stock, over and above the per-share price you pay. The cost depends on how and where your order is filled. Sometimes the "cost" of trading involves paying a higher price for your shares because your broker failed to route your order to the market with the best selling price. Higher trading costs also result if your broker, or the exchange he sent it to, delayed filling your order and the share price moved against you. Other times your broker may send your order to a market that doesn't have the best price because he received a payment to do so.

Did you ever stop to ask who pays for the army of people buzzing about the NYSE floor every day? Or for the thousands of people working behind the scenes at Nasdaq? If you think it's your brokerage firm or some other third party, wrong again. As an investor, you pay for all the middlemen, floor clerks, and telecommunications and other electronic apparatus that make markets run smoothly. The cost may not be apparent. It may be hidden in the commission you pay your broker, or disguised in the somewhat higher price you pay for your shares. But it's there.

Both cases—the cost of not finding the best match for your order and the cost exacted by the exchange and its various middlemen who handle your trade—are called transaction costs. They are costs over which you have little control. But that is changing. Transaction costs are the cause of much debate and controversy today, and the root of an immense struggle pitting the NYSE against Nasdaq; both established exchanges against new electronic networks; large investment banking firms against the exchanges; and small investors against institutional investors.

In this chapter, you'll learn all about transaction costs and how they affect you. You'll also learn about recent structural changes in the stock markets, some of which have been revolutionary, that affect trading costs. I'll explain the differences between the NYSE and Nasdaq; the role of middlemen, such as NYSE specialists and Nasdaq market-makers; and the importance of newfangled systems called electronic communication networks, or ECNs. In short, this is where you'll learn about the stock market's plumbing.

Knowledge Is Power

Why should you care? One reason is that understanding how all this works is the first step to making the stock trading system work for you. As an ordinary investor, your interests are not always uppermost in the minds of exchange officials who oversee the trading process. The exchanges, frankly, operate to benefit listed companies and the middlemen, such as the NYSE seat holders and specialists and Nasdaq dealers, because these are the people who handle your trades and interact with the exchange.

You should also care because the stock transaction process, much like the plumbing in your own home, can cost you dearly if you don't pay attention to it. Individual investors pay higher transaction costs because no one is paid to look out for their interests. There was even a long period when investors were routinely cheated by corrupt practices among Nasdaq dealers. Dealers were able to get away with this behavior because few investors understood the business of trading stocks. A group of NYSE floor brokers in 1998 also were found to be taking unfair advantage of their customers by trading ahead of their orders. If you understand the basic mechanics of how stocks trade, you'll be better equipped to watch out for your own interests.

Some of the changes we'll discuss in this chapter were forced on the stock markets by Congress and the SEC, such as the switch in 2001 from quoting prices in fractions to dollars and cents. The exchanges, on their own, adopted other measures to survive an onslaught of competitive pressure. With each new change in market structure, the individual investor has been a major beneficiary. My hope is that the more you understand this, the more you'll want to keep pressure on the markets.

Transaction costs today are a lot lower than they were just five years ago. Nasdaq and the NYSE have adopted new trading technologies and their middlemen have eliminated markups that increase investor costs. Quoting prices in decimals instead of fractions alone has saved investors billions. But while both markets have made huge strides, more can be done, especially at the New York Stock Exchange, which has resisted trading technologies that would erode the franchise of its specialists and floor brokers. The evolution of our markets is like the nine innings of a baseball game—and we're only in the top of the third inning.

The Buttonwood Tree

To understand the stock markets of today, it helps to understand the origins of the NYSE. On May 17, 1792, twenty-four commodities merchants and traders signed a pact to trade securities, at fixed commissions, under a buttonwood tree facing 68 Wall Street. At the time, about the only securities that traded were government bonds issued to pay for the Revolutionary War and stocks issued by the Bank of the United States. But soon there were more bank stocks and shares issued by insurance companies and railroads. The issues were sold in a central auction, where auctioneers received a commission for every security sold. A customer's agent, called a broker, would also receive a per-share commission.

By 1817, the stock market had adopted a constitution and the formal name of the New York Stock and Exchange Board. Only members were allowed to trade. A list of stocks to be auctioned was read aloud each day, and members put in bids (to buy) and offers (to sell) while seated, which is why an NYSE member today is said to have a "seat" on the exchange. In 1871 the exchange introduced continuous floor trading, and in 1903 it moved to its present location at the corner of Wall and Broad Streets.

The NYSE has held on to many cherished traditions. It continues to trade what are called "listed" stocks, or those that meet the exchange's current listing requirements. Today that means an NYSE company must have three years of profits, a market value of at least $100 million, and a minimum of 2,000 shareholders and 1.1 million shares outstanding. The NYSE still conducts trading in an auctionlike setting, where buy and sell orders meet in a central location on the floor, called a trading "post." Each stock still has its own auctioneer; today this person is called a specialist. And the NYSE floor is still an exclusive club available only to members who own a seat. The NYSE has 1,366 members whose seats can be bought and sold. At the end of 2001, a seat was worth $2.2 million.

The NYSE, also known as the Big Board, operates at times more like a country club than a quasi-public utility. It is captive of the seat holders, specialists, and floor brokers who dominate the floor action. And like a country club whose management is torn between its tennis players who want more tennis courts and its golfers who want new golf carts, the NYSE is riven by conflict.

The NYSE membership is divided among three types of people: floor specialists and two kinds of brokers. There are "house brokers" who are employed by the giant investment banks and brokerage firms of Wall Street (firms such as Merrill Lynch, Goldman Sachs, and Morgan Stanley) to execute their own firms' trades and those of their customers. And there are independent floor brokers, also called "two-dollar brokers," who handle trades for some institutional investors such as mutual funds, and smaller brokerage firms. The name comes from the commission fee of $2 per 100 shares that members once charged one another.

The 480 specialists and roughly 400 independent floor brokers together make up the majority of the NYSE's membership, placing the floor brokers employed by the major firms in the minority. This is an important point to remember. It will help you understand why the NYSE is reluctant to introduce changes, such as matching shares by computer instead of by humans. While that would cut costs for investors and the Wall Street firms, it would also reduce the role, and the profits, of the middlemen. More automation could make many specialists and floor brokers redundant, but before that happens, the middlemen themselves would have to vote in favor of it. The possibility of that happening is even more remote when you consider that 66 percent of the NYSE's seats are leased from retired or absentee NYSE members, who nevertheless retain the right to vote and have little incentive to cut off a lucrative source of income.

What's So Special about Specialists?

On the NYSE floor on any given day, you'll see the specialist standing in front of a bank of electronic screens, surrounded by a crowd of people shouting out numbers. He keeps an electronic book of orders, and from this book he matches the buys and sells. Orders arrive at the specialist's post through various routes. One of these is the NYSE's SuperDOT (for Designated Order Turnaround) system, which transmits orders electronically from member firms. Orders can also be hand-carried by floor brokers to the post. The specialist's job is to conduct a fair auction. Sometimes he does this by using his own money to trade shares, when, for example, there are too many sells and not enough buys. Specialists receive a commission every time they act as agents on behalf of an incoming order. In other words, they get a cut of each transaction in their stock, unless it's for their own account.

Specialists are in business for themselves, and they often buy and sell shares for their own accounts. Unlike other types of auctioneers, the specialist is allowed to bid for shares while conducting the auction. If you think a specialist's ability to see incoming orders gives him a built-in advantage when trading for himself, you're right. It's like being in a card game in which only one of the players gets to see everyone else's hand. Specialists exploit that advantage, too: in late 2001, they were accounting for about 32 percent of all the shares traded. And the work can be very lucrative. In 1999, when LaBranche & Co., a large specialist firm, went public, its prospectus revealed that senior partners each earned about $1.7 million. Naturally, specialists don't want to see their roles reduced in any way.

There is one more powerful group that interacts with the NYSE that you need to know about. To cater to institutional investors, such as pension funds, mutual funds, and insurance companies, the large Wall Street firms started what are called block-trading desks in the 1960s. Some of the traders on these desks sit in offices literally above the NYSE trading floor, and thus are called "upstairs" traders. They match buy and sell orders from institutions, and sometimes use their firms' capital to take the other side of an order when a buyer or seller can't immediately be found. Completed trades are then reported to the NYSE, which then makes the trade public by printing it on what is called the consolidated trade tape. This is the same ticker tape that runs across the bottom of financial news shows and on Web sites (usually delayed by fifteen minutes).

Today, about 20 percent of the NYSE's daily volume, which has ballooned from an average of 179 million in 1991 to 1 billion in 2000, consists of block trades, defined as 10,000 or more shares, that are handled upstairs and never make it to the NYSE floor. The big firms have calculated that upstairs trading costs less than sending an order to the floor. Their large customers, mutual funds such as Fidelity Investments, have noticed the difference, too. And they have noticed that the new electronic communications networks (ECNs) can execute trades for even less. This is true especially for highly liquid stocks, or those shares for which there are enough buyers and sellers to allow trading without excessively moving the price. Institutional investors are attracted to any trading mechanism that cuts costs, since investment returns are highly dependent on transaction costs.

The big firms' fear is that the NYSE will fall behind technologically, and that the ECNs and other innovative trading systems will eat into their business, possibly undermining their franchise for bringing companies public through initial public offerings. For decades, exchange middlemen were an acceptable cost of doing business. That's no longer true. The dominant member firms, including Merrill Lynch, Goldman Sachs, and Morgan Stanley—sometimes together called MGM for short—and their institutional customers have become impatient with the high cost of trading. They may not have a majority of the votes at the NYSE, but they have leverage: the top ten firms account for about one-half of the orders at the NYSE. They are convinced that costs could be much lower if the exchange were more automated.

Before we get to that, let's discuss how the other major stock exchange, Nasdaq, works. It's an entirely different animal from the NYSE. In fact, it's not really an exchange at all, though it's seeking SEC approval to become one. Still, Nasdaq serves the same function as an exchange in that it's a place where buyers and sellers meet. If the NYSE is the home of the older, more genteel corporate establishment, then Nasdaq represents the cool, entrepreneurial cutting edge. It's a fairly recent creation, begun in 1971 by the National Association of Securities Dealers as a trading venue for companies that failed to meet the NYSE's strict listing standards. Small technology companies that sprouted in the 1980s, including Apple, Microsoft, Cisco Systems, and Intel, did not qualify to list in New York, but they found a warm welcome at Nasdaq. Instead of "graduating" to the NYSE once they met the listing requirements, they and most other tech companies have chosen to stay with Nasdaq.

Nasdaq: The Underdog Market

The acronym "Nasdaq" stands for National Association of Securities Dealers Automated Quotations, but today the term has taken on a meaning all its own as the brash young upstart that challenged the staid NYSE and, by some measures, even beat the Big Board.

The boom years of the 1990s were especially good to Nasdaq, when many individual investors flocked to Nasdaq's high-tech companies.

Nasdaq certainly has suffered since the technology boom faded, when some of its superstar companies lost 90 percent of their value. Still, at the end of March 2002 it had 3,994 member companies, versus the NYSE's 2,784. Its average daily share volume of 1.7 billion regularly beats the NYSE's 1.2 billion shares per day. Nasdaq, however, lags the NYSE in market value: Nasdaq companies were capitalized at $2.7 trillion versus the NYSE's $12 trillion, also as of March 2002.

Unlike the NYSE, Nasdaq is not an auction market that sends orders through a single specialist. Instead, multiple dealers openly compete against one another for investor orders by quoting two prices: a lower bid price at which they are willing to buy shares and a higher ask price at which they are ready to sell shares. The dealers, also called market-makers, specialize in a handful of stocks. They provide buy and sell quotes—and must honor those quotes by filling orders at those prices—not on a central floor but over an electronic network. One way to differentiate between the two markets is to view the NYSE as an auction house where buyers and sellers meet at a designated place. Customers bid against one another with an auctioneer (the specialist) acting as a referee. Nasdaq, on the other hand, is much like a flea market. A collection of independent dealers gathers in one place (in cyberspace over the Nasdaq network) and customers interact with those dealers rather than one another.

A Nasdaq market-maker takes the other side of three-fourths of every Nasdaq transaction, so that if you buy 100 shares of Microsoft, the shares most likely will come from a market-maker. They help smooth out the flow of orders, since an order to buy 100,000 shares of Microsoft won't always arrive at the same time as an order to sell 100,000 shares in the software company.

Today, there are some five hundred Nasdaq market-makers; each stock has at least three and some have up to forty market-makers quoting prices in competition against each other. They do not collect fees or commissions, as on the NYSE (although that could change soon, as you'll learn below). Instead, they make their profit from the spread, which is the difference between the price they pay for shares from a seller and the price at which they later sell those shares to another buyer. The wider the spread, the greater the market-maker's profit.

At age thirty, the underdog exchange has proven to be a nimble competitor to the mighty NYSE, and yet it almost suffered a fatal blow in the 1990s. In 1993, I heard market gossip that some Nasdaq dealers were keeping spreads artificially wide. As I explained, spreads are the market-maker's bread and butter—the wider the better. When I was chairman of the American Stock Exchange from 1978 to 1989, it was common knowledge that Nasdaq investors were paying abnormally wide spreads, but no one was able to show outright collusion. Amex calculated that Nasdaq investors were penalized by $2 billion a year because of wide spreads. Nasdaq officials dismissed the report out of hand.

But the rumors continued. They were fueled by a May 1994 academic study by William G. Christie and Paul H. Schultz, who analyzed years of trading data and found a suspicious lack of trading in odd eighths, such as $30⅜ (share prices were quoted in fractions of a dollar until 2001). By quoting only in even eighth increments, market-makers were achieving two goals. With such a yawning gap between buyers and sellers, investors were forced to use an intermediary to bring them together. And as long as prices were quoted in even eighths, market-makers could guarantee themselves a one-quarter spread, or a hefty profit of 25 cents per share. The study, along with several investigative news stories, prompted class-action lawsuits and a Justice Department antitrust probe. As I settled into my new duties at the SEC, I knew the agency had to take a look at whether dealers were ripping off investors.

The Nasdaq Case: Shameful and Shocking

What we found was shameful and shocking. We were able to document that some Nasdaq market-makers were secretly agreeing to keep spreads wide. They were fixing prices in violation of antitrust laws—to the detriment of investors. Market-makers who tried to narrow the spread by quoting prices in between the acceptable even-eighths gap were verbally harassed or ostracized. Some market-makers conspired with other dealers against their own customers. Or if a customer's limit order—an order to buy or sell a stock at a specific price—would have narrowed the spread, market-makers routinely withheld the order by not displaying it to the rest of the market. And many market-makers were failing to honor the prices they quoted—a practice that violates one of the basic rules of market-making—as well as reporting completed trades hours after the fact, so as to mislead the rest of the market. When you added it all up, it was clear that the Nasdaq pricing process had become corrupted.

At first, some of the staff in the Division of Market Regulation, which is the part of the SEC that oversees exchanges, didn't want to believe the allegations. We had let ourselves, as regulators, get too cozy with the stock market we were supposed to be watching over. In particular, we failed to see that the NASD had gradually been taken over by a cabal of dealers who used the NASD's disciplinary process to punish certain players, such as day traders, while failing to prosecute serious infractions by market-makers.

The corruption and price-fixing became all too clear when the agency's enforcement division subpoenaed tapes of phone conversations between dealers. Firms routinely make such tapes in case of a dispute between trading parties. The very first tape to arrive at the SEC showed evidence of collusion, as did subsequent ones. Traders knew they were being taped, but the collusion had become so accepted, they showed no fear.

Here's an example of one such taped conversation. A market-maker we'll call Trader 1 is looking to unload a substantial quantity of shares in a company called Parametric Technology Corp. Minutes earlier, another market-maker had raised his bid price (the price at which he's willing to buy shares) on Parametric to $26¼. But Trader 1 needs another market-maker to follow suit, thus creating the appearance that demand for the stock is rising. Trader 1's hope is that he'll get more for his Parametric shares by selling into a rising market. So Trader 1 calls Trader 2 and asks him to raise his bid. Trader 2 is willing—and together they agree to a side deal of 2,000 shares to cover their tracks. Here is their conversation:

Trader 1:   Are you doing anything in Parametrics?

Trader 2:   Ah, running for the hills, bro.

Trader 1:   Okay, can you . . .

Trader 2:   What can I do for you?

Trader 1:   Can you go a quarter bid for me?

Trader 2:   Yeah, sure.

Trader 1:   If you want, I'll sell you two at a quarter, just go up there. I'm long and I want it going.

Trader 2:   Yeah.

Trader 1:   Okay, I sold you . . .

Trader 2:   Two. That would be great.

Trader 1:   I sold you two at a quarter. Just go there, okay?

Trader 2:   I'm goosing it, cuz.

Trader 1:   Thank you.

Beyond confirming the dealer collusion that many had long suspected, the investigation brought into sharp focus a basic flaw that had developed: Nasdaq had become a two-tiered market. One tier, the official Nasdaq dealer network with its wide spreads, was the sucker's market for small orders, mostly placed by individual investors. The other tier was an electronic market called Instinet, majority-owned by Britain's Reuters Group PLC. Because spreads were narrower on Instinet, it was the market of choice for mutual funds and other institutional investors. But it was off limits to individuals.

It was also off limits to day traders, folks who weren't dealers but acted like them by trading stocks all day long, searching out small ticks in price from which they could profit. They often used a Nasdaq network called the Small Order Execution System, or SOES. SOES was set up in 1984 to give small investors quick execution for orders up to 1,000 shares. Since the 1987 market crash, when individual investors were unable to get their brokers on the phone and Nasdaq market-makers failed to honor their quotes, market-makers have been required to fill orders that come to Nasdaq via SOES. Day traders learned that they could take advantage of market-makers' failure to update quotes when the market moved, and so they developed their own electronic ordering systems to swiftly get their orders executed on SOES. Irate, the Wall Street firms' market-makers referred to them as "SOES bandits," and tried to put them out of business. They even used the NASD's disciplinary process to harass the most active day traders. But the SOES bandits knew that market-makers were fixing spreads, and helped uncover the collusion that was taking place by working with Justice, the SEC, and plaintiffs' lawyers. The day traders not only exposed Nasdaq's flaws, but they also were the source of much innovation. Such ECNs as Island and Archipelago largely grew out of day-trader demands for quicker executions.

After two years of investigation, Justice in 1996 settled a civil antitrust case against twenty-four dealer firms. But that was just the opening salvo in what would turn into a three-year legal nightmare for Nasdaq, its parent group, two dozen firms, and about fifty individual dealers in those firms. First, plaintiffs' lawyers filed on behalf of investors class-action lawsuits against the firms, including such powerhouses as Merrill Lynch, Salomon Smith Barney, PaineWebber, and J. P. Morgan. Those cases were settled in 1998 for $1 billion. At the SEC, we pursued a three-pronged remedy that included a censure of the NASD, civil cases against the firms and individuals involved, and new rules to make sure the abuses couldn't happen again.

One of the most disappointing aspects of the Nasdaq case was our finding that the NASD, which owned the Nasdaq market and was its primary regulator, for years knew about many of these transgressions and had turned a blind eye. Why? Because, we learned, Nasdaq market-makers had undue influence over the NASD's oversight and disciplinary committees. The inmates were running the asylum.

Every stock exchange must act as its own self-regulatory organization, or SRO, to enforce the securities laws. The philosophy behind this is that an exchange knows intimately what takes place within its own walls, and thus is in a better position to police itself. The SEC, with its limited resources, can monitor the SRO to make sure it has rules that prevent investor fraud and market manipulation, and that promote fair trading practices. The SRO must make sure that price quotes are fair and informative and not misleading or fictitious. And when someone is alleged to have stepped out of line, the SRO must have procedures to investigate the charges and, if necessary, take disciplinary action.

Sadly, the NASD's position as a self-regulator was seriously compromised. The NASD board, however, was in denial. It appointed a commission to recommend changes, which I considered window dressing. The NASD's directors refused to accept that they were overseeing an organization whose core was rotten. In one of the most tension-packed moments of my life, I appeared before the board, in private, and read from prepared remarks. I laid out what my enforcement crew had uncovered, and what we wanted them to do. I said they had an obligation to the investing public to adopt sweeping changes in the way they operated. If they refused, the SEC would have no choice but to force their hand. They listened politely, asked a few questions, and dismissed me.

When the NASD refused to accept the remedial actions I proposed, I had to conclude that the group was incapable of reforming itself. In August 1996 we made public what is called a 21(a) report—named for the investigative powers granted the SEC in the Securities Exchange Act of 1934—that explained what we had learned from our probe. In a highly unusual and controversial step, we then censured the NASD and issued a detailed list of remedies. We placed the NASD on probation for three years, forcing the group to answer to an outside monitor.

Parts of the industry, fearing expensive litigation from investors if they admitted guilt, were willing to fight to the death. Dan Tully, the CEO of Merrill Lynch and a longtime friend, mediated between this faction and the SEC enforcement staff. At a marathon, twenty-hour session at SEC headquarters, Tully moved back and forth between my office and the firms' representatives huddled two floors below, and worked out a settlement.

We made them clean house. They had to change the makeup of various NASD and Nasdaq boards and create an independent subsidiary, called NASD Regulation Inc., to separate market surveillance from stock trading. We laid out strict requirements to make sure that everyone from independent board members to hearing officers who preside over disciplinary cases had no conflicts of interest. And we required them to spend $100 million over five years to install new audit systems to detect late reporting of trades and other rule violations.

I also insisted on new management at NASD and Nasdaq, and recruited Frank Zarb for the job. Zarb and I had worked together at Shearson Hayden Stone in the 1960s, and I knew I could trust him. From 1997 to 2001, when he served as chairman and CEO of both NASD and Nasdaq, we worked closely together as he steered a severely wounded and demoralized organization back to health.

Because of the overwhelming evidence of collusion in the tapes, we also brought civil suits against twenty-eight companies and fifty individual dealers. Those were all settled on the same day in 1998, with PaineWebber agreeing to pay the largest fine—almost $7 million. None of the firms or their traders admitted or denied guilt, but their civil penalties added up to $26 million.

Order-Handling Rules: The Big Bang

Separately, we dealt with the price quotation flaws and the two-tiered market with a new rulebook, issued in late 1996, called order-handling rules. We didn't realize it at the time, but these rules would trigger a big bang in the Nasdaq market, and eventually the NYSE.

The order-handling rules require that market-makers display— on Nasdaq or any other market center, such as an ECN—any limit order (an order that specifies a price) that improves their buy or sell quote. This stopped market-makers from hiding limit orders from the rest of the market to keep spreads wide. A second requirement forces ECNs, such as Instinet, also to publish their quotes. This eliminated two-tiered markets—a superior one for institutions and an inferior one for retail customers. The rules also place new obligations on market-makers and brokers to obtain what is called "best execution" for their customers. This means that it's not good enough just to fill an order; dealers must also try to get their customers a better price, a concept known as price improvement.

Some of these ideas, such as the limit order display rule, had been kicking around internally for a decade or more, but previous commissions rejected them as overly intrusive. The package was largely devised over the summer of 1995 by Bob Colby, the number-two person in the Division of Market Regulation; Mark Tellini, one of my legal counsels; and Rich Lindsey, then the chief economist for the SEC and later the head of Market Regulation. But I don't think even they knew they were about to set off a chain reaction of seismic proportions.

And this is where the market structure story gets very interesting. New rules of fair play and new technology came together to transform Nasdaq. The rules, for example, gave individual investors an equal footing against Nasdaq dealers who had been taking unfair advantage of their orders by executing them only when it was profitable for the dealer. But once retail investors could see their orders displayed in the Nasdaq system, dealers could no longer ignore them or trade around them.

The result? Spreads narrowed by 30 percent, saving investors $25 billion in the first year. Simultaneously, the roaring bull market and the advent of online trading were luring millions of individual investors into the market for the first time. Their business grew to rival that of institutional investors, and many of these new orders were being funneled to ECNs. Already, ECNs had gained new business as market-makers began sending them orders to satisfy the limit order display rule. The obscure ECNs were now a force to be reckoned with.

ECNs and Wholesalers

What, exactly, are ECNs? In short, they are electronic dating systems that match buyers and sellers. Remember earlier when I said that the NYSE is much like an auction, and that Nasdaq resembles a flea market? Well, ECNs are akin to eBay, the Internet auction company that lets buyers and sellers meet directly in cyberspace. ECNs are cheaper because they are designed to cut out the middlemen. This is what the fancy term "disintermediation" means. Investors, through their brokers, send ECNs their orders, and within seconds they appear on the ECN's screen, along with many others'. The ECNs are transparent because they aren't looking to hide orders, or to trade on the knowledge gained from an advance peek at orders, as middlemen sometimes do. ECNs, therefore, don't use your order as a weapon against you. They make their money by charging a per-share fee. At the end of 2001, ECNs had captured 42 percent of the share in Nasdaq market-making, and had just begun moving in on the NYSE.

The ECNs weren't the only force pushing Nasdaq and NYSE into a competitive corner. There were also wholesale market-makers, such as Knight Trading Group in Jersey City, N.J., and San Francisco's Schwab Capital Markets, owned by the same Charles Schwab who pioneered discount brokerage. Knight grew rapidly because it paid brokers for orders—called payment for order flow—while Schwab engaged in a practice called "internalization," in which buy and sell orders are matched internally. Both practices are problematic. Payment for order flow gave brokers an incentive to search out the highest bidder for their customer orders, rather than the market center that offered the best possible execution of investor orders. And internalization means that a large chunk of orders is cordoned off from the rest of the market, possibly denying investors a more favorable execution in another location. In both cases—payment for order flow and internalization—the market-makers were matching, but rarely beating, the market's best advertised price. These practices met the letter, but not the spirit, of the best-execution rule.

In a short period of time, the wholesalers began to dominate the flow of orders. They had become money-making machines. Knight grew to handle about 20 percent of the volume in the most active Nasdaq stocks by mid-1999. And Schwab Capital Markets was raking in almost half a billion dollars a year in market-making revenue. Neither contributed much to the crucial process of price discovery—the result of order interaction over the Nasdaq network or the auction taking place on the floor of the NYSE. But with a guaranteed flow of orders, and most customers not knowing where their orders were ending up, there was little reason to send orders elsewhere to get price improvement.

This development worried me. I was concerned about fragmentation, which is what happens when markets are divvied up into smaller market centers. While ECNs and the wholesale marketmakers had introduced much-needed competition and vitality to the business of trading stocks, they also made it tougher for buyers and sellers to meet in a central place. When that happens, it's hard to know what the "true" price of a stock is. Fragmentation can result in buyers paying more and sellers getting less for their shares. It can mean waiting longer to get orders filled. And it can result in Balkanization: a buyer in one market paying a different price from a buyer in another venue, even though they traded the same shares at the same moment.

Fragmentation of the markets was just one of many structural issues that I became obsessed with, almost from the moment the last Nasdaq case was settled to when I left the SEC three years later. In the summer of 1999 I learned that my concern about fragmentation was magnified in the boardrooms of the major brokerage firms, and not just because orders sent to one location weren't interacting with orders at another location. Sure, that caused them to worry, but not as much as the challenge that wholesalers and ECNs posed to their highly profitable initial public stock offering (IPO) business, which depends on the ability to predict demand for new issues of stock. Knowing the level of demand ahead of time allows the underwriting firm to price IPO shares more accurately. But with about one-half of orders being diverted to wholesalers, the brokerage firms worried that they could not predict the demand for retail orders, and that could cause them to lose their iron grip on the lucrative IPO business.

How the Virtual CLOB Was Born

A late-summer meeting in the dining room of Hank Paulson, the chairman and CEO of Goldman Sachs Group, convinced me that the time was ripe to lay down some markers on how the markets should evolve. Paulson relayed his frustration with the NYSE, which was brushing off his concerns that the Big Board was falling behind technologically. It lacked the automation and anonymity of ECNs. Because only the specialist could see what was in the order book, it lacked transparency. And fragmentation was growing— there was no competition among the orders that market centers were receiving. To fix this, Paulson endorsed an idea that had been floating around for years: a central limit-order book, or CLOB, which is a fancy term for collecting all orders in a single clearing-house, for all investors to see. Order-matching would take place on a first come, first served basis.

The major firms very much wanted a CLOB because they thought it would get them closer to their goal of faster, cheaper transactions without middlemen, as well as protect their premier role in the IPO business. It also solved the problem of orders being isolated at separate market centers. I was taken aback by the extent of the unhappiness with the NYSE, and promised to work with the firms and the NYSE to address their concerns.

The CLOB was an interesting concept, but it raised almost as many questions as it answered. In a September 1999 speech at Columbia Law School, I said that I wanted more such ideas to flourish. A virtual book of orders connecting all markets was a con-cept worth exploring, I said. But the model that the large firms leaned toward, an execution utility—a monopoly, in other words— was out of the question. At the same time, I encouraged the exchanges to shed their cumbersome governing board structures and pushed them to reduce the role of their middlemen. I also tried to foster competition by allowing the ECNs to exist with as little regulation as possible, and even to become exchanges on their own, if they wished. To avoid fragmentation, I urged the ECNs and the wholesalers to establish links with other market centers.

The CLOB, however, made some powerful enemies. The NYSE took issue with the idea because it would have gradually eroded the auction model. The most vocal opponent, however, was Charles Schwab & Co., which thought a CLOB would stifle competition and hurt the profitability of its market-making subsidiary, Schwab Capital Markets. When retail orders to buy or sell shares come through Schwab's online accounts, its discount brokerage branches, or from some two hundred other outside brokers, Schwab Capital Markets matches them. By doing so, Schwab keeps the profits from the spread.

Jousting with Phil Gramm

Schwab and other CLOB detractors ginned up opposition on Capitol Hill, primarily from Senator Phil Gramm. The Texas Republican then chaired the Senate Banking Committee, the panel that oversees the SEC. Gramm, a former professor of economics who announced his retirement from the Senate at the end of 2002, is by nature regulation-averse, and the CLOB opponents found in him a kindred spirit. Gramm called me into his office shortly after I gave the Columbia speech, having been told, wrongly, that I had endorsed a central order facility that would stifle competition among ECNs, wholesale market-makers, and the exchanges. I went to see Gramm, along with Annette Nazareth, the head of Market Regulation, and got an earful from him on the harmful effects of regulation. While we were worried about fragmentation—the lack of interaction among orders—he was most concerned about the opposite, that we might not allow competing market centers to flourish. The tension between those seemingly contradictory goals—better prices through more order interaction versus competition among multiple market centers—was the subject of dozens of meetings and phone calls Nazareth and I would have with Phil Gramm over the next eighteen months.

At first, I thought Gramm and I would come to blows. We hail from vastly different traditions. I grew up in a household that viewed government regulation as necessary to protect the weaker guy. And while I believed in free markets—after all, I had been chairman of Amex and president of a major brokerage firm—I didn't think they were foolproof. Besides, our markets sometimes only had the veneer of fair competition, as the cases against Nasdaq and NYSE floor brokers demonstrated. The SEC also brought charges against the four options markets, which for decades had colluded to maintain exclusive listings for their options. By agreeing not to compete with one another, the four exchanges caused investors to pay higher spreads, which narrowed as soon as the exchanges began competing for options listings in August 1999.

On the other hand, Gramm, with his Southerner's mistrust of big government, believes that markets, left to their own devices, eventually will find the most efficient way of bringing together buyers and sellers. "Unless the waters are crimson with the blood of investors," he exclaimed in one meeting, with a finger in my chest, "I don't want you embarking on any regulatory flights of fancy." I grew to enjoy my intellectual jousts with Gramm. Over time, Gramm and I discovered that we shared a number of common beliefs about the stock market. For example, we agreed that an execution utility with monopolistic powers was the wrong way to go. We agreed that the SEC should move cautiously, whatever course it chose, to avoid unintended consequences. Banning payment for order flow and internalization, then, were out of the question. Putting a finger in that dike would just cause a leak to spring up elsewhere, as ever-creative market-makers figured out a way to get brokers to send them orders one way or another.

Gramm and I also saw eye to eye on the rise of the ECNs and the introduction of such new technologies as online brokers that made stock markets more accessible to the retail customer. And we agreed that transparency of transaction costs was a goal to work toward. This is an important point. Transparency means that the customer knows where her order was executed and why, at what cost, what she may have given up in price improvement to get a speedy execution, and whether her broker took the time to make sure she got the best execution possible. None of this was happening, and as a result, investors were losing money.

Toward the end of my tenure, the SEC proposed rules that required market centers to provide monthly information on how well they executed orders. For example, they must reveal, on a stock-by-stock basis, how often they obtained price improvement for customer orders, versus how often they simply executed orders by using the best quotes available at a competing market. Brokerage firms, too, must make public, once a quarter, where they send customer orders, and whether they receive payment for order flow or have any other financial arrangement. This was the least intrusive of all the solutions we had proposed to deal with market structure issues. Gramm didn't exactly support the new rules, but he didn't stand in our way, either.

In the end, the CLOB didn't stand the test of time. What it gained in efficiency, it gave up in competition and innovation. A central book with one-size-fits-all rules probably would have stifled the entrepreneurial instincts of the people behind the new trading styles and technologies that had blossomed in the last several years. It became clear to me that a centralized order book would suffocate any incentives to be more nimble and more responsive to investors. Gramm and other market participants were right: the cure for fragmentation was worse than the disease.

The CLOB also fell victim to brokerage firms, such as Schwab, that internalized small customer orders, and the major Wall Street firms that internalized large customer orders. The giants of Wall Street, it turned out, had no intention of sending to the CLOB the large block trades that their upstairs trading desks were matching.

But the real reason the CLOB died was less the political power of Schwab, or the arguments of Phil Gramm, or even the New York Stock Exchange's opposition. It was decimals.

The SEC, with lots of prodding from Congress, forced the exchanges to switch to trading in dollars and cents instead of fractions. Surprisingly, most of the impetus came from two Republicans, who never again advocated a pro-investor position while I was at the SEC: Representative Tom Bliley, the House Commerce Committee chairman, and Representative Mike Oxley, who led the panel's securities subcommittee. The two Republicans were convinced that trading in fractions was causing investors to overpay on every trade. They were right. But because Nasdaq was still reeling from the price-fixing scandal and was technologically incapable of making any immediate switch, we had to delay the change for more than a year. The NYSE went first, beginning the transition in late 2000 and completing it early the next year. Nasdaq followed suit, completing its switchover in April 2001. The effects were immediate. We thought that stocks would mostly be quoted in increments of nickels and dimes. We were wrong. Almost overnight, most stock quotes went from sixteenths of a dollar to pennies. For example, IBM's stock was quoted not at $75\frac{5}{16}$ to buy and $75\frac{9}{16}$ to sell (a spread of 6.25 cents), but at $75.31 to buy and $75.32 to sell (a penny spread).

The Switch to Decimals

Decimals have been a godsend to retail investors. Not only are they easier to understand, but they also have narrowed spreads by 50 percent and more—even beyond the narrowing that took place in Nasdaq stocks after the order-handling rules took effect.

Like those order-handling rules, decimals have changed the economics of trading. While retail investors have clearly benefited, as have ECNs, others are screaming. Institutional investors, for example, have been hurt by a practice known as "stepping ahead" or "pennying." Here's an example of how it works. A specialist has a customer limit order to buy AT&T at $20.10. A market order from another customer comes in to sell AT&T. Remember, a market order doesn't specify a price, but rather is an instruction to obtain or sell shares at the best available price. The specialist can match the limit order to buy with the market order to sell. Or, if the specialist (or a floor broker in the crowd) thinks the market is moving up, he can grab the market order by buying the AT&T shares for his own account for $20.11—exactly one cent ahead of the limit order.

By stepping ahead of an existing limit order by one penny, the specialist leaves the limit order unmatched, while filling the market order. If the specialist was wrong and the market moves down, he still has that unfilled limit order he can sell to. All he has risked is a penny a share. Previously, when shares were quoted in sixteenths, the risk to the specialist was a much higher 6.25 cents per share, and thus stepping ahead was not economical.

The large Wall Street firms' trading desks also have suffered under decimals, but no one has been hit as hard as the wholesale market-makers. These are the companies, such as Schwab and Knight Trading, that had nearly cornered the market in order flow. Suddenly, orders are less valuable now that spreads have shrunk to a penny—and sometimes even less on ECNs. This, in turn, has caused payment for order flow to decline. The result is that Knight, Schwab, and others are now doing the opposite of payment for order flow and are asking brokers to pay *them* a commission to execute their orders. In a matter of months, the wholesalers went from being kings of the hill to having to rethink their business models.

If market-makers earn a commission rather than profit from the spread, that could be a positive development. It means that trading costs are more visible, and investors can make easier comparisons between market centers. At the same time, however, retail investors soon may have to pay higher commissions, especially when using an online broker, now that brokers aren't getting paid for sending orders to a market center. At online broker E*Trade, for example, payment for order flow totaled 15 percent of revenues at the height of the stock market boom. Without that revenue stream, E*Trade will have to find other sources.

At the same time, the switch to decimals has made order flow less transparent. Transparency is the measure of trading interest at any single price point. Transparency has declined because quote sizes—the number of shares that are on offer, or that will be purchased, in any one order—have shrunk almost as quickly as spreads have narrowed. At the NYSE, for example, quote sizes have fallen by 66 percent since the introduction of decimals. On Nasdaq, it's 75 percent.

One big reason for reduced transparency is that penny pricing has created more, and quicker, fluctuations in prices, and investors don't want to commit to paying a set price for a large order when the market price is constantly changing. Another reason is that submitting a limit order is an open invitation for someone to step ahead of your order by a penny.

Exchanges Acting More Like ECNs

It's probably too early to draw many conclusions about decimals—except that they're here to stay, and the economics of stock trading will never be the same. The exchanges, meanwhile, are working to counter some of the negative effects. Decimals and other changes have forced the NYSE and Nasdaq to think the unthinkable. They have begun changing their balky ownership structures to be able to respond faster to competitive pressures. Both exchanges floated the idea of selling shares to the public, forming their own ECNs or acquiring one, and even the possibility of merging with one another. They began exploring links with overseas exchanges, and trading around the clock.

The NASD dealt with its competitive problem by doing a number of things. First, it sought to consolidate its position as the high-tech exchange by designing a new order display system, called SuperMontage, which was expected to be up and running in mid-2002. ECNs caused a fragmentation of Nasdaq's market into many submarkets, forcing investors to check several places for the best prices and the most liquidity or for expressions of interest in trading a particular stock. So SuperMontage is Nasdaq's attempt to get some of its market share back. The aim of SuperMontage is to reaggregate those orders in a central place. The system will show not just the best bid and ask prices, but also the amount of trading interest at those prices, and the next four increments away, just like an ECN. This is called market depth; knowing the depth of a market helps investors make better trading decisions.

A more radical move was NASD's decision to spin off Nasdaq, with the NASD continuing as the self-regulatory organization for the stock market. First, NASD sold shares in Nasdaq through a private placement, raising $318 million. The new owners include many of the major Wall Street firms, technology vendors, and even some of the companies that trade on Nasdaq. Now Nasdaq is seeking SEC approval to become a stand-alone exchange. As of mid-2003, the SEC had not given its consent. Once that occurs, Nasdaq may consider an IPO to raise further cash, and could merge with an overseas exchange, such as the London Stock Exchange.

Not to be outdone, NYSE chairman and CEO Dick Grasso rocked all of Wall Street in July 1999 when he predicted that his exchange would go public by Thanksgiving that year. Well, that was mighty ambitious, and even Grasso now concedes that probably was not the wisest move. All kinds of thorny issues needed to be sorted out, including how a for-profit exchange would meet its expensive, but crucial, self-regulatory obligations.

An IPO now seems out of the question, but Grasso has unveiled two new initiatives that, combined, will make the NYSE more like an ECN. First, he has introduced a new product, called OpenBook, that reveals the orders in the specialist's book, similar to the way ECNs reveal theirs. The OpenBook shows, for example, the total number of orders at each price point, thus unmasking the depth of interest in a particular stock that decimal quoting forced into hiding. But the NYSE will not allow data vendors, such as Bloomberg and Reuters, to commingle the NYSE order book with orders from other markets, which limits its usefulness. Another problem: Open-Book is not real-time but is delayed by ten seconds, thereby preserving the specialist's privilege of seeing orders before the rest of the market.

The NYSE's second initiative is called NYSE Direct+ (pronounced *direct-plus*). This allows brokerage firms or their customers to automatically execute orders of 1,099 shares or less against the latest NYSE quote, without any specialist intervention. The turnaround time on a Direct+ execution is just 1.7 seconds, versus the 15 to 22 seconds it takes to execute an order via the floor. Sound familiar? Sure—this is exactly what ECNs and the wholesale market-makers do, except that they don't limit you to 1,099 shares. Even if all the NYSE's limit-order customers took advantage of this new feature, it would represent only 8 percent of total volume.

The NYSE is innovating, but keeping a lid on it, so as not to undermine the specialists. Still, some of its protectionist barriers have come tumbling down like the Berlin Wall. The most controversial was the NYSE's Rule 390, which kept its member firms from trading stocks of companies that listed before April 1979 anywhere but at the exchange. I had hinted several times to Dick Grasso that Rule 390 was anticompetitive, but he clung to it—under pressure from his seat holders. Rule 390 worked well: by the time of my 1999 Columbia speech, ECNs were handling about 25 percent of Nasdaq orders, but less than 1 percent of NYSE orders. I said in the speech that Rule 390 was on its ninth life, and publicly threatened to force Grasso to get rid of it. Privately, I gave him until January 2000 to eliminate it. Grasso had no choice but to tell his members that the rule had to go, and his board voted to eliminate it in December 1999.

So far, there hasn't been much erosion of the NYSE's market share. Neither NYSE nor Nasdaq sold shares to the public in an IPO, and the NYSE floor remains intact—and as busy as ever. In 2001, the NYSE's market share in its listed stocks remained steady at nearly 85 percent. And despite my initial enthusiasm for a centralized virtual book, even I backed away from the concept. So did all our efforts come to nothing? Not at all. It's fair to say that we laid the groundwork for a process that is still unfolding today. For example, once Nasdaq becomes a stand-alone exchange, Wall Street firms might start sending orders to trade NYSE stocks to Nasdaq instead. Soon, ECNs could also start eating away at the NYSE franchise. They proved their usefulness on November 28, 2001, when credit rating agencies downgraded Enron's debt to junk status, sending the company's stock into free fall. The NYSE halted trading because of an order imbalance—there were far more sell orders than buy orders and the specialist handling Enron couldn't keep an orderly market. Other markets, however, can keep on trading if a halt is due to an order imbalance, and they did so. The NYSE specialist shut down his post, but ECNs traded more than 10 million shares as the stock went from $2.60 to $1.10 over the next thirty minutes. The specialist then resumed trading at prices the ECNs had reported—a blow to the mighty NYSE specialist system.

Execution Quality: Buzzwords du Jour

Market centers now compete against each other to attract customer orders on the basis of greater execution speed, better chance of price improvement, more efficient linkages with other markets, the ability to trade large orders, or the cloak of anonymity. Different investors have different needs. Some want speed, above all. But retail customers might want to hold out for a better price than the one being quoted, rather than grab the fastest possible execution.

Many challenges remain before we reach the ideal market structure. One is the lack of connections between markets. The NYSE needs to upgrade its connections to Nasdaq and other market centers—a task that's easier said than done, for political reasons. Several of the ECNs have begun to address this issue on their own and have installed high-speed connections between one another's networks. When the Archipelago ECN receives an order, for example, its system is programmed to search the order books of Island and Instinet to see if they can offer a better match. One problem: ECNs charge market-makers and other market centers fees to access their systems. If those fees continue to rise, as they have been, they could become an obstacle to the goal of competing but interconnected markets.

At the end of 2001, the exchanges, ECNs, and Wall Street firms were busy digesting all of this. The recession and the terrorist attacks of September 11 temporarily lifted the pressure from the NYSE to move swiftly. But no one doubts that more change is around the corner. My own guess is that we will not end up with a single, monolithic market, but a network of electronically connected markets. They will compete for investor orders as well as listings. The market that fills orders not just at the fastest rate, but also at the lowest cost, will have a competitive advantage.

And while there will be fewer middlemen, they will continue to play a role. The NYSE trading floor will not disappear, but it will gradually lose business, especially in cases where specialists don't add value. Some shares are thinly traded, and need an intermediary willing to commit capital to keep the shares trading smoothly. At the other end of the spectrum, mutual funds sometimes need to unload millions of shares very quickly, and intermediaries can help there, too. But highly liquid stocks—those for which there is a lot of trading interest all day, every day—hardly need the help of a dealer to step in between investors and exact a toll for doing so.

What You Can Do

As an individual investor, you might be tempted to say that none of this is important to you. Not true. Once you understand market structure, you can direct your broker to send your order to the one offering the most liquidity, the fastest matchups, and the lowest transaction costs. But how would you determine that?

Well, new SEC rules require all market centers and brokers to report on Web sites how well they execute customer orders. This information will be most useful to individual investors who want to know how their orders are filled and at what cost. One set of data will come from market centers—NYSE floor specialists, Nasdaq market-makers, and ECNs—and will reveal the average spread at that market center, the speed of matchups, whether investors are getting prices that improve on their orders, and the number of orders that go unfilled. Each market center must provide this information on a monthly basis. These figures can help you decide which market center is best for you. The data are just now being produced. Brokers and market centers are now figuring out how they rank against one another, looking for competitive advantages in the data. When it does, you can compare across all markets the last month's buy/sell spreads for the stock you are interested in.

You can also compare the market center reports to see which ones fill orders the fastest and which ones delay executing orders to make a quick buck or two. For example, say you put in a market order to buy 2,000 shares of Home Depot, and the best quoted offer at the time is $35.10. The market-maker who received your order thinks the market is going up, so he delays your fill by twenty seconds. Sure enough, the price jumps to $35.20, and only then is your order filled. The market-maker has just walked off with $200 ($0.10 × 2,000 shares) of yours.

A second set of data from brokerage firms will disclose, on a quarterly basis, what percentage of customer orders they send to each market center. Brokerages also must disclose whether they have any financial arrangements with market centers to which they route orders, and whether they internalize orders by sending them to a market-making subsidiary to be matched. Firms can post these data on their Web sites.

Let your broker know that you expect him to get the best execution possible. Remember: best execution is a legal duty, not just a lofty goal. Ask your broker where he will be sending your next order, and why. Make sure he's looking out for your best interests by searching out the exchange or the ECN with the lowest transaction costs. Be sure to ask your broker for a customized report showing where your orders were routed, whether you got price improvement, and the time it took to fill the order. Your broker, after all, is charging you a commission. Make him earn it.

When buying or selling shares, use limit orders (those specifying a trade at a definite price or better) rather than market orders (those not specifying a price but directing the market center to find the best price currently available in the market). A limit order protects you against a sharp fluctuation in the price between the time you place your order and the time it gets executed.

But keep in mind that while limit orders can save you from paying far more for your shares than you expected, you also risk not getting a fill. A quoted price on the Nasdaq or an ECN screen may look attractive, but it's only available for a limited number of shares. Be ready to make a trade-off between getting the price you want and getting the shares you want. If you really want those shares, put in a limit order that is priced aggressively to boost your chances of getting it filled.

If speedy executions are your goal, then you are probably giving up the chance for price improvement. Many brokers today consider that they've met their best-execution obligations if they've executed your order at high speed—or under fifteen seconds. The Island ECN, for example, doesn't charge customers if it can't execute a trade within sixty seconds. But don't be seduced by speed if you would rather have the chance of price improvement. Make sure your broker knows which is more important to you—speed or a better price than the one he is quoting you. And make sure your broker explains his firm's choice of market center by backing up his routing choice with statistics from the order execution data.

ECNs offer the fastest executions, without any middleman taking a cut. But ECNs charge fees and have less liquidity in many of the stocks they trade than do the established exchanges. If you want an ECN to fill your order, choose one, such as Archipelago, whose system sends your order to another market center if it can't find you a match. Island's system does not have this feature.

If you are really curious about how your orders are being filled, monitor your trades. Some brokers offer their customers streaming quotes that adjust with each successful trade. You can see your order in the quote, and watch how it's executed.

Payment for order flow has declined because of decimals, but be sure to ask your broker if his firm is receiving any payments or other inducements to steer orders to a particular market center. If so, ask your broker to justify why that market center is superior to others. Also, ask your broker why he's not rebating some or all of that payment to you, the customer. At the very least, you should expect your broker to try to get you a better price on your limit order in exchange for the payment for order flow. After all, it's your money that's being kicked back.

Finally, if you think you got a poor execution, contact your brokerage firm's customer service department and complain. If you don't get a satisfactory response, make sure the customer service rep knows that you've been paying attention to the plumbing. Remind him that his firm has a legal duty to get you the best execution possible.

Now I've probably told you more than you care to know about the infrastructure of our stock markets. Relax. You don't have to be an expert in market structure to trade stocks. But it sure helps to know who the hidden players are, what their motives may be, and where to apply the pressure so your interests take precedence.

CHAPTER EIGHT

CORPORATE GOVERNANCE AND THE CULTURE OF SEDUCTION

Ever since I owned my first Macintosh in 1984, I have been addicted to Apple computers. I now have six Macintoshes and an iPod digital music player, and I occasionally go to conventions of Mac users. I guess I might be called an Apple junkie. You can imagine my delight when Apple CEO Steve Jobs invited me to join his board once I left the SEC in February 2001. At least I was under the impression that he invited me.

I flew to San Jose to meet Jobs for breakfast in mid-January. We then went to Apple headquarters, where he introduced me to his management team. After a series of meetings with department heads, Chief Financial Officer Fred Anderson briefed me on the company's finances, the responsibilities of various board members, and the dates of upcoming meetings. As I was leaving, I gave Anderson a copy of a speech I had recently made on corporate governance. I thought it might be useful to the company as it planned the board's agenda for the coming year. The next day I was Apple's guest at the annual Macworld trade show in San Francisco, where, with his rock-star presence, Jobs unveils new Apple products. By the time I left, I considered myself part of the Apple family and looked forward to my first directors' meeting with enthusiasm.

It was not to be. The very next day, Jobs disinvited me. "Arthur, I don't think you'd be happy on our board and I think it best if we not invite you," he said over the phone. "I read your speech and, frankly, I think some of the issues you raised, while appropriate for some companies, really don't apply to Apple's culture."

I was floored. What radical ideas in that speech had set him off? Turns out, Apple's board did not meet a number of the good governance litmus tests I had highlighted. It did not, for example, have a separate compensation committee (although it does now). Instead, important executive pay issues were referred to the full board, which could hardly give them the attention they deserved, or be as objective as a subcommittee of independent directors. One director, Oracle CEO Larry Ellison—Jobs's close friend—was invited to join the board in 1997, even though he warned the company that he would not attend most meetings. After joining, Ellison attended a little less than half of Apple's formal board meetings, an abysmal record. (After serving on Apple's board for five years, Ellison resigned in September 2002, citing a lack of time to devote to Apple matters. Former vice-president Al Gore replaced Ellison on Apple's board.)

One member of Apple's audit committee, Jerome York, is the CEO of MicroWarehouse Inc., whose Mac Warehouse catalog was responsible for nearly $150 million of Apple's $5.4 billion in 2001 sales. York is eminently qualified to sit on Apple's board: He is a former chief financial officer of both IBM and Chrysler. And when he joined Apple's board in August 1997, he was not involved with the Mac catalog. But when he became CEO of MicroWarehouse in 2000, York's relationship as a major reseller of Apple products meant that he could no longer be considered an independent board member. And yet he is one of three directors on Apple's audit committee, despite a Nasdaq rule that requires audit committee panelists to be independent. Apple gets away with this because the Nasdaq rules have a loophole: One nonindependent audit committee member is allowed "under exceptional and limited circumstances." If a company invokes the exception, the board must disclose why it's in the best interest of the company and its shareholders to have a nonindependent on the audit committee. Apple's explanation? Its proxy statement says only that, considering York's expertise, the board finds that his audit committee service "is in the best interest" of Apple.

To me, the Apple board has even more flaws. The chairman of

Apple's audit committee is former Intuit CEO Bill Campbell. Not only is Campbell a former Apple marketing and sales executive, but Apple in 1990 bought out the software company, Claris Corp., that Campbell started after leaving Apple. Under the current stock exchange listing standards, Campbell qualifies as an independent director because his Apple ties ended more than three years ago. But no matter how conscientious a director is, it's difficult to switch loyalties from one's former colleagues to shareholders. It's even more difficult not to feel beholden to the acquirer of your own company. Campbell and York, along with Genentech CEO Arthur Levinson, not only make up the audit committee, but they also are the only three members of Apple's compensation committee—the two panels that most governance experts agree should be truly independent of management.

None of this would matter were it not for the fact that Apple's tight-knit board has only six members, one of whom is Jobs. Because Ellison missed more than half the meetings, only four outside directors were regular attendees, and one of them clearly was not independent while a second arguably is not.

Like many CEOs, Jobs had carefully hand-picked his own board. His directors are highly qualified, prominent members of corporate America. But it's plain to me that Apple's board is not designed to act independently of the CEO. Clearly, my speech signaled that I would not fit that mold.

To his credit, Jobs has turned Apple around since his 1997 return to the company he founded two decades earlier. He has restored the company's image through innovation and cost-cutting. Today, Apple's product lineup is on the cutting edge technologically and aesthetically. And despite the audit committee structure, Apple has never had to restate its results or been subject to a Securities and Exchange Commission probe.

So what's the problem? Small, insular boards lack the outside perspective that is necessary in case a company finds itself in trouble. Especially when the CEO is as charismatic as Jobs, it's crucial to have independent thinkers who do not act as an extension of management.

Not surprisingly, Jobs disagrees. He says that when there was no compensation committee, the full board found the time to have "vigorous and full discussions" about pay packages. Despite Ellison's failure to show up for more than half the board meetings, Jobs insisted that his friend's informal consultations were so valuable that his absences were tolerable. To me, that relationship made Ellison more of a management consultant than an independent overseer. Jobs also says that his board members have a "stunning amount of experience, judgment, and concern for Apple." No argument there. But if something goes wrong with the company's strategy or its execution, it seems to me that this board would not buck Jobs and insist on a midcourse correction.

As you can probably tell, independent boards are a passion of mine. I have sat on many, both before I came to the SEC and now. I don't think it's proper for the CEO to make important decisions, such as the choice of his successor, how much compensation he and his management team will receive, and whether the financial statements reflect the company's true status, without vigorous board discussion and approval. Nor am I comfortable when matters that have been decided prior to a board meeting come up for the directors' rubber-stamp approval. What may have passed muster several years ago is no longer acceptable in a post–Enron environment. Investors have lost faith in corporate managers and boards, and that means companies must work harder to prove that their boards provide the strongest possible checks and balances. It is essential that CEOs recognize that they do not own the companies they run and that they are ultimately responsible to shareholders. The past few decades have brought dramatic improvements in most boards, and the seriousness with which they take their jobs, but, as recent corporate failures make clear, much work remains to be done.

The Sarbanes-Oxley law should shift the balance of power to shareholders from management, but the shift will take time. The law requires public companies to adopt important corporate governance changes by the time of their 2004 shareholder meetings. These include naming only independent directors to audit committees and revealing whether the audit panel has a financial expert—a person with experience in the nitty-gritty detail of preparing or interpreting financial statements. The law makes the audit committee, not the chief executive or chief financial officer, responsible for hiring and firing the auditor, reviewing the financial statements, and approving, in advance, any consulting service by the auditor. The stock exchanges, in addition, are proposing that a majority of board members be independent. That means no business ties whatsoever to the company or its management.

When added up, the changes could amount to a seismic shift. But it's up to investors to make sure the changes are more than cosmetic. Boards should be commended not because directors show up at meetings, write fancy ethics codes, or check off boxes to prove they're complying with the new rules. Instead, they should be commended for showing a willingness to challenge management, take on tough issues such as CEO succession, and make sure executive pay hinges on measurable performance standards. In the end, the attitude of directors must change from "I'm here on behalf of management" to "I'm here on behalf of shareholders." And when shareholders don't see that change in mindset, it's their job to vote directors out.

What Is a Board of Directors?

A board of directors is usually composed of well-educated, accomplished individuals, elected by the shareholders annually or every few years. One of its responsibilities is to advise the CEO and the top executive team with impartial common sense and various kinds of expertise. The board should meet regularly to discuss such issues as the ongoing health of the business, the current management team and its performance, the compensation of the top executives, and the future outlook of the company. A board's most important job is to make sure the company has the best CEO it can find. Corporate boards should have a nominating committee, composed of independent directors, to review candidates to replace the CEO in case of retirement or resignation, and to help choose new board members.

If problems arise, it's the board's responsibility to address them before the situation spins out of control—ideally before investors take a beating. After all, in a bankruptcy, shareholders get what's left after everyone else gets paid. And that's usually nothing.

At major public companies, boards are made up of a combination of insiders—senior executives at the company—and others from outside the company, such as other chief executives, scientists, educators, and civic leaders. At smaller companies, boards often include the venture capitalists who funded the company or other financiers, such as the local banker.

The board's mandate is to oversee management as a representative of the shareholders. The board is not the same as the management and does not have the same responsibilities. Management makes most of the company's day-to-day operating decisions, but major strategic issues, such as whether or not to buy another company or to enter a new line of business, require the board's participation and approval.

Most boards are subdivided into committees, each of which focuses more directly on parts of the business. Some of them, such as a corporate governance committee, are optional. But stock exchange rules require publicly traded companies to have an audit committee to oversee how the management team prepares the company's financial statements and to make sure that internal controls are working properly. Most companies also have a compensation committee to determine the salaries and bonuses of top management.

A board's makeup is vital. If you think a director is not doing her job, or if you feel a director's business interests could create a conflict, it's your right—your duty, really—to vote against her, using the ballot that comes with your proxy statement. Unfortunately, removing unacceptable directors from a board isn't easy. Large shareholders, such as pension and mutual funds, tend to vote with management unless the company's share price has plummeted. Boards of directors also are often presented as one slate; you vote for all or none. But as activist shareholder groups and the financial media frown on this practice as a management-protection ploy, companies increasingly are putting individual directors up for annual reelection by shareholders.

Why Should You Care?

I believe a company's corporate governance is one of the most important factors to consider before investing in a company. Put simply, corporate governance is the relationship between the investor, the management team, and the board of directors of a company. Each of these groups has different rights and responsibilities. When the three groups are able to communicate openly and independently, we can say that a company is exhibiting good corporate governance.

This does not mean that the board second-guesses every decision made by the top executives of a company. Rather, a board should provide careful oversight of a company's activities, drawing on its members' expertise in areas such as marketing, finance, or technology. A board can help solve problems by sharing its own experiences with similar matters. A board should add value to an already strong executive team.

How can you recognize a good board from a bad board? Outside board members should be free of connections or business interests that make them feel beholden to the CEO or undermine their responsibility to make decisions in the interests of shareholders. Ideally, fewer than half the directors should be employed by the company or have other connections that hinder independence. And I use the most rigorous definition of "independence": those directors should not be family members, former employees, the company lawyer or investment banker, or even someone who represents an institution that has received donations from the company. They should not be paid consulting fees or receive exorbitant perks. All board members should have a hefty stake of their own in the company. A bad decision should sock them in the wallet, too.

Caring about governance does not guarantee that a company will outperform others in its industry, but there is ample evidence that paying attention to governance issues leads to better financial results. One study, by Wilshire Associates, examined the performance over five years of sixty-two companies named by the California Public Employees' Retirement System (CalPERS) as poor performers. While the stocks of these companies trailed the S&P 500 by 89 percent in the five-year period before CalPERS singled out the companies, the same stocks outperformed the index by 23 percent in the following five years.

That's not to say that companies will fail unless they have a model board of directors. Take Warren Buffett's Berkshire Hathaway Inc. Among the seven directors are his wife, his son, longtime business partner Charlie Munger, a partner at his company's law firm, and a coinvestor with Berkshire Hathaway in another company.

When a corporation is in trouble, it often becomes clear that the board failed in some way. A landmark case brought by the SEC in 1998 against chemical company W.R. Grace illustrates my point. As the company foundered, the board allowed CEO J. Peter Grace to negotiate a retirement package that included such generous perquisites as the use of a corporate jet and a company-owned apartment. The perks were valued at $3.6 million. W.R. Grace was also planning to sell a small subsidiary to the ex-chairman's son.

Clearly, good corporate governance means not letting a former CEO walk away with a private jet when the company has hit the skids. Yet it wasn't strictly illegal. What got Grace's board in trouble was its failure to disclose these and other matters to shareholders in its 10-K annual report and proxy statement. Although one member of the board led the negotiations for the retirement package and another was aware of the negotiations for the subsidiary's sale, neither required Grace to inform its shareholders. The negotiations were not fully disclosed or described, as the law requires, in any SEC filing. Indeed, the company's filings contained only the briefest description of the retirement perks, and never mentioned any proposal to sell a subsidiary.

After reviewing the case, the commission concluded that not only the company but also several W.R. Grace directors bore responsibility for these failures. Each of them knew about the deals and should have known that such sensitive matters would not sit well with shareholders. The company settled the SEC case, without admitting or denying guilt, by consenting not to further violate securities laws.

What is obvious in hindsight can be avoided through foresight. In practice, this simply means that boards must be equipped with an effective system to monitor management. But directors can't stop there. If they have reason to know something doesn't seem right, they cannot avert their gaze. Every time directors demand a tough disclosure or ask a difficult financial question, thousands of shareholders benefit. So there must be an atmosphere that encourages directors to be active—to avoid the trap of believing that they must go along to get along.

Sometimes boards make sensible decisions, but wait far too long. In November 2001 the board of apparel company Warnaco replaced longtime CEO Linda Wachner, who had driven the company into bankruptcy while still managing to be one of the nation's better-compensated executives with a salary exceeding $2 million, plus generous stock options. But for years the board had tolerated Wachner's poor management skills. Under Wachner, Warnaco became mired in litigation with its biggest licensor, Calvin Klein, for trademark violations. And at one point Wachner spun off a company, Authentic Fitness, but remained its CEO while also serving as Warnaco's CEO. Later she sold the company back to Warnaco. She made millions, but Warnaco's shareholders lost money in the transaction. Warnaco's share price slid 92 percent between 1995 and 2001, leading the company to declare bankruptcy in June 2001. But even then the board did not remove Wachner for five more months.

Such governance failures have led to calls for increased board accountability and caused quite a bit of upheaval as directors second-guess management and shareholders second-guess directors. At company annual meetings, for example, shareholders increasingly are turning to shareholder resolutions, which also appear in the proxy, to force change. To bring a shareholder proposal to a vote, there must be some logical relationship between the proposal and the company's business. Proposals can't involve "ordinary business," or issues considered part of a company's normal day-to-day affairs. If a company wants to disqualify a proposal as ordinary business, it must notify the SEC, which makes the final decision.

To offer a proposal, a shareholder must have owned $2,000

worth of a company's stock for the past year. If a resolution fails, it must have received at least 3 percent of the votes cast to be eligible for the ballot the next year. You can find more detail on shareholder proposals at the SEC's Web site, *www.sec.gov*. Once there, click on the "Division of Corporation Finance," then "Staff Legal Bulletins," then "SLB 14."

Shareholder proposals are now a favorite tool of governance activists. Pension funds, mutual funds, labor unions, social activists, corporate gadflies, and ordinary investors use the shareholder proposal system hundreds of times each year to promote their view of good governance. After the Enron calamity, one popular cause is auditor independence. Consider how this issue played out at Disney's February 2002 annual meeting. A union-owned mutual fund pushed for a shareholder vote on a resolution directing Disney to stop awarding consulting contracts to PricewaterhouseCoopers, its auditor. Disney was vulnerable on this point: the previous year it had paid PwC $7 million in audit fees, but more than four times that for such services as financial systems design and tax preparation.

Disney management fought to keep the resolution off its proxy statement. It asked the SEC to strike the proposal because, Disney claimed, it dealt with "ordinary business" and therefore was in violation of SEC rules. But the SEC disagreed, and allowed the resolution to be put to a vote at the annual meeting. CEO Michael Eisner then had a change of heart—or else he wanted to avoid an embarrassing loss. Weeks prior to the meeting, he preempted the resolution and announced that Disney would no longer use PwC's consulting services. By then it was too late to remove the resolution from the proxy; it won 43 percent of the vote—not enough to force Disney's hand, but a powerful sign of shareholder resolve. Rarely do resolutions garner more than 20 percent of the vote the first time around.

Another popular shareholder concern is the overuse of stock options as compensation. What began as an incentive to keep or reward extraordinary talent has now become routine. Dot-com executives especially made eye-popping sums of money from their options in the late 1990s. Cisco Systems CEO John Chambers received $150 million on top of his base pay and bonus of $1.3 million in 2000.

As generous as that seems, it doesn't compare to Steve Jobs's options and bonus awards that year. In January 2000, Apple's board awarded Jobs 20 million shares, worth $550 million if the share price increased just 5 percent a year over ten years. The board also authorized the company to spend $90 million to buy Jobs a Gulfstream V corporate jet. When Apple's share price declined the next year—pushing Jobs's options underwater (that's when the exercise price exceeds the current market price)—the board simply granted him 7.5 million more options at a much lower exercise price. At the time, Apple shares were underperforming other computer hardware stocks by 28 percent—hardly a ringing endorsement. When boards reprice stock options or, as Apple's board did, issue new ones at a lower price, they undercut the use of stock options as an incentive for management to try harder. By lowering the bar, boards send a clear signal that management will not be held accountable.

Pension funds and other institutional investors are taking umbrage at stock option abuses, and are turning to the proxy system for relief. When a board approves stock option grants, the company often must issue new stock to cover the grant, thus watering down, or diluting, the outstanding shares. Like it or not, that means that your shares lose value every time a stock option is awarded. And academic studies have begun to cast doubt on just how much retention and incentivizing power stock options really have. This is where the shareholder proposal process enters the picture. Shareholders have begun to offer resolutions that, if approved, would require companies to obtain their approval for new option grants or to reprice options that are underwater. Many investors are registering their disapproval of new option grants. In 2000, 22 percent of shareholders who voted said no to stock option plans, according to the Investor Responsibility Research Center, a Washington, D.C.–based corporate governance research outfit.

The back-slapping, smoke-filled, fraternal boardroom is hard to find these days, in large part because of a series of corporate meltdowns and the outcry they caused. The first corporate disaster to really strike a chord with the public came after the merger of two railroads, New York Central and Pennsylvania Railroad, in 1968. The resulting company, Penn Central, was the corporate equivalent of the *Titanic*: it hit an iceberg because its captains, the directors, weren't paying attention. Actually, it was worse than the *Titanic,* because Penn Central's captains effectively stole away on the lifeboats and left the rest of the company to a watery grave. While debt soared and working capital deteriorated, Penn Central's board was busy enriching itself and approving dividend payments of more than $100 million. Everyone and everything associated with that company sank in 1970, when Penn Central, one of the country's largest companies, declared bankruptcy.

Penn Central's board was not unique. A Harvard Business School study at the time concluded that the modern firm's board of directors had ceased to function as a meaningful check on the CEO. A senior partner in a consulting group reported in the same study that he didn't know of a single board that really dug into the strategy of the business or held management accountable for results. Remember that word: accountable. The job of a board member is to monitor management and hold it accountable for its decisions. At Penn Central and thousands of other corporations, no one was doing this.

Slowly, investors began to realize they could do something. In the 1970s and '80s, activist religious and political groups began using company annual meetings to push shareholder proposals that denounced investment in apartheid South Africa as well as companies dealing in weapons and tobacco. Shareholder groups also began invoking federal securities laws in place since the 1930s to support their corporate governance struggles.

Corporate Raiders and Poison Pills

The biggest boost for corporate governance, however, came in the 1980s, when corporate raiders and leveraged buyout firms vied for control of struggling corporations. Many companies resisted being taken over, and enacted protections such as special share-voting devices and poison pills. The share-voting devices block hostile takeovers by, for example, providing for super-voting rights to be cast in favor of management when an unwanted suitor appears on the scene. Poison pills are slightly different in that they grant existing shareholders (but not the unwanted suitor) rights to buy additional shares at a deep discount, thus diluting any potential acquirer's ownership stake and thwarting his efforts to control the company. These takeover defenses are not shareholder-friendly. They entrench the current management, even when it's doing a poor job. They water down shareholders' votes and deprive them of a meaningful voice in corporate affairs. And they deprive investors of a contest for their shares—and the possibility that they will receive a premium price from a new owner.

Numerous courtroom battles were waged over poison pills and other antitakeover measures. The corporate raider era shook up many complacent management teams and corporate boards, which often were smack in the middle of these legal dramas. The mergers-and-acquisitions divisions of Wall Street firms became more profitable than their brokerage departments. But overall, the 1980s "was a mixed bag" for governance, says Harvey Goldschmid, a former securities law professor at Columbia University. "There was increased pressure on management to look after the interests of shareholders, because a raider could come along if the stock was too low," says Goldschmid, who would later become the SEC's general counsel, and then an SEC commissioner. "On the other hand, there was a lot of funny money going around, and a lot of questionable people and motives involved."

The raiders—people such as Carl Icahn, T. Boone Pickens, and Saul Steinberg—caused much bitterness, and not just among unhappy managers turned out of their corner offices. Dozens of acquired companies were broken up and sold in pieces, thousands of people were laid off, suppliers and customers were disrupted, and local communities were torn apart.

The corporate raider movement caused governance experts to look for better ways to improve corporate performance, but with far less turmoil. Goldschmid and others focused on forcing directors to switch their allegiance from management to shareholders. And that gave rise to a new and powerful special interest group: activist shareholders. Institutional pension funds began to use their considerable leverage to pressure companies to get rid of poison pills and take other steps to improve performance. Among the most active were TIAA-CREF (the country's largest private pension fund, formally called the Teachers Insurance and Annuity Association–College Retirement Equities Fund) and CalPERS (the nation's largest public pension fund). Together, they manage hundreds of billions of dollars' worth of retirement and savings funds on behalf of teachers and state employees. The pension funds became empowered and soon realized that they could change corporate practices that weren't in the interests of investors.

Awake, Slumbering Boards

In the 1990s, the idea that a board of directors should be an independent and active steward of investors' money really began to take hold. The business press also began exposing the clubbiness of some boards—in a quite unflattering way. Then, just before I joined the SEC in 1993, the agency required companies to make public more information on executive pay packages. The SEC also made it easier for shareholder groups to communicate with each other by liberalizing the rules governing the proxy system. This is the process by which a company informs shareholders of its performance over the past year and solicits shareholder approval of changes to its bylaws, board slate, and any proposals.

All this information is contained in a proxy statement, an important document that companies must send to every shareholder annually. More than any other filing, the proxy statement reveals the inner workings of a company. It lists each board member, along with a short biographical sketch. It says which directors serve on which committees, such as compensation and audit, and if they attended 75 percent of board meetings. It must say whether management has reviewed the company's financial statements with those board members who serve on the audit committee. The proxy statement also discusses the stock's performance over the past five years and compares the share price to a relevant index, such as the Standard & Poor's 500. It must reveal the compensation of the five top corporate officers. And it must explain any proposals that shareholders will be asked to vote on at the annual meeting. A ballot is provided so that shareholders can vote without having to attend the annual meeting in person.

When added up, the changes that took place in the 1980s and 1990s were sweeping. Directors knew that shareholders could, in effect, gang up against underperforming CEOs—and the boards that protected them—so they had to act before the shareholders did. Corporate boards suddenly began ousting longtime CEOs. In quick succession, board putsches ended the careers of IBM chairman John Akers, Westinghouse Electric chairman Paul Lego, and General Motors chairman Robert Stempel. At the time, all three companies were losing money.

Then, in February 1993, the board of American Express (AmEx) shocked corporate America when it forced out CEO James Robinson III. Robinson had been chairman and chief executive for fifteen years, and had appointed fifteen of the seventeen outside board members. These included close personal friends Henry Kissinger, the former U.S. secretary of state; Drew Lewis, the CEO of Union Pacific Corp., on whose board Robinson sat; and superlawyer Vernon Jordan, Jr., who stretched himself thin by sitting on nine other boards. These individuals had ties to AmEx that could conflict with their role as shareholder advocate. Robinson awarded Jordan's law firm a retainer, for example. Kissinger's international consulting firm received $350,000 in annual fees to advise Robinson and a brokerage subsidiary, Shearson Lehman Brothers, on overseas matters. Not only did Drew Lewis once run AmEx's cable-TV business, he also employed Robinson's wife while there. AmEx had invested $1 million in a partnership in which Lewis's son owned a major interest. At Union Pacific, Robinson sat on Lewis's compensation committee, helping to determine his pay. What director would revolt against the guy who sets his pay? The icing on the cake: all

AmEx directors were eligible for retirement and life insurance benefits after serving five years. This board personified the culture of seduction.

During Robinson's reign, however, American Express's financial condition deteriorated because of numerous strategic errors. Robinson tried but failed to merge AmEx with Disney, the Book-of-the-Month Club, and McGraw-Hill. He sold off companies, such as the cable-TV business, just before cable company prices shot through the roof. And in 1989, AmEx had to apologize publicly to international banker Edmond Safra, as well as give $8 million to charities he named, as compensation for allegedly engaging in dirty tricks to discredit Safra as he tried to set up a bank to compete with American Express. Altogether, AmEx lost some $4 billion in shareholder value under Robinson.

Shareholder protests at first fell on deaf ears until a small handful of dissident board members began pressuring Robinson to step down. Robinson finally agreed to give up the CEO position. But rather than step down entirely, he tried to maneuver himself into the chairman's office—a ploy that had worked for many a disgraced CEO in the past. Not this time. Institutional investors and even some of Robinson's own management team protested. The board had no choice but to force Robinson out completely. An era of greater board vigilance was beginning.

SPRINTING FOR OPTIONS

Shareholders of Sprint Corp., the long-distance and wireless telephone company, used the shareholder process to register their disapproval when company executives awarded themselves millions of stock options. In 1997, Sprint's shareholders approved a stock option plan that allowed company executives to exercise all their options as a form of severance payment if the company changed hands. Sprint's board, however, quietly approved an amendment to the plan the next year that allowed executives to exercise options once shareholders approved a merger, rather than when a merger was actually completed. The company filed a notice about this seemingly minor change with the SEC, but few people noticed. Now fast-forward to 2000: Sprint shareholders approved a merger with telecom rival WorldCom Inc. But months later, regulators at the Justice Department and in Europe blocked the deal for antitrust reasons. The company's stock crashed from $61.50 in April to $25 by December. Now here's the catch: even though the WorldCom merger had to be called off, the board amendment allowed $1 billion in Sprint stock options to vest right away. Numerous top managers took advantage of the loophole by cashing in their options and resigning from the company.

Angry shareholders reacted by filing lawsuits alleging that the Sprint board and chairman William Esrey violated their fiduciary duty to shareholders and unjustly enriched themselves. While Esrey did not cash in his options, valued at $400 million, the board granted him 3 million more options in Sprint stock and its wireless tracking stock, Sprint PCS, in exchange for not doing so.

Rubbing salt in shareholders' wounds, the Sprint board in October 2000 also approved a plan that would allow thousands of employees to turn in their underwater stock options, only to have them reissued by the company six months and one day later. By doing so, Sprint was helping employees out of a pickle. Their options were originally priced at an average of $59 and thus were worthless. The "six-months-plus-one-day" ploy also lets Sprint skirt an accounting rule that requires companies to treat repriced options as an expense, if those options existed anytime in the last six months. Since Sprint launched its faux repricing plan, numerous other companies have copied the six-months-plus-one-day scheme. At all these companies, the employees now have an incentive to keep the share price as low as possible, in opposition to shareholder interests. Why? When the options are returned to them in six months, it's in the workers' interest to have a new exercise price that is as low as possible.

No wonder Sprint shareholders are unhappy. To register their dissatisfaction, they offered two resolutions at Sprint's 2001 annual meeting. One, offered by Amalgamated Bank of New

York, which is the trustee for some 600,000 Sprint shares held in labor union pension funds, called on Sprint to seek shareholder approval for any future severance agreements such as the one that allowed Sprint managers to cash in their options early. It won 48 percent of the votes cast. The other resolution, sponsored by the New York State Retirement Fund and the International Brotherhood of Electrical Workers, called on the board not to reprice (or terminate and regrant) options without the prior approval of a majority of stockholders. It got 36 percent. Most shareholder resolutions fail the first year they are offered, but can pick up steam when proposed in subsequent years. At least that's what the sponsors of the Sprint resolutions are hoping.

Bolstering the Audit Committee

Although many boards of directors continued to improve, scandals involving overstated earnings and accounting chicanery at such companies as Waste Management, Sunbeam, and Cendant kept cropping up throughout the late 1990s. Some even involved allegations of fraud on the part of management. Something was wrong with the way companies were reporting their earnings, and it was natural to look to the board of directors for answers.

It didn't take much research to realize that there was a gaping lack of oversight on many boards, and it was right in the middle of the most important committee—the audit committee. Many of them had directors with some connection to management, such as a consulting contract. Still others had members who didn't know how to read a balance sheet. How could an audit committee spot a problem if it didn't even know the right questions to ask? Most audit committees rarely met with the outside auditors, and if they did, the CEO or other top executives were usually present to discourage any probing questions. I felt strongly that audit committees needed to be reinvigorated. These committees should be able to question auditors not only on the acceptability of a company's financial reporting, but on its quality as well. That means directors must always be ready to ask simple—but sometimes unsettling—questions. They must ask whether management's approach to a particular accounting principle is aggressive or conservative, compared to best practice. Directors also must understand the quality of financial reporting and disclosure practices so they can influence those practices when, in their judgment, they fall short of meeting investors' needs.

In the summer of 1998, the senior staff of the SEC went on a retreat and decided that one of the best things the agency could do to put an end to earnings manipulation was to reform the audit committee. The staff felt that audit committee members at least had to be financially literate and had to have the kind of independence that could challenge management in constructive ways.

Rather than decreeing this ourselves, we decided that new rules would be more widely accepted if the private sector came up with them and the stock exchanges enforced them as one of their listing requirements. So in September 1998 I gave a speech at New York University's Stern School of Business. Called "The Numbers Game," this address brought all of these brewing issues to a boil. I called for the establishment of a blue-ribbon committee to evaluate the effectiveness of corporate audit committees and to recommend changes to the listing requirements of the stock exchanges.

The Numbers Game speech brought a hailstorm of criticism from some of corporate America's top executives: a phone call from Disney CEO Eisner and a letter from IBM CEO Lou Gerstner saying I was misguided. And my former business partner, Sandy Weill, now CEO of Citigroup, cornered me at a meeting of the Business Roundtable, a trade association of the country's top corporate leaders, and gave me an earful. But I found their arguments unpersuasive. At first, I wasn't certain that the blue-ribbon committee idea would fly. So I asked to speak to the Business Roundtable. I made my pitch by explaining that audit committees had become paper tigers, and warned that the capital markets were losing faith in company financial statements. I thought I would get frosty stares from this elite group—after all, I was attacking their boards. But soon after, I learned that more than half the group favored my proposal—perhaps knowing that strong, independent boards inspire investor confidence. I knew I was on to something.

We set to work putting together the panel with Dick Grasso and Frank Zarb, the chairmen, respectively, of the New York Stock Exchange and the National Association of Securities Dealers, overseer of Nasdaq. With some cajoling, they agreed to sponsor the group. Blue-ribbon committees succeed only if they include well-respected members of the profession whose behavior you're trying to influence. To that end, I invited Philip Laskawy and Jim Schiro, the CEOs of accounting firms Ernst & Young and Pricewaterhouse-Coopers, respectively. If there was any industry I hoped to change, it was accounting, so I was elated when they agreed to participate. The panel was led by Ira Millstein, a governance expert and a senior partner at the law firm Weil, Gotshal and Manges, and John Whitehead, the retired cochairman of the investment bank Goldman Sachs.

After three months of deliberation, the panel recommended that audit committees be composed solely of independent directors. It also said the audit committee must have at least three people, all of whom should be considered financially literate, but one of them must have specific expertise in accounting and finance. The panel also urged audit committees to have a formal written charter that explains their purpose. The outside auditor, the panel recommended, should be accountable to the board and the audit committee, and replaceable at their discretion. The proxy statement should include a section saying whether the audit committee has reviewed the company's financial statements and other key areas, such as the independence of the outside auditor. The committee should analyze not just the numbers, but also the quality of the accounting. It should ask, for example, if the company is abusing the spirit of the accounting rules, even if it's not technically in violation. These were bold ideas.

On December 14, 1999, the stock exchanges adopted the panel's recommended listing requirements almost to the letter. I believe the blue-ribbon committee did more to change the culture of corporate governance than almost anything else we did at the SEC. Since the report, I have seen a shift of responsibility to the audit committee. Today, most committees have members with financial experience who ask smart, probing questions. They don't have to be CPAs, but they do have to know enough to understand where problems may exist. A July 2001 study published by *CFO* magazine found that audit committees were meeting an average of 4.6 times a year, up from 3.5 in 1998. And while 28 percent of companies in 1998 had at least one audit panelist who was not independent, that number fell to 13 percent in 2001.

By now that number should be zero because of the June 2001 effective date of the requirement that all audit committee members be fully independent. But the stock exchanges, which set many of the corporate governance rules that companies must follow, haven't been as tough about enforcing the rules as their public relations literature implies. For example, the listing standards allow companies to have one nonindependent audit committee member "under exceptional and limited circumstances, provided that the board determines it to be in the best interests of the corporation and its shareholders," and discloses the reasons in the company's next annual proxy statement. While numerous companies made use of this loophole, they no longer can do so under the Sarbanes-Oxley law, which mandates that all audit committee members be independent.

Now that my SEC term is over, I've been asked to sit on several boards. I currently serve as a director at Bloomberg L.P.; M & T Bank of Buffalo, N.Y.; fund management company Neuberger Berman; and U.S. Investigation Services. I take my corporate governance duties seriously.

How Do I Find Out Whether a Company Has Good Corporate Governance?

You, too, should care deeply about the governance of the companies in which you invest. But how do you know whether a company practices what I preach?

It's easier than you think, because the most important information about the board is in the annual proxy statement. This document must be mailed to every current shareholder. It tells you which items, such as the slate of directors, require investor approval, and gives instructions on how to vote your shares.

You may not think this is important, but it is. Investor groups are banding together to oppose certain corporate decisions, and they can make a difference. I think it's your responsibility as an owner of a company's shares to express your opinion whether or not you support the company's actions. Like democracy, corporate governance works only when you exercise your right to vote.

You may also think that as an individual investor, there's little you can do to change corporate governance. Yet you have powerful allies in the form of large pension funds and mutual funds, known as institutional investors. They collectively vote the shares of millions of people who, like you, have invested in these funds through their company pensions and 401(k) retirement accounts. Not all institutional investors care about corporate governance, but some of the very biggest ones are passionate about it—and can flex a lot of muscle. Among the most active, besides TIAA-CREF and CalPERS, is the AFL-CIO's Office of Investment, which sets voting guidelines for $450 billion in union pension fund investments. For the labor federation, the treatment of workers and executive pay are critical issues, in addition to increasing return on investment. The AFL-CIO has spoken out publicly against the governance practices of many companies, and has won several victories that would have been unimaginable a short time ago. In 2001, thirty-two labor-backed shareholder proposals received an average of 34 percent of the votes cast—a far cry from the 1 percent that dissident groups typically were able to muster just a decade ago.

Different groups have different objectives. For CalPERS, increasing shareholder returns, and thus improving the standard of living for California state retirees, is paramount. In 1993, CalPERS began pressuring underperforming companies to change their board composition, but soon became more directly involved in removing poor managers. They were instrumental, for example, in persuading the board of General Motors to oust its CEO in 1992, the year GM lost $7 billion. Based on that success, CalPERS created a list of governance principles, and asked 200 other companies in which it had invested to adopt similar standards. Among the principles: a majority of directors should be from outside the company, and they should meet separately from the CEO three times a year; the board should perform an annual assessment of its own performance; and directors should have access to senior executives beyond the CEO.

Every year, CalPERS identifies companies in its portfolio that have underperformed the market for the past three years. Then its executives meet with the directors of each of those companies to talk about performance and governance issues. Those companies that also have poor governance end up on what is called the CalPERS Focus List, which can be found at *www.calpers-governance.org*.

TIAA-CREF spends over $2 million a year on governance issues. It, too, draws up an annual list of poor-performing companies and the governance changes it would like to see. But TIAA-CREF prefers to work behind the scenes before resorting to the more shame-oriented tactics of CalPERS, as by discreetly sending one or two retired CEOs on its staff to meet with the company and present its viewpoint. That's when most changes are made, says TIAA-CREF chairman John Biggs.

If you do not already own shares in a company, you can still access its proxy statement on the Internet at the SEC's Web site, *www.sec.gov*. Once there, click on "EDGAR," then select "DEF" (for Definitive Proxy Statement) in the box marked "form type." Then enter the company name and the year, and press "search." The proxy statement comes out in preliminary form (PRE 14A) and final form (DEF 14A) once a year. Look for the most recent filing; it usually appears in the spring for companies with a calendar fiscal year. You can also have any proxy statement sent to you by calling the company's investor relations number.

A number of other Web sites devoted to corporate governance are worth investigating. They'll give you a sense of how governance activists are voting on various proxy proposals, and point out egregious conflicts of interest in some companies or great governance examples in others. I recommend *www.thecorporatelibrary.com*, an overall resource on CEO contracts, pay, director independence, and other issues; and *www.iss.cda.com*, the Web site of Institutional Shareholder Services, a proxy monitoring organization that recommends how its clients—major investment firms—should vote. I also like the site of the Council on Institutional Investors, *www.cii.org*, which represents pension and mutual funds. Then there are the sites of TIAA-CREF, *www.tiaa-cref.org*; CalPERS, *www.calpers.org*; and the AFL-CIO, *www.aflcio.org/paywatch*, all of which have loads of helpful info on compensation, current issues, shareholder proposals, and much more. The AFL-CIO site has a handy executive compensation worksheet that can help you calculate how much a CEO is paid, including stock options. Sprint Corp. chairman and CEO Esrey, for example, took in $109.5 million in salary, bonus, and stock options, according to the site, in 2000.

A GOOD BOARD: TRANSPARENCY IS PART OF THE CULTURE AT PFIZER

If you're looking for an example of a company practicing good corporate governance, consider Pfizer Corp., a pharmaceutical company that has really pushed the envelope. In 1992, Pfizer became the first company to name a vice president for corporate governance, and today remains one of the few companies with such a position. It also has a corporate governance committee, in addition to the standard audit, compensation, and executive committees. And its proxy statement lists the company's corporate governance principles. Companies don't have to do this, says Peggy Foran, the company's current vice president for corporate governance. "But Pfizer makes an extra effort to be open, in the belief that it leads to better investor relations," she says.

The job of the corporate governance committee, according to Pfizer's 2001 proxy statement, is to "make recommendations to the board concerning the appropriate size and needs of the board." Like the audit and compensation committees, the corporate governance committee is made up entirely of independent directors.

Pfizer's proxy statement has another advantage: it's written in clear, basic English. Most other companies' proxy statements are written in confusing legalese, making it difficult for shareholders to understand what's really going on. That's just the way some companies like it. "Transparency is part of our culture," says Foran. "I do this for a living and I can't understand a lot of [corporate material] on the first read. We believe in plain English, and we give a lot of information that's not required. Pfizer tries to put itself in the shoes of the investors."

Now let's take a look at Pfizer's board. In 2000 it met twelve times. That's three times the number I recommend as a minimum, although it's worth noting that Pfizer has had plenty of business to discuss since it acquired Warner-Lambert in 2000. The recent merger also explains why it has nineteen directors, which is more than the ideal number but understandable considering that two companies were bolted together. All of the directors attended at least 75 percent of the full board and committee meetings during 2000—another sign that the board really cares. And the audit committee alone met six times. Five of the six audit committee members are current or former CEOs. That's a good sign that they actually understand numbers.

Each committee has a charter, which appears in the proxy statement. Only the audit committee is required to do this under SEC rules. The charter explains each panel's specific responsibilities. Again, this is unusual and worth reading to see how a committed board conducts its affairs. The corporate governance committee explicitly says it works on succession issues—a key matter for any board, but one that many ignore until it's too late.

Directors at Pfizer are paid in a combination of cash and a form of restricted stock. I would prefer to see them paid in stock alone, which would give them more of a stake in the company's performance. Pfizer doesn't require its directors to own Pfizer stock, as some companies do, but it expects them to hold a significant amount.

Only three of the nineteen board members are current or former executives: Bill Steere, the former CEO; Hank McKinnell, the current CEO; and John Niblack, who would succeed McKinnell in an emergency situation and therefore must be comfortable with Pfizer's board. This means that only 15 percent of the board are insiders—below the average of 22 percent.

Pfizer's board is extremely involved in the company's affairs. It regularly takes trips to Pfizer facilities in other parts of the world, such as Latin America and Asia, to meet with the executives there and understand all parts of Pfizer's business.

Yet Pfizer also monitors its directors to make sure they're not sitting on too many other boards. Each time a member is invited to join another board, he or she must submit an application to the corporate governance committee, which makes sure there are no overlaps or conflicts of interest before giving its approval. Also, when board members change jobs, they must resign from the board. The corporate governance committee then has the option to retain them or find new ones.

Although Pfizer could make improvements, such as not staggering directors' terms and beefing up the stock ownership of some directors, the company is an example of what good governance is all about. I urge you to read Pfizer's proxy statement. It's also worth noting that $100 invested in Pfizer stock in 1995 would have returned $450 by the end of 2000, a 450 percent return compared to the 300 percent of Pfizer's peer group over the same period.

A Governance Checklist: What to Look For

Board Independence   Who's on the board? How many are outsiders (meaning people who don't work at the company) and how many are insiders? According to Spencer Stuart, the average board in 2001 had 77 percent outside members and 23 percent insiders. Even if your company matches this profile, take a closer look. Read the proxy statement to see how many of the outsiders are actually independent. I think that the majority of the board should have no ties of any sort to the company. The only connection to the company should be their board service. If you see any commercial relationships, such as real estate deals, legal fees, or consulting contracts, that means a director is not truly independent.

Also be wary of family relationships that could compromise the independence of outsiders. At Hillenbrand Industries, for example, five of the eleven board members are Hillenbrand family members, and another is related by marriage. And watch out for interlocking directorates, or when CEOs serve on each other's boards. This could be an indication of mutual back-scratching.

Look carefully at the audit committee. Did any audit committee members ever work at the accounting firm that's been chosen to do the audit? This is a danger sign, because an audit committee member must question whether the auditor is doing a good job—yet it's human nature to give your former colleagues some slack.

Is there any mention of the board meeting periodically without the CEO present? If so, this is a true sign of independence. If the CEO is always around, it's a safe bet that no one's really conducting a no-holds-barred review. Another positive sign: boards that have lead directors who can call all the others together without the CEO's permission.

Board Overcommitment   How often does the board meet? It should meet four times a year at a minimum, and preferably more often. The average S&P 500 company met eight times in 2000. The various committees should meet at least as often as the full board, particularly the audit committee. Did the members attend at least 90 percent of the meetings? The proxy statement must list the directors who attended less than 75 percent of the scheduled meetings. If some didn't, that's a possible sign that they are not paying close attention.

Make sure that the directors aren't so busy serving on other corporate boards that they don't have time for the company whose shares you own.

Vernon Jordan, for example, now serves on eleven different

boards. Former Senate Majority Leader George Mitchell, a Democrat, sits on twelve boards. But Jack Kemp, the 1996 Republican vice-presidential candidate, takes the cake: he sits on twenty-one boards. If a board member has a demanding job, such as the CEO of a separate company, he should serve on no more than two or three other boards. The Council of Institutional Investors recommends five boards as the maximum that any one person can serve on properly.

Board Size   According to executive search company Spencer Stuart, the average board today has eleven members. The Council of Institutional Investors recommends that boards have between five and fifteen members. Too large a board can be unwieldy, while too small a board robs a company of the different perspectives and skills it needs. During the dot-com craze, many start-up companies, such as Yahoo!, insisted on iconoclastic boards with six to eight members, preferably with some tie to management. As we've seen from the performance of numerous dot-coms, they were misguided.

Board Compensation   In 2001, according to Spencer Stuart, the average board member was paid $92,452, in a combination of cash and stock. Is your company's board paid considerably more than the average? If so, is there a good reason why? (Some companies, such as General Electric, pay their directors more because they meet more often—ten times in 2000—and must understand numerous industries.) Small companies with revenues under $500 million should pay their boards less. Keep an eye out for any extreme variations from the average. It could signal a fat and complacent board, or, at the other extreme, one that isn't paid enough money to take its role seriously. Make sure that board members get at least a portion of their compensation in stock. Like you, they should be at risk if the share price plummets.

Board Perks   Remember my term "the culture of seduction"? In the old days, it was common for directors to collect a goody bag of perquisites in addition to their salaries. It once was common for a company to offer its directors a pension after retirement—despite the fact that most directors already have a handsome pension from serving as a top executive at another company. Ten years ago, more than three-quarters of S&P 500 companies offered director retirement plans. Now only 6 percent of companies offer this perk. If you see it in the proxy statement, beware.

The same goes for board meetings held at deluxe resorts and other "sweetheart deals" that may compromise directors' independence. Read your proxy statement to find out whether directors get perks such as free use of the company jet, or whether philanthropic contributions are made to their pet causes. Companies may not report all of this information, but the governance Web sites mentioned above often have information about these enticements.

Succession Planning   A board's most important duty is choosing the CEO. Every board should make sure there is a succession plan in place should something happen to the chief executive. Johnson & Johnson is an example of a company that makes succession planning an explicit part of the board's responsibility. Read the board's description of its duties carefully, and look twice at any company whose board doesn't take an active role in succession. It could mean that the CEO has cowed the board into submission.

Executive Pay   One of the most critical issues in governance is how executive compensation is determined. Read the compensation committee's report to make sure that it uses a clear, performance-driven standard for paying the chief executive. Simply put, the CEO should be paid generously only if he deserves it. If the company's share price is sinking or long-term performance targets are repeatedly missed, he should take a hit, with smaller stock option grants, a reduced or no bonus, or some other penalty. Look for any indication that the board decided to pay the CEO the full compensation package despite not meeting the agreed-to goals.

Stock options are another sensitive issue. They are a popular way to pay executives because they tie the performance of the company to the share price. That's good, in principle. Yet if a CEO is awarded too many stock options, he can become wealthy beyond all justification if the stock moves up just a dollar or two. Too many options allow managers to underperform their peer group and still make a hefty profit when they cash in their stock options. Stock options also create more shares of stock over time, which waters down the value of your shares. Remember: it is shareholder money that officers and directors are using to pay themselves. Look for a compensation committee that understands this.

Annual Board Elections   In my view, it's best for the investor if the entire board is elected once a year. But about 60 percent of company boards have staggered terms. Usually this means that each year, one-third of the directors are elected to three-year terms. In the era of hostile takeovers, this made it easier for companies to deny predators the opportunity to replace a board all at once. But it also means that shareholders have far less control over who represents them. Look for companies whose boards are elected annually. In 1998, Disney ended the staggered terms of its directors and required them to stand for election as a single slate every year. Staggered boards aren't always bad. Pfizer, for example, has a staggered board, and its governance practices are otherwise exemplary. But it's a good rule of thumb to support companies that give shareholders more control over choosing directors.

Poison Pills   Poison pills were of most concern in the 1980s and early '90s, when hostile takeovers were hot. But be on the lookout, because poison pills are making a comeback now that share prices are depressed. Silicon Valley execs are especially keen on having poison pills in their arsenal now that their shrunken share prices have left them vulnerable. Poison pills make it easier for incumbent management to retain control. But they also prevent shareholders, and the overall market, from exercising their right to discipline management by turning it out. I think the market should have its say. Look in the proxy statement to see whether there are any proposals to adopt a pill. If so, and you think the company might do better under new management, you might want to skip this stock.

A BAD BOARD: THE POWER FAILURE AT ENRON

Look for a train wreck of a company and chances are the vital checks and balances that active boards provide are missing. That appears to be the case at Enron.

Enron's finances, especially its many off-balance-sheet partnerships, were incomprehensible even to the smartest analysts on Wall Street, who recommended Enron's stock anyway. Why? Because it delivered glowing results: revenues in 2000 came to $101 billion, and its stock market value topped $75 billion. In early 2001, its future looked bright, too.

But almost at once, everything came unglued. Enron's overseas projects were losing money, as was a $1.2 billion investment in a fiber-optic network, which came online just as the country faced a glut of fiber-optic capacity. Enron's stock, too, suffered along with most other companies' in the recession that began in March 2001. But the biggest blow resulted from Enron's use of accounting tricks, which auditors at Arthur Andersen and the board of directors should have known about and stopped.

Why didn't the board act? Sadly, the directors appear not to have asked the right questions, and accepted Enron's financial alchemy without really understanding it. Twice in 1999 the board waived the company's code of ethics, which normally would have prohibited CFO Andrew Fastow from managing partnerships that placed his personal financial interest above Enron's. The audit committee was especially remiss in not noticing that Fastow and other employees were enriching themselves at Enron's expense, Fastow alone by at least $30 million, through the off-balance-sheet deals. Nor did the audit committee notice that many of the partnerships were designed to make the financial statements look good, not to achieve bona fide economic objectives.

A report by a special investigative committee of the Enron board said that the entire board, despite its financial sophistication, had failed in its oversight duties. It especially failed to make sure that Fastow followed procedures set up to protect Enron from potential conflicts. In essence, Fastow was allowed to sit on both sides of the table, without anyone looking over his shoulder, while negotiating over huge sums of money that passed back and forth between Enron and the partnerships he managed. The special committee wrote that the board "can and should be faulted for failing to demand more information, and for failing to probe and understand the information that did come to it." For example, although the board compensation committee was supposed to review the money Fastow received from the partnership deals, no such reviews ever took place. And on May 5, 2000, when the board was told that one transaction with a Fastow partnership raised the risk of "accounting scrutiny," the board never acted. Instead, it relied on assurances that auditor Arthur Andersen was comfortable with the deal.

Robert Jaedicke, the retired Stanford University accounting professor who led the audit committee, defended his stewardship of Enron before Congress: "We do not manage the company. We do not do the auditing. We are not detectives." In other words, he should be able to rely on the word of Enron management and its auditor. If only that were so. When a company's dealings are as complex as Enron's were, the board should seek outside advice, at the very least. In Enron's case, it should also have required Fastow to back up his claims about the merits of the off-balance-sheet entities, and to report back each quarter on how they were performing. The board should not have accepted at face value what Enron management told them. If the board, for example, had demanded to see the paperwork for the partnership transactions, they would have spotted suspicious activities, such as the movement of assets back and forth, that would have raised many questions about financial manipulation.

Michael Miles, who was chairman and CEO of Philip Morris Cos. from 1991 to 1994, names four attributes all board members must have. They should be engaged, meaning they should be willing to commit their time and energy. They should know how the "game" is played, and by that he means the best directors are former CEOs with a sophisticated understanding of the dynamics of business. Directors should not be shy; they should ask inconvenient questions and not worry whether the CEO considers them polite or likable. And finally, directors should have a very keen bullshit detector so they know when someone is selling them a bill of goods. "My sense is these characteristics were missing at Enron," says Miles.

Conflicts of interest among board members may also have played a role in the board's lack of vigilance. Two Enron directors, one of whom sat on the audit committee, had consulting contracts with the company. Two other audit committee panelists worked for institutions that received substantial donations from Enron. One of those institutions, the University of Texas M.D. Anderson Cancer Center, alone received $1.8 million from Enron and related foundations over an eight-year period.

And where were the institutional investors and other shareholder advocates? Even the most activist of shareholder groups did not oppose Enron's opaque financial reports or its board structure. Indeed, one of Enron's biggest shareholders was CalPERS, the California pension fund whose $146 billion in assets now includes 3.5 million nearly worthless Enron shares. CalPERS also was a partner in two of Enron's off-balance-sheet deals, a transaction that produced a handsome gain of 62 percent a year for CalPERS over eight years. When Enron sought CalPERS's participation in a later off-balance-sheet deal, the pension fund balked when advisers warned it about Fastow's conflicting fiduciary relationships—exactly the conflict that Enron's board did not see. But CalPERS did not publicize the problems at Enron, nor did it complain to Enron's board, even though CalPERS was also a major Enron shareholder. Why not? "We cannot read tea leaves," CalPERS's director of corporate governance, Ted White, told a House committee. "It's impossible for anybody to have forecast that those relationships would mushroom and that Enron basically would commit fraud." True enough; hindsight is always twenty-twenty. But I can't help feeling that CalPERS could have used its corporate governance expertise and its credibility to make sure Enron stopped its risky practices. Sometimes even watchdogs fall asleep.

CHAPTER NINE

HOW TO BE A PLAYER

During my seven and a half years in Washington, I was constantly amazed by what I saw. And nothing astonished me more than witnessing the powerful special interest groups in full swing when they thought a proposed rule or a piece of legislation might hurt them, giving nary a thought to how the proposal might help the investing public. With laserlike precision, groups representing Wall Street firms, mutual fund companies, accounting firms, or corporate managers would quickly set about to defeat even minor threats. Individual investors, with no organized lobby or trade association to represent their views in Washington, never knew what hit them.

The Washington I came to in mid-1993 was a highly partisan place. A Democrat, Bill Clinton, was in the White House, but his party would control the House and Senate for only eighteen more months, when a Republican revolution would sweep the GOP into complete control of Capitol Hill. With a more sympathetic GOP chairing Hill committees and setting the agenda, the business community, already a commanding presence, consolidated its power.

Among the capital's competing centers of influence, business's clout is considerable. That's not necessarily bad. The private sector creates jobs and fuels economic growth, and that helps us all. If we didn't have thousands of successful corporations, we wouldn't have robust stock and bond markets, and without them, none of us would be able to invest and prosper. But the interests of corporations and those of people who work for them, buy their products, and own their shares is a constant source of tension. In the Washington lobbying hierarchy, the corporation is by far the most muscular power center, followed by workers (in large part because of the efforts of organized labor) and consumers. Shareholders, and especially individual investors, come last. There is no one, in fact, who represents individual investors full-time. They are the most overlooked and underrepresented interest group in America. My job at the SEC was to bring some equilibrium to the equation.

Business spends many millions of dollars supporting trade associations and issue-oriented think tanks in the nation's capital. CEOs use these groups to promote and protect free enterprise, but also sometimes to enhance their own prestige. The most powerful of these are the Business Roundtable, which represents large companies; the U.S. Chamber of Commerce and the National Federation of Independent Business, both of which represent small business; and the National Association of Manufacturers, which as its name implies represents nonservice companies that make things. They all vigilantly watch out for their members' interests as Congress and executive branch agencies increasingly set the rules under which companies may operate—rules that dictate everything from which companies are allowed to merge to what products they can sell overseas and how much they must pay in taxes.

Often these groups take different positions on such issues as tax cuts and international trade, but when their interests intersect, they can be a potent force. And when business groups use all the tools at their disposal—campaign contributions, phone calls from high-profile CEOs, advertisements on local TV, op-ed pieces in major newspapers, and visits from lobbyists who once worked for the very lawmakers whose arms they are twisting—the business point of view trounces everything else.

When an issue does not concern the at-large business community, but just a slice of it, specialized trade groups dominate. On investor issues, these include the Securities Industry Association, which represents the major Wall Street investment banking and brokerage firms, such as Merrill Lynch, Salomon Smith Barney, Goldman Sachs, Morgan Stanley, and Credit Suisse First Boston. The SIA also represents hundreds of regional and discount brokerage firms, such as Edward Jones and Charles Schwab. Altogether, the SIA has some 675 member firms employing 750,000 people and producing $200 billion in annual revenues.

The American Institute of Certified Public Accountants is another major player on investment issues. It represents 330,000 individual CPAs but is dominated by PricewaterhouseCoopers, KPMG, Deloitte & Touche, Ernst & Young, and what's left of Arthur Andersen. It has a $140 million budget and employs fourteen lobbyists, three of whom lobby full-time, but the real source of its clout is a widely dispersed membership. Every Congressional district is home to hundreds of CPAs who are often prominent members of the community. They frequent the local golf course, are active in local business clubs, and contribute to local politicians. I saw the AICPA unleash this grassroots force when the SEC was pursuing stiffer auditor independence rules. The SEC and Congress within weeks heard from thousands of accountants. Many of their written comments were suspiciously alike; the AICPA had mass-mailed sample letters, and members dutifully copied them and sent them under their own names. The same goes for the letters the SEC received from Capitol Hill. Lawmakers put their own signatures on letters that were word-for-word the same, written by accounting lobbyists.

Corporate managers also support legions of lobbyists and public relations experts, who act as a company's eyes and ears and alert it when any issue arises that ultimately might affect profits. Hiring the right lobbyist can help ensure that the CEO has access to powerful lawmakers when he needs it. Campaign contributions also open doors. Many CEOs donate their own money to elected officials, and some also form political action committees to which employees can donate funds, and which the lobbyist can then distribute, with strict limits, to helpful lawmakers.

I explain all this not to offer great new insight into how Washington operates, but to show how sophisticated the business lobby is. By contrast, individual investors lack a power base in Washington. And that's exactly how the business community would like to keep it. I know from my own experience that when investors do find their voice, business groups too often succeed in drowning them out. One way they do this is by assiduously courting the lawmakers who chair the panels that oversee the SEC. Increasingly when the agency makes a move they disagree with, business's hired guns go directly to Capitol Hill, bypassing the SEC.

"Arthur, I wish you'd play more golf," Representative Tom Bliley, the courtly, bow-tied Virginia Republican, told me plaintively. "Every time you give a speech, I get bombarded with complaints." Like clockwork, Bliley, the chairman of the House Energy and Commerce Committee until his retirement in 2000, was on the phone. It was late September 1999 and I had just delivered what I hoped would be a provocative speech in which I outlined my idea of what the stock market of the future should look like. Whenever I pursued new initiatives to make the securities industry more transparent to investors, Bliley rang. He let me know that his district's brokerage firms, banks, and businesses alerted him to my every move. He hated Regulation Fair Disclosure, and he bitterly opposed my pursuit of auditor independence rules. This time, Bliley accused me of meddling with the capital markets, which he thought functioned just fine without any interference from the SEC.

I explained to him why the SEC needed to guide the development of new, electronic exchanges to make sure they were properly integrated into the existing market structure. I promised that his constituents would have ample opportunity to opine on whatever SEC initiative might result.

While I liked Bliley, who firmly believed that he was doing the right thing for his constituents, it occurred to me that not once did he call to remark on how our various efforts might help the tens of thousands of individual investors in his district. They were his constituents, too, but they never appeared en masse in his office, contributed to his campaigns, or gave his former top aides high-paying lobbying jobs. Bliley, like too many of his colleagues, seemed only to speak for the special interest groups—the accountants, lawyers, brokers, investment bankers, and corporate managers—because they were in regular contact. And he didn't just react to the business leaders in his own district, though he was extremely responsive to them. Because he chaired an important committee, Bliley was one of the accounting and securities industries' "go-to" guys, lawmakers they knew they could count on to fight their battles. They had his ear because they attended Chamber of Commerce lunches with him and regularly visited him in his Capitol Hill office to explain why this legislation or that rule was bad for their industry. They provided "talking points" that he could refer to in his own SEC communications. They understood how to work the legislative machinery, and they made sure they were among his biggest campaign contributors. In short, corporate lobbyists have a special relationship that ordinary investors just don't have.

Bliley wasn't the only one, of course. Wall Street and other investment-related groups make sure they have access to numerous other lawmakers. Prominent among them is Representative Billy Tauzin, the cagey Louisiana Republican who became chairman of the House Energy and Commerce Committee after Bliley's retirement. This may surprise you, since Tauzin held the most aggressive investigation, by far, of the dozen Congressional inquiries into Enron's collapse. And the indignation he showed Enron and Arthur Andersen officials called to testify before his panel sure looked sincere to the folks watching the televised hearings back home. But when the cameras aren't on, Tauzin doesn't always carry the investor torch. In the spring and summer of 2000, when our auditor independence rules were being hotly debated, Tauzin was relentless. He sent three separate letters warning the SEC to back down. One five-page letter, which Bliley also signed, demanded answers to sixteen questions on such matters as the SEC's statutory authority to issue the rules, the empirical evidence that rules were necessary, and whether SEC employees were subject to the same stock-owning restrictions as accountants. While I can't prove that the letter was written by lobbyists from the Big Five accounting firms, it strains credulity that Tauzin or his staff could have written such a detailed letter on their own. He sent a second letter on July 20, 2000, demanding that the SEC delay the rule making because the accounting industry needed more than the seventy-five-day comment period we had allotted to analyze the proposal. Tauzin's strategy was obvious: any delay would push the process past the November election, and a George W. Bush win would likely mean the demise of our rule. To prove his clout, Tauzin sent this letter with signatures from twenty other House colleagues, but his name appeared prominently at the top.

Tauzin also tops the list of recipients of accounting industry largesse, though the Congressman strongly denies that campaign contributions influenced him in any way. Since 1995, Tauzin has received nearly $150,000 from the accounting industry.

I'm sure Tauzin believed that the SEC was pursuing rules for which there was no demonstrated need, and that he found it unfair that a regulator might try to rein in accounting firms' money-making ability. After Enron collapsed and its top auditor admitted shredding documents, Tauzin, to his credit, conceded the need for tougher enforcement of independence rules and a more vigilant oversight body to replace the AICPA. Senator Mike Enzi, a Wyoming Republican who also happens to be an accountant, opposed the SEC's auditor independence rules on the grounds that they would harm small accounting practices. This was nothing but a distraction. We studied the possibility and found that, because most public company audits are done by one of the Big Five, small firms would not be affected much. After the Enron collapse, however, Enzi supported legislation to create a new board in place of the CPA trade association to oversee and discipline the accounting profession.

I don't mean to single out just Republicans. Sometimes Democratic lawmakers who are otherwise diligently pro-consumer are surprisingly effective in representing business interests. Democratic senators Chuck Schumer of New York, Evan Bayh of Indiana, and Bob Torricelli of New Jersey all signed letters urging me to back down on auditor independence rules, or else delay the rule-making process until after the 2000 elections. Like Tauzin, they failed to see the need for such a radical step as banning accounting firms from doing consulting work for their audit clients. But none was a more formidable foe than Senator Joe Lieberman of Connecticut.

The former vice-presidential candidate now chairs the Senate

Governmental Affairs Committee, one of the twelve panels investigating the fallout from Enron's collapse. It was Lieberman who sponsored the 1994 Senate resolution that urged the Financial Accounting Standards Board to withdraw its proposed stock-option rule. The Lieberman resolution was nonbinding, but politically very effective. The Senate adopted it by an 88–9 vote. The message was that Lieberman had the power to clip FASB's wings if it pursued the rule.

No group cheered Lieberman louder than the high-tech industry—the biggest users of options and the source of millions in campaign contributions. Lieberman was doing exactly what lawmakers are elected to do: push for policies he believes to be in the national interest. In this case, his aim was to foster the growth of struggling tech start-ups, which claimed they wouldn't be able to attract talented workers if they had to pay normal salaries and bonuses. Stock options allowed them to promise rich rewards down the road in exchange for salary sacrifices today.

But I believe the senator also unwittingly promoted the interests of corporate executives who wanted the benefits of overly generous compensation packages for themselves, without the responsibility of disclosure to shareholders. Full and fair disclosure is a bedrock accounting principle. And once the FASB retreated on stock options, the door was open for more such Congressional meddling. For the next eight years, the FASB would shy away from controversial issues because it feared setting off more political firestorms.

Indeed, the FASB backed down again in 2001 when Michigan Republican senator Spencer Abraham, along with Lieberman and about a dozen others, opposed yet another rule meant to stop companies from abusing the "pooling-of-interests" accounting treatment for mergers and acquisitions. Abraham is now President Bush's energy secretary. Once again, the lawmakers acted on behalf of Silicon Valley, for which retention of pooling accounting was a top priority. Pooling allowed companies to combine their assets without declaring any goodwill, which is the amount of the purchase price above the fair-market value of the acquired assets. Because goodwill had to be amortized, and amortization lowers earnings, pooling was the accounting method of choice. The FASB eventually abolished pooling, but Lieberman & Co. got the result they wanted when the standard-setters ruled that companies didn't have to amortize goodwill anymore.

I don't quarrel with the duty of elected officials to act when they believe any group, even a private-sector body, is about to cause grave damage to the economy. And they rightly insist that no organization fulfilling a quasi-public responsibility—not even the privately funded FASB—should be immune from Congressional oversight. But I can't help but wonder if some of their arguments would survive close inspection by millions of individual investors.

The pols' position on accounting rules can be boiled down to this: standards must reflect the special interests of the country's promising young tech companies, for whom existing rules would reduce earnings and depress share prices. But if it's in the national interest to protect budding enterprises, why not bend other rules for them, by not requiring, for example, that cash compensation count against earnings? If they knew all the arguments, and had a forum in which to express their opinion, I think most investors would conclude that accounting rules should not bend to the agenda du jour, because that will never serve the long-term national interest of honest, transparent accounting.

The Honor Roll of Investor Champions

Happily, I know a handful of lawmakers who are consistently pro-investor, and you should consider them your staunchest allies. If I had to list the legislators who would make my honor roll of investor champions, Senator Carl Levin, a Michigan Democrat, would be one of them. Every time a legislator fought a tough accounting standard, Levin fought back. More than most, he understands the importance of an independent FASB. Well before the Enron disaster, he saw the fiction that corporate financial statements had become: companies technically were in compliance with accounting rules, and yet their financial statements were hiding huge debts and other liabilities. From his position as ranking

Democrat on the Senate Governmental Affairs Committee's Permanent Subcommittee on Investigations, Levin uses his broad authority to pursue pro-investor causes.

Levin's GOP colleague on the investigations subcommittee is Senator Susan Collins, a low-key legislator from Maine. As Maine's former commissioner of professional and financial regulation, Collins knows how vulnerable investors can be. She vigorously pursues securities and Internet scam artists who prey on uninformed investors. As a fierce proponent of investor education, Collins was one of the most receptive lawmakers when I looked for hosts and support for my SEC town meetings.

Collins's New Hampshire neighbor and fellow Republican, Senator Judd Gregg, would also make my A-list. As the chairman of the Senate appropriations subcommittee that determines how much the SEC can spend each year (the panel's formal name is the Senate Appropriations Subcommittee on Commerce, Justice, State, and the Judiciary), Gregg was always extremely helpful in making sure the agency received adequate funding.

Maryland Democratic Senator Paul Sarbanes also deserves credit. As chairman of the Senate Banking Committee, Sarbanes beat the odds in the summer of 2002 and pushed through legislation to establish a new accounting oversight board. He did so despite heavy opposition from both the accounting industry and the SEC, which favored a weaker House version.

But when it comes to investor advocacy, no one beats two House Democrats, Representatives John Dingell of Michigan and Ed Markey of Massachusetts. Whatever issue I was pursuing—better disclosure of mutual fund fees, greater bond market transparency, getting rid of corrupt practices in the municipal bond business, improving auditor independence—Dingell and Markey were with me every step of the way. While I saw many lawmakers take knee-jerk positions in support of their wealthy campaign contributors, Dingell and Markey are instinctively pro-investor.

Because they are not organized into a dues-paying group, ordinary investors are rarely, if ever, heard from and therefore don't flex their political muscle. They are the most undersupported and underrepresented constituency in the country. It's always been my belief that investors could form a powerful special interest group if they spoke up. The characters and plot lines in Washington change often, but it's really not that difficult to follow along. You don't have to hire an expensive law firm to represent you, and you don't even have to know how to lobby. Your power rests on the fact that you are one of 79 million individual investors, and that you are able to express an informed opinion (and cast your vote) on matters affecting your financial well-being.

The New Investor Class

The Federal Reserve Board's 1998 Survey of Consumer Finance (the Fed will next update this survey of household wealth in 2003) showed that 49 percent of all households owned stock, up from 32 percent in 1989. The Investment Company Institute and the Securities Industry Association, the trade associations that speak for mutual fund companies and securities firms, respectively, concluded in a separate study that 79 million individuals owned stock in 1999, up from just 42 million people in 1983. Of those 79 million, 85 percent owned stock through one or more mutual funds and 54 percent owned stocks directly.

Americans who own stock are no longer just the wealthiest among us. Most investors today are solidly middle-class. The typical stock owner has a household income of $60,000 and total household assets of $85,000—not exactly the country club set.

There's no disputing that stock ownership has become as common as the two-car garage, and that there is a new investor class in America today. One of my goals as chairman was to give voice to this new silent majority. I viewed the individual investor as my most important constituent, and set out to realign the power structure in Washington between small investors and the politically well-connected Wall Street firms and accounting firms.

To make the agency more approachable, we revamped the SEC's Web site. The new site (*www.sec.gov*) helps investors follow our rule-making process, and makes it possible for them to electronically express their opinions. By clicking on "EDGAR" at the site, investors can access the thousands of filings—annual and quarterly reports and proxy statements, among others—that public companies file every year.

We also pushed an initiative to require companies to file certain SEC documents using plain English rather than the legal jargon that only securities lawyers understand. I made it my personal crusade to get people who represented the investing public on the governing boards of corporations, stock exchanges, and the Financial Accounting Standards Board. In addition, I held forty-three investor town meetings across America, at which I explained the SEC's agenda. Then I invited investors to ask me, or any of the specialists I brought along, any question they wanted. My goal was to get investors excited, or mad, about what was happening in Washington, and to coax them out of their shells.

My efforts were not exactly embraced on Wall Street, where the heads of large investment banks at first complained about my activities, or on Capitol Hill, where some lawmakers let me know in no uncertain terms that I was overstepping the boundaries that most SEC chairmen observed. That's when I knew my efforts were paying off. By going over their heads and speaking directly to investors—their customers and constituents—I was hoping to create a new grassroots force.

As an investor, you can and should do more to make sure your point of view is heard in Washington. I'm not suggesting that you mimic the groups that represent Wall Street interests in Washington. They have far greater resources and far more access to powerful lawmakers than you will ever have. They call on personal relationships, built up over many years, with influential legislators or policy makers. They also have the ability to gain access through campaign contributions to key lawmakers, and to combine that with well-timed e-mails, phone calls, and personal visits from important figures in the industry. They are able to create the appearance of a groundswell of opposition to whatever they are looking to defeat. More often than not, they are successful.

Instead, you can tap into the wealth of information available over the Internet to keep up with hot issues and the activities of Congress, the SEC, and the special interest groups. By doing so, you can be just as informed as the well-paid lobbyists roaming the corridors of Capitol Hill. Once you know the important issues, and take the time to understand the pros and cons, you can speak with authority. You can weigh in at the SEC with your comments in support of, or against, a proposed rule. Or you can write letters or e-mails to the House and Senate members who sit on the committees considering legislation that could affect your finances. In short, you can be a player in Washington. All it takes is a little effort.

The Key Hill Committees

What are the key Congressional committees to watch? On the Senate side, the most important is Senate Banking, which oversees the SEC and all financial institutions, determines the agency's funding level, and confirms SEC commissioners nominated by the president. The full committee, now chaired by Alabama Republican Richard Shelby, also has an important Subcommittee on Securities, now chaired by Wyoming Republican Mike Enzi.

The Senate Commerce Committee, with its broad authority over interstate commerce, occasionally gets involved in securities matters. The panel's current chairman, Republican John McCain of Arizona, has helped small investors in his own unique way.

McCain spent seven years trying to rid the campaign finance system of soft money. He achieved his goal in March 2002 when President Bush signed legislation banning soft money, which consists of large checks that wealthy individuals, labor unions, and corporations write to political parties and that often result in favors in return. The securities industry gave $39 million in soft money to party campaign committees in the 2000 election cycle, on top of the $53 million it gave to individual candidates, making it the third most prolific giver across all industries, according to the Center for Responsive Politics, which tracks campaign giving. The much smaller accounting industry, consisting mostly of the Big Five firms and the AICPA, gave $39 million from 1989 to 2001, of which $6 million was soft money.

Such huge sums of money explain why Wall Street and accounting executives have easy access to members of Congress. It's hard for lawmakers to turn down a request from individuals or groups that have helped them raise thousands of dollars. Hopefully, the new campaign-finance law will return some balance between individual investors' ability to be heard and the carte blanche granted to big check writers.

You can keep track of who's giving to whom at the Web site of the Center for Responsive Politics (*www.opensecrets.org*). Once there, you can look up who's giving money, sorted by industry, individual, political action committee, or lobby group. Or you can look up who's getting money, sorted by candidate or party organization. You can see how much a particular company or lobby group, such as the securities industry or the accounting firms, spent lobbying Congress in the past year. The center calculated, for example, that six companies now awash in scandal—Adelphia Communications, Enron, Arthur Andersen, Global Crossing, WorldCom, and Qwest Communications—gave nearly $13 million in soft money to political parties between 1992 and 2002. You can even familiarize yourself with the basics of campaign finance law, and especially the new limits on campaign giving as the result of the passage of McCain's legislation.

On the House side, the jurisdiction is divided. The Energy and Commerce Committee, now chaired by Tauzin, oversees accounting issues and the Financial Accounting Standards Board. The Financial Services Committee, whose current chairman is Representative Mike Oxley of Ohio, watches over financial institutions, financial products, and the stock exchanges. Oxley was among the House members who opposed me on a number of SEC initiatives, especially auditor independence.

You can view any committee or member Web site by going to *http://thomas.loc.gov*. There you can access hearing schedules, witness lists, names of committee and subcommittee members, and information on how to contact them. If you missed an important hearing, most (but not all) committee Web sites will post a hearing transcript. By calling the committee, you can request copies of testimony and, with a few weeks' delay, a copy of the full hearing record.

The Key Special Interest Groups

Congress isn't the only Washington institution you need to follow. You should also keep an eye on the lobbyists and the special interest groups that play a major role in shaping our laws. As I explained, three of the most active groups are the Securities Industry Association (SIA), the American Institute of Certified Public Accountants (AICPA), and the Investment Company Institute (ICI).

The SIA, with offices in New York and Washington, D.C., performs multiple tasks. It sponsors conferences, conducts research on industry trends, and compiles statistical information, including an annual yearbook. In Washington a government and regulatory affairs staff keeps track of legislation and rule making, and seeks to influence the outcome in favor of SIA member interests. The SIA's Washington office has a $19 million budget and employs about thirty people, of whom sixteen perform at least some lobbyist functions. The Washington office also hires outside lobbyists with special expertise, as in tax issues. The SIA's New York office, in addition, has a 100-person staff and about a $22 million budget.

The SIA's Web site, *www.sia.com,* explains the group's mission in detail, and you can explore it even if you're not an SIA member. For example, click on the "How to Lobby" site, and up pops a useful guide on how to conduct yourself in a person-to-person meeting with a lawmaker. The SIA site explains the basics of how legislation is produced and the different roles that Capitol Hill aides play. The site also has a section on investor education, including calculator tools to explain the mathematics of investing.

The SIA claims to represent individual investors, but the truth is more complicated. Often, the SIA's interests deviate from those of individual investors. Regulation Fair Disclosure is one example. The SIA vigorously worked to defeat Reg FD, the rule that put an end to the whisper game, in which companies leaked quarterly earnings and other market-sensitive information to selected analysts. I believe the SIA was trying to protect the lucrative franchise Wall Street had on market-moving data that its members used to their advantage, to the detriment of small investors.

But something unusual happened in the summer of 2000, shortly after the SEC proposed Reg FD. Thousands of individual investors flooded the SEC with e-mails and letters in support of our proposal. It was an outpouring of support from ordinary people the likes of which the agency had never seen before. The letters weren't exactly spontaneous. The Motley Fool, the Internet-based, pro-investor advisory service, used its Web site to promote the benefits of Reg FD, and urged its followers to write to the SEC in support. The strategy worked. Commissioner Isaac Hunt was having a hard time deciding whether to support the proposal. But when he saw how many individual investors had weighed in, he was swayed to vote yes. (His vote was not firmly secured, however, until I agreed to make several changes to the original proposal.) For the first time in my memory, small investors played a role in getting a rule adopted that benefited them, over the protests of Wall Street's biggest players.

The conflicts of research analysts are another example. The SIA did not outright oppose rules requiring analysts to reveal the banking fees their firms received from companies whose stocks they were recommending. But the SIA tried to get away with the weakest possible set of rules. My point is not that the SIA is the enemy, but that individual investors' interests and those of the SIA sometimes are at odds. Unless you speak up on your own behalf, the SIA will be able to get away with the claim that it speaks for you.

The AICPA is another important Washington special interest group. The CPAs conduct some 17,000 annual audits of publicly traded companies. The AICPA has a staff of more than 600, of which about 40 work in Washington, and the trade group, along with the Big Five firms, spent $12.5 million on lobbying in 2000 alone. The AICPA's Web site is *www.aicpa.org*.

Unlike the SIA, the AICPA is more than just a trade association; it is also a self-regulatory organization. Congress could soon shrink that role, however. The AICPA currently polices the conduct of accountants who perform audits of publicly traded companies. It develops the standards that auditors must use when conducting audits, and it enforces those standards by monitoring their application and disciplining accountants who violate them.

My view is that the AICPA has neither served the public nor its own members well. The AICPA's performance as a regulator leaves much to be desired, and it has done its members a disservice in its role as a trade group by impeding reforms. Over the decades, the AICPA has disciplined few accountants. No Big Five firm has ever failed a peer review by one of the other Big Five firms, even though such peer reviews are the industry's main way of ensuring the quality of audits. And despite growing evidence of auditor misbehavior, the AICPA has stubbornly resisted change.

True, it has appointed study commissions to examine industry-wide problems, but in the end, the thick reports that these blue-ribbon panels produce get relegated to the bookshelf. Because the AICPA has fallen down on the job, Congress and the SEC should take away the group's self-regulatory responsibilities. In mid-2002, plans were under way to create an independent oversight body, which I wholeheartedly support. Congress must give it broad standard-setting, investigative, and disciplinary powers, and its funding must be totally independent of the AICPA. Anything less and the group could fall, like others before it, under the accountants' thumb.

The third major special interest group you should keep an eye on is the Investment Company Institute (ICI), the Washington-based trade association that represents mutual fund companies. The ICI has a 170-person staff, of which twenty-four work in regulatory affairs and another ten in legislative affairs. It employs four lobbyists. In 2002 it had an annual budget of $34 million. Its Web site is *www.ici.org*.

The ICI represents mutual fund companies, not mutual fund shareholders. Sometimes their interests intersect, as when the ICI lobbies Congress to allow fund shareholders to put off paying taxes on capital gains distributions until they actually cash out of a fund (rather than the current requirement that they pay capital gains taxes annually whether or not they cash out). If funds could defer the reporting of capital gains distributions, that would benefit them (less paperwork, lower costs) and their shareholders (lower or at least deferred taxes).

But the ICI's and investors' interests sometimes split. One example is the ICI's active lobbying campaign in favor of legislation that would allow mutual fund companies both to offer their funds to 401(k) plans and to give investment advice, for a fee, to the same 401(k) plan participants. Certainly, employees are in dire need of investment advice, but I have reservations when that advice comes from the very same mutual fund company whose products are for sale to a plan's participants. One of my bedrock principles of investing is that advice should come from neutral parties with no ax to grind.

Mutual fund companies want this legislation because the Employee Retirement Income Security Act of 1974 prohibits them from both offering their funds and giving investment advice to the same plan participants. The legislation would give them access to a new and potentially very lucrative source of revenue—the $1.8 trillion in employee 401(k) accounts, 40 percent of which is invested in mutual funds.

But my main complaint about the ICI is that it doesn't do enough to educate mutual fund investors, and therefore squanders an opportunity to communicate vital information to millions of mutual fund shareholders. The group produces brochures and pamphlets on investing, and its Web site has an informative investor education section. But the ICI could do a lot more. For example, it could spend some of its money on advertising campaigns aimed at educating investors on the role that fees play in reducing overall investment returns, or why some fund investors get hit with capital gains taxes and how they are calculated. The possibilities are endless. The ICI also was conspicuously quiet as Congress considered post-Enron reforms. While none of the proposals directly affected mutual funds, the ICI should have taken pro-investor positions and lent support to the measures that would have prevented future Enrons.

While its focus is not primarily financial, TechNet is another lobby group you may want to keep your eye on. This Palo Alto (Calif.) organization represents some 300 CEOs and other top officials from the country's largest technology companies. It prides itself on aggressive advocacy of policies to strengthen the New Economy, such as tax credits for research and development, education reform, and permanent trade relations with China. But sometimes TechNet's advocacy is not pro-investor, such as its strenuous lobbying to prevent Congress or accounting standard-setters from requiring companies to deduct the cost of stock options from earnings. TechNet argues that expensing stock options would all but eliminate their use in recruiting and compensating rank-and-file employees of high-tech companies, many of which use stock options as an alternative form of pay. But it's my belief that stock options, the bulk of which are awarded to top executives rather than ordinary workers, have created perverse incentives to keep the share price high, even if it means falsifying the numbers. And that's hardly in the interests of investors.

Whom Can You Trust?

Because of Enron, investors may have a wealth of new ways to pass judgment on which members of Congress deserve their support and which ones they should work to defeat. Watch how Congress votes, for example, on legislation to create an independent oversight body for the accounting industry. The pro-investor legislator will push to make any new accounting oversight body free of AICPA control and will seek to give it strong investigative and disciplinary powers. The pro–accounting industry lawmaker will want accountants to occupy as many seats as possible on the new board and will try to restrict the board's ability to investigate.

One way to test whether a special interest group takes to heart the interests of individual investors is to examine its governance. Does the group have individual investors, or someone representing the public interest, on its board? If the directors come from Wall Street firms only, or mutual fund companies only, then it's a safe bet that that organization thinks first and foremost about the well-being of those companies, and not you. For example, the ICI has forty-six directors on its board, but only six of them are so-called independent board members who specifically represent the public interest. It's hard to imagine that those six can sway the other forty on anything important. But at least that's better than the SIA, whose board has no independent members.

Another key question to ask: Who funds the group? The source of the money behind an organization will tell you who calls the shots and where the loyalties lie. The SIA, AICPA, and ICI are 100 percent industry funded. But some special interest groups, such as the Consumer Federation of America, Consumers Union, the AFL-CIO, and the AARP (formerly the American Association of Retired Persons), are not. These groups represent individual consumers, union workers, or seniors, and are less apt to be compromised by financial considerations. And while none is primarily investor oriented, each one occasionally takes on pro-investor projects.

The AFL-CIO, the 13-million-strong labor union federation, has been especially active in taking on individual investor causes. Corporate accountability is more than a slogan at the AFL-CIO. To better safeguard $400 billion in union-sponsored fund investments, the AFL's Office of Investment takes positions on many investor-related issues in Washington and it promotes the use of shareholder resolutions to bring about corporate governance changes. Because union members' retirements are at stake—union pension funds that invested in Enron lost $1 billion—the AFL-CIO has long opposed overly generous executive stock option grants and the use of outside auditors as company consultants. In 2002, the labor union pushed shareholder resolutions at twenty-six companies. At the annual meeting of EMC Corp., for example, a union-sponsored resolution urging the data-storage company to name a majority of independent directors to its board won 56 percent of the vote. The resolution also calls on the company, whose stock lost more than 75 percent of its value in 2001 because of declining market share and other problems, to name independent board members to the audit and compensation committees, the panels that have the greatest ability to prevent accounting abuses and curb excessive pay. While such resolutions are nonbinding, many executives find it difficult to ignore them when a majority of shareholders vote yes.

Under director Bill Patterson, the ten-person Office of Investment petitioned the SEC to bar Enron directors from ever again serving on a corporate board. Patterson's office has sent experts to testify before several Congressional committees in search of stronger protections for employee 401(k) accounts. They will also monitor the post-Enron legislation that Congress will consider over the coming years. You can count on the union viewpoint not to parrot the Wall Street line. The AFL-CIO's advocacy positions can be found at *www.aflcio.org*.

The Consumer Federation of America, under its chairman Howard Metzenbaum (the former Democratic senator from Ohio) and its director of investor protection Barbara Roper, has taken a keen interest in investor issues. Its Web site (*www.consumerfed.org*) has a special section devoted to investor protection issues. The CFA was very supportive of my efforts to adopt Regulation FD and is now pushing for strong auditor independence rules.

State securities regulators are also active champions of investor interests. Their Washington organization, the North American Securities Administrators Association, or NASAA, keeps an updated list of state regulators and telephone numbers on its Web site (*www.nasaa.org*). State regulators license brokers and investment advisers, investigate complaints, and often work together to push industrywide reforms. NASAA, for example, has been an outspoken advocate of ending research analyst conflicts. NASAA also provides investor education, such as its well-designed brochure, released in 2002 in cooperation with the SIA, to explain in plain English how to read a monthly brokerage statement.

The AARP also has been active in investor causes, especially by helping seniors understand how to better manage their retirement accounts and how the broker compensation system causes conflicts between brokers and their clients. The AARP's Web site is *www.aarp.org*.

Another organization that champions individual investors— really a one-man show—is Fund Democracy. Mercer Bullard, formerly a lawyer in the SEC's Division of Investment Management, is the individual behind Fund Democracy. His Web site, *www.funddemocracy.com*, keeps mutual fund shareholders informed of hot regulatory and legislative issues. Bullard isn't just an information conduit, however. He also takes on causes, such as his successful crusade to get the SEC to crack down on mutual funds' misleading names. Bullard petitioned the SEC to force funds to have names that match their portfolio holdings. This resulted in new SEC rules that require funds to have at least 80 percent of their money invested in securities that match their name. The T. Rowe Price Small-Cap Stock Fund, for example, must have at least 80 percent of its assets in small-cap stocks. While Fund Democracy began as a hobby for Bullard, he plans to convert it to a nonprofit membership organization engaged in fund shareholder activism.

Beyond Capitol Hill and the lobby groups, a handful of well-respected, trustworthy personalities are worth your attention. Warren Buffett, the Berkshire Hathaway chairman, has been an avid champion of plain English SEC documents, more-transparent accounting, low-cost mutual funds, and many other pro-investor initiatives. His annual report to shareholders is a model of how companies should communicate with their investors. You can read it at *www.berkshirehathaway.com*. Vanguard founder John Bogle has been a thorn in the side of the mutual fund industry for fifty years. He is convinced that the lower fees, lower portfolio turnover, and fewer capital gains distributions of index funds make them the best possible investment for individuals. He makes a compelling case in his speeches, books, and other publications, all of which can be found on the Vanguard Web site (*www.vanguard.com/bogle*).

Another staunch investor champion is pension fund giant TIAA-CREF (formally the Teachers Insurance and Annuity Association–College Retirement Equities Fund). TIAA-CREF's leaders were frequent allies of mine at the SEC. The pension fund believes in strong corporate governance, greater transparency, and increased accountability—all of which investors need to safeguard their money. The group leverages the $280 billion it controls by pushing companies it invests in to adopt pro-investor policies. You can learn more about TIAA-CREF's investing philosophy on its Web site (*www.tiaa-cref. org*).

To sum up: Gaining access to elected officials and policy makers doesn't mean that you have to make campaign contributions or hire an expensive law firm. Instead, you can play the influence game by keeping yourself informed and by expressing your views to the right person at the right moment. If you show Washington officials that you care by commenting on SEC proposals and sending letters or e-mails to the right lawmakers on investor legislation, you will be doing your small part to influence the outcome. Multiply that by 79 million people, and you will see how powerful individual investors can be. In Washington, money may talk, but when millions make their voices heard, they can drown out the narrow special interests.

CHAPTER TEN

GETTING YOUR 401(K) IN SHAPE

In the late 1970s, a benefits consultant named Ted Benna was designing a retirement plan for a client when he came across section 401(k) of the 1978 Tax Reform Act. The little-noticed section gave workers a tax break if they set aside some of their earnings in a savings account and didn't spend it until they reached retirement age. Searching for a way to help wage earners who had no pension plan and didn't make enough money to save on their own, Benna came up with the idea of company-sponsored accounts in which employee contributions and a matching amount from employers would be made with tax-deferred dollars. The icing on the cake: all taxes on earnings in such accounts would also be deferred until retirement.

In 1982 the Internal Revenue Service gave Benna's plan the green light, and the 401(k) was born. While they took a few years to catch on, the 401(k)'s tax benefits and the company match have made these retirement plans wildly popular in recent years. In 2001, 42 million Americans had accumulated $1.8 trillion for their golden years through these accounts. The average 401(k) account had about $50,000 in it. Some 42 percent of participants had account balances of less than $10,000, while 15 percent had balances greater than $100,000. The split is predictable: younger workers have less, older workers more.

For many companies, the 401(k) is preferable to traditional employer-sponsored pensions, which are more costly to administer and don't come with as many tax incentives. For many workers, 401(k) savings will represent the biggest component of their net worth when they retire. If managed properly, those savings should far exceed their monthly Social Security check as a source of retirement income.

As beneficial as they are, though, 401(k)s have created new headaches. In just two decades, the country's retirement savings system has gone from one that is professionally managed by corporations on behalf of their employees to one that is managed by individual employees. No longer are most workers guaranteed a set monthly income, depending on their years of loyal service. It's now up to each individual to save and invest wisely.

You may think a 401(k) means freedom of choice. True, it gives you the power to decide how much to save and where to invest. Like most 401(k) participants, you probably face a bewildering assortment of investment options. But no one is watching to make sure you make the right choices in order to have enough money to retire on. Most workers, in fact, are woefully in need of reliable information about how to invest their 401(k) assets. When in doubt, many choose their company's stock, sometimes on top of the company shares they get as matching contributions. In doing so, employees and their companies are violating the three most important tenets of modern portfolio theory: diversify, diversify, diversify. Indeed, recent events at Enron and several other troubled companies raise serious questions about whether the country is ready for do-it-yourself investing.

A Recipe for Disaster

Nothing demonstrates the dangers better than the swift collapse of Enron. A few months before the company declared bankruptcy in early December 2001, Enron seemed to be in the peak of health. Its employees never imagined that they could lose $1 billion worth of Enron stock in their 401(k) plans, which they were about to do.

The trouble started years before, when Enron designed its 401(k) plan to reward employees with its high-flying stock. It matched every dollar of employee contributions with fifty cents in Enron stock, up to 6 percent of salary. Moreover, it prohibited employees from moving their 401(k) assets out of Enron stock until they reached age fifty. On top of all that, Enron offered its stock as one of many investment options into which employees could funnel their own contributions. Thousands chose this option, believing Enron's use of its own shares as the company match to be an implicit endorsement of the stock as a wise investment choice for their personal contributions. By the time Enron's problems surfaced, more than 50 percent of employee 401(k) assets were tied up in company stock. That was just dandy—as long as Enron shares kept appreciating, as they did for five years.

Unbeknown to these employee-shareholders, much of Enron's success was fake. It had created off-the-books partnerships—that is, they were privately held and so their accounts were not available for review by Enron investors and employees. The meltdown began in mid-October 2001 when Enron announced a huge third-quarter loss of $618 million, due to partnership losses, and a reduction in shareholder equity of $1.2 billion. Within weeks, the share price plunged from $60 to less than $1.

Employees couldn't react fast enough to save their disappearing nest eggs. For one thing, they couldn't sell their Enron shares unless they were over fifty years of age. To add insult to injury, Enron locked up all its 401(k) accounts for two weeks during the crisis to switch plan administrators. In the end, some four thousand employees not only lost their paychecks, they also lost most of their retirement savings.

In hindsight, we now see that Enron's 401(k) was poorly designed. Matching contributions in company stock, restricting sales of that stock, and then allowing further investments in company stock are a recipe for disaster. Unfortunately, Enron isn't the only company that makes it difficult for employees to diversify and reduce risk. According to consulting firm Hewitt Associates, about 215 companies offer their stock as an investment option. About 100 of the 215 require employees to accept company stock as the matching contribution. And of those, about 85 restrict the sale of company stock before a set number of years or before reaching a specific age (usually fifty). Gillette, Coca-Cola, Procter & Gamble,

Qwest Communications, Lucent Technologies, and Nortel Networks all have plans with one or more of these features. Nationwide, workers have 19 percent of their 401(k) assets in company stock. But when a company matches contributions with its own stock, 33 percent of employee contributions are also invested in company stock. That's far too much concentration for any portfolio, no matter how much risk you think you can tolerate.

Put the SEC in Charge

As SEC chairman, I found it frustrating that I had no jurisdiction over 401(k) plans. That job belongs to the Department of Labor's Pension and Welfare Benefits Administration, which uses most of its resources to prevent companies from defrauding workers out of their pensions, not to educate employees on how to invest wisely. The Labor Department has never viewed itself as a source of investment information. Companies, too, have been slow to educate employees, partly because federal law forbids them from recommending specific investments and partly out of fear they'll get dragged into court for offering advice that causes workers to lose money.

Because of the Enron tragedy, I believe it's time for Congress to give the SEC the authority and the resources to start a massive 401(k) education program for workers. The Labor Department could continue to oversee the registration and administrative functions granted to it under the Employee Retirement Income Security Act of 1974, or ERISA, the main law governing retirement plans. But the SEC and its Office of Education, which already has taught millions of investors about the hidden dangers of mutual funds, online trading, and broker compensation, is in a far better position to reach 401(k) investors.

Congress could help, too, by amending ERISA so that companies are subject to fiduciary rules when making matching contributions. A fiduciary has a legal obligation to make investment decisions that benefit the recipient. Because such contributions are strictly voluntary, Congress never brought them under the protective arm of

ERISA. It also did not subject 401(k)s to diversification rules that traditional, defined-benefit plans must follow. In such plans, company stock cannot exceed 10 percent of total assets. Companies in the past have fought such diversification rules, arguing that it's good policy to align their employees' interests with those of the company, and the best way to do that is to require employees to own stock in the company. Some companies also have argued that matching funds are not required by law, so Congress shouldn't restrict the form or the amount of those contributions. If it does, some companies have warned, they will stop making matching contributions altogether.

Each of those arguments contains a nugget—but only a nugget—of truth. Corporations can make stakeholders of their workers without overloading their 401(k)s with company stock. And companies that stop making matching contributions are likely to find it difficult to recruit and retain talented workers, who will seek out employment opportunities elsewhere. Employers also fail to point out that they get something in return—a tax deduction—when they make matching contributions. Congress should pass legislation that reduces that tax break when contributions are in the form of the company's own stock, and when more than 20 percent of any 401(k) plan's investments are in the company's shares. Even a 20 percent cutoff is probably too high; my own advice is that you should not let company stock exceed 10 percent of your 401(k) assets.

Save More—Starting Now

Overconcentration of 401(k)s in company stock isn't the only problem we face. Many workers are also falling short in saving for retirement, now that the bull market is no longer doing the job for them. After eighteen years of rising markets, during which time it was easy to accumulate assets in a 401(k) account, many savers suffered their first losses in 2000 and 2001, and now must learn to set aside more of their income. Even worse, millions of workers who are eligible to participate in a 401(k) are not doing so, either because they must take care of more immediate needs or because they think there will always be plenty of time to save for retirement.

In passing President George W. Bush's 2001 tax-cut bill, Congress allowed workers to shelter more of their income through tax-deferred 401(k) contributions. But if employees don't take advantage of these opportunities, especially now that the baby boom generation is nearing retirement and the Social Security system may become strapped, many could find themselves in severe financial straits in old age.

This chapter is designed to help investors understand the complexities of 401(k)s. My hope is that you will avoid some of the common mistakes people have made in managing their accounts. Whether you are a rank beginner or already know the 401(k) ropes and need a refresher course, this chapter can help you. To make it easier to follow, the information appears in question-and-answer format.

What Is a 401(k)?   Essentially, a 401(k) is one of the federal government's major incentives to get Americans to save more for retirement. You can steer a portion of your compensation to a retirement plan as a deduction from your salary. Your contribution automatically is deducted from your paycheck and is then invested in financial assets, most likely a mutual fund of stocks or bonds, or a combination of these and other options. Because your contributions are a deduction from your taxable income, they are called "pre-tax" contributions. The contributions, plus any investment earnings, are taxed only when withdrawn, presumably when you are older and subject to a lower marginal income tax rate. Pre-tax contributions may also lower your taxable income enough to bring down the tax you pay on the rest of your salary.

How Do 401(k)s Differ from Old-Fashioned Pension Plans?
There are two types of retirement plans: defined-benefit and defined-contribution. A defined-benefit plan promises an employee a specified monthly benefit at retirement. Typically, the benefit is calculated

through a formula based on salary and service. For example, for every year of service, a worker might receive 1 percent of average salary for the last five years of employment. Whatever the benefit or how it's calculated, the key feature is that it is a specific amount, identified and guaranteed to workers in advance.

On the other hand, a defined-contribution plan, such as a 401(k), does not promise a specific benefit. Instead, it is the periodic contributions from workers and employers that are specified in advance. Rather than get a specific retirement benefit, workers accumulate a balance in their account, based on contributions and investment gains or losses. Because investment performance cannot be predicted in advance, the future value of an employee's account balance is unknown, and monthly retirement payments cannot be specified in advance.

Some people prefer the predictability of a defined-benefit plan, while others prefer to direct their own investments, as a 401(k) plan allows. In any case, defined-benefit plans are more expensive for employers to offer; thus many have replaced them with 401(k)s.

How far has the balance tipped today? Very far. Overall, about three-fourths of American workers with retirement plans are covered by a defined-contribution plan, such as a 401(k), reports the Employee Benefits Research Institute (EBRI), a Washington-based think tank. Defined-contribution plans are a major reason why retirement program coverage has been increasing. Of course, higher retirement coverage doesn't necessarily mean a higher level of benefits.

The trend away from defined-benefit plans is even creating a change in the lexicon of retirement. Before the explosion of defined-contribution plans, the term "pension" almost universally referred to defined-benefit plans. Today, however, "pension" is often used interchangeably among defined-benefit and defined-contribution plans—even though the level and certainty of benefits can differ significantly.

How Much Can I Contribute? Under President Bush's tax-cut legislation, passed by Congress in 2001, the contribution limit for an individual is $12,000 as of January 1, 2003. This limit will rise by $1,000 annually until reaching $15,000 in 2006. Today, the average worker's 401(k) contribution is 8.6 percent of salary, according to the Spectrem Group, a consulting firm.

The new tax-cut law also allows those age fifty and over to "catch up" and make extra contributions. The extra amount is $1,000 for 2002, rising to $5,000 extra in 2006, and adjusted for inflation thereafter.

The same law also requires faster vesting, shortening the early years of participation during which companies don't allow workers to take company matching funds with them if they change jobs. Until 2002, companies could stretch the pre-vesting period to seven years, but now that period is limited to five years.

As Congress considered the tax-cut legislation, some groups expressed concern that its benefits were tilted too far in favor of higher-income workers. For instance, only those able to afford to contribute the maximum amount will typically be able to put away even more under the new limits. These workers are likely to be higher-, not lower-, paid. To defuse political opposition, the act added a new tax credit for certain low- and middle-income individuals who contribute to 401(k)s or other plans. The tax credit, ranging from 10 percent to 50 percent, depending on salary, is on contributions up to $2,000, for income below $25,000 for singles, $37,500 for heads of households, and $50,000 for married couples filing jointly. The credit is not available to students or dependents. You should find out if you qualify and make sure you take advantage of these tax credits if you do.

If you are contributing the maximum and you want to save even more, you may be able to make after-tax contributions as well. While the earnings on after-tax money will grow tax-deferred, the contributions aren't likely to be matched by your employer. And if you choose to withdraw your after-tax contributions early, you must also withdraw a proportionate amount of the earnings the money has generated—and you'll have to pay taxes, plus a 10 percent penalty, on the earnings (though not on the after-tax contributions themselves).

Is My Employer Required to Match My Contributions? No, but most do. The consulting firm Hewitt Associates reports that 97 percent of employers provide some form of match or contribution to employees' 401(k) plans. Typically, employer matches are set as a percentage of worker contributions, or based upon company profitability. Many companies, for example, put in fifty cents for every dollar of employee contributions; other companies match dollar-for-dollar, and some even match two-for-one.

Six years ago, the William M. Mercer benefits consulting firm found that 85 percent of plans with some form of employer contributions matched at least one-half of worker contributions. By 2000 that number had risen to 89 percent. But in response to the slower economy, lower profits, and cost-cutting pressures, many companies contributed less money to 401(k) programs in 2000 than in 1999.

Can I Access My Money Before I Retire? Once you set up a 401(k), the money is generally off-limits to you and you will not be able to withdraw it penalty-free until you reach age fifty-nine and a half. Before then, penalty-free withdrawals are allowed only if you become fully disabled, you die and a beneficiary inherits your account, your medical bills exceed 7.5 percent of your income, or a court requires you to give money to a dependent or divorced spouse.

You can withdraw money penalty-free from your 401(k) if you reach age fifty-five and you lose your job or take early retirement. This rule, however, applies only to funds in a 401(k) that was sponsored by the employer for whom you worked when you turned fifty-five, and not to funds that may have accumulated at a previous job. And even if you meet these conditions, you will still have to pay federal, state, and local taxes on the amount withdrawn.

If you don't meet any of the above requirements but you still withdraw the money because of a financial hardship, you must pay all applicable taxes plus the 10 percent penalty. A financial hardship occurs when you need to pay college tuition for yourself or a dependent; you need to make a down payment on a primary residence; you must pay unreimbursed medical expenses; or you are in danger of a bank foreclosing on your home or a landlord evicting you.

Your employer may also allow you to borrow from your 401(k), but more on that below.

Who Decides How My Money Will Be Invested?   Once money starts flowing into your 401(k) account, it needs to be managed. You should play an active role in deciding how that is done. Many studies show that workers aren't doing a terribly good job with their 401(k) investments. A recent John Hancock survey offered these scary statistics: Nearly half of 401(k) participants thought stocks are included in money market funds (they aren't). About 80 percent didn't know that the best time to buy bonds is when interest rates fall. One-half expected stocks to average an astounding 20 percent annual return over the next twenty years. Most experts believe that stocks are likely to produce less than half that. Since 1926, stocks have returned 10.7 percent a year, according to Ibbotson Associates, a Chicago-based research firm. It's no wonder that many employees, unsophisticated about financial markets or just plain too busy to educate themselves, have had trouble making sound investment choices.

In the 1990s, many employees depended too much on technology stocks or else their own company's stock. They failed to rebalance—that is, readjust their investment mix to meet the goals they had set—after market fluctuations threw their allocations out of whack. If you chose an investment mix of 60 percent stocks and 40 percent bonds in 1990, by 2000 that would have become a portfolio with 75 percent stocks and 25 percent bonds.

What Happened to 401(k) Assets in the 2000–2001 Bear Market?   The bull market of the late 1990s covered a multitude of 401(k) investor sins, and it wasn't hard to be a big winner. In fact, about 80 percent of the growth in 401(k) assets from 1995 to 2000 was due to market appreciation, according to consulting firm Cerulli Associates. Today's market leaves no room to hide.

In March 2003, EBRI and the Investment Company Institute, the

Washington, D.C.–based trade group for mutual fund companies, reported that the average 401(k) account balance declined by 4 percent in 2001, to $43,215. This is an addition to a 12 percent decline in 2000—the first-ever across-the-board decrease in 401(k) assets.

Why Can't I Just Lock in My Gains by Cashing Out When the Market Is Turning Down, Then Get Back in When the Market Is Turning Up?   This is called market timing, and it rarely works. When investors try to get all the upside and none of the downside, they usually end up buying high and selling low—not a very savvy investment strategy. Markets are unpredictable, and even the smartest market watchers can't predict sudden rallies and declines.

The dangers of market timing are especially true when your 401(k) assets are in mutual funds, as they should be. For example, if you switch your 401(k) assets out of a small-cap mutual fund and into a large-cap fund because of an attractive rally in large-caps that day, you may already have missed the action. That's because mutual fund shareholders get a price, called net asset value, or the value of one share in the fund, that is calculated at the end of the trading day. Instead of getting in on a rally, you may be buying after it, at the peak. Similarly, you may have sold the small-cap shares just as they were about to head up.

Ibbotson Associates calculates the effects of market timing this way: If you had invested $1 in an S&P index fund in 1980, that $1 would have been worth $18.41 at the end of 2000. But if you had missed just fifteen of the best days in those twenty years, you would have had only $4.73. It's impossible to predict which fifteen days out of 5,200 will be the best. Jumping in and out of the market is likely to cause you to be out of the market precisely when you need to be in it.

So How Should I Be Investing My 401(k) Money?   Only you can answer this question. But forget about trying to make a killing in the market because of a well-timed purchase of a hot stock or a well-placed tip. You may as well expect to win the lottery. And just owning a bunch of investments is not the same as having a retirement strategy. Only a well-planned strategy will see you through economic good and bad times and help you build a nest egg that will support you to the end of your life.

To get started, you must decide two basic things: in how many years will you retire, and what is the minimum income you can get by on in your retirement years? For many, the answers will be educated guesses, but that's better than nothing. A good goal to aim for is having a nest egg that provides you with 70 percent to 80 percent of the salary you were receiving at the time of retirement.

Here's an example. Bob is now thirty-five. His annual salary is $45,000. He has $20,000 in an Individual Retirement Account. And he expects to receive about $14,500 a year from Social Security after retirement. His hope is that he can retire at age sixty-five with about $40,000 a year in retirement income. What will he need in his nest egg at retirement? The answer: $378,000. To get there, Bob will need to save about $7,500 a year. You can do a similar calculation by going to the American Savings Education Council Web site, *www.asec.org*. Click on the "Ballpark Estimate" retirement planning worksheet, and plug in your own numbers.

Now you're ready to take the next crucial steps: determining how much risk you can tolerate and how to allocate your funds among the many investment options. Risk tolerance and asset allocation go hand in hand. Risk is the possibility that your investment won't produce the level of returns that you were expecting. All investments are risky, and some are riskier than others. But in general, the higher the risk, the greater the potential reward. Higher risk also carries higher potential for loss and greater uncertainty about the level of return. The opposite is also true: the lower the risk, the lower the potential return. And low risk carries lower potential for loss and more certainty about level of return.

Asset allocation is the process by which investors find the best possible returns for the level of risk they are willing to accept. In general, stocks are riskier than bonds, and thus have greater potential returns. Because younger people have a longer time horizon before retirement and can thus accept higher levels of risk, they should allocate a greater percentage of their overall portfolio to stocks. If you are near retirement age, and can't afford to risk much of your savings, then you will want to allocate more of your portfolio to bonds.

There are rules of thumb to help you allocate your assets. Here's one: subtract your age from 100, and put whatever the answer is into stocks. So if you are thirty-five, you would put 65 percent into stocks and 35 percent into bonds. But such rules of thumb are not foolproof and are meant only as rough guides.

After deciding how much to allocate to stocks and to bonds, make sure that you diversify within those asset classes so that you aren't overexposed to one particular industry. The sudden downturn in the high-tech sector, for example, took many 401(k) participants by surprise in 2000 because they were not properly diversified.

When you own mutual funds, the intellectual work involved in making sure you are diversified is done for you. Well, mostly. Diversification means balancing the high-risk, high-return potential of a small-cap stock fund with the steady-as-she-goes growth of a blue-chip fund, though even blue chips can lose value, as we have seen in recent years. Diversification means that if you own a fund that specializes in stocks that appear to be undervalued—so-called value stocks—you might want to balance that with a fund that looks for stocks likely to generate above-average earnings—so-called growth stocks. Because fund names can be misleading, it's important to review the underlying stocks that make up a mutual fund to make sure it's doing what its name advertises. If you are investing in a bond fund, diversification means choosing bonds that have different interest rates and maturity dates. Remember: diversification helps you reduce risk by balancing investments that perform poorly with those that produce solid earnings.

Stocks versus Bonds: How Do I Decide Between Them?   Historically, stocks have outperformed bonds. As I explained earlier, the stocks that make up the S&P 500 have achieved an average annual return of 10.7 percent since 1926. Long-term corporate bonds, on the other hand, have returned about 6.5 percent. Treasury bills have achieved average annual returns of only 5 percent. Among stocks, small-cap stocks have done the best historically, and among bonds, corporate bonds have done better than government bonds.

Statistically speaking, stocks have been the best-performing investment over the past seventy-five years. But in the short term, stocks can disappoint. Plenty of people found this out in 2000 and 2001, when the S&P 500 lost about 30 percent of its value, and 401(k) plans lost money for the first time in their twenty-year history. But if you aren't retiring for another twenty to forty years, you can afford a few stormy years in the stock market. Not only do you have many more years to make up for any losses, but you also have the luxury of being able to make adjustments in your portfolio.

In fact, one of the problems many participants face with their 401(k) accounts is the tendency to invest too conservatively. To avoid the ups and downs of stocks, they are seeking the safety of bonds, slow-growing money market funds, and so-called stable value funds, which invest in guaranteed investment contracts, or securities offered by many insurance companies with a low fixed rate of return. While such fixed-rate investments have a place in your portfolio, you might not have enough money on which to retire if you altogether avoid the higher returns of equities.

What New Types of Plans Are Being Considered to Help Workers Make Smarter Choices? In the early days of 401(k) plans, choices were slim. A company might offer a handful of simple investment choices—perhaps a bond fund, a money market fund, and a general-purpose equity fund. Today, the average 401(k) participant can choose from at least ten investment options. But as the number of defined-contribution plans grows, so too do concerns over whether they place too much risk and responsibility on workers' shoulders.

To address this, 401(k) experts have been busy devising new types of plans that essentially take choice out of the equation. For workers intimidated or confused by the many options they face, these new accounts could relieve anxiety and boost participation. "The biggest change over the next five years will be the emergence of what I call the final choice—delegating asset allocation to someone else," says David Wray, director of the Profit Sharing/401(k) Council of America, an industry-funded association.

One such development is the so-called life-cycle fund. Rather than offering a confusing menu of investments, these options offer preset mixes of securities aimed at making it easy for workers to match investment choices to age and risk tolerance—that is, to their place in the life cycle.

Such funds are professionally managed, with adjustments in portfolio holdings made over time, as appropriate. For example, a life-cycle account for younger investors, who can afford to be more aggressive, would hold more stocks than an account for workers nearing retirement. But as the worker ages, the proportion of stocks would decline while the proportion of bonds would grow. If you aren't interested in learning about asset allocation and diversification, and don't have time to read prospectuses and quarterly statements, you may want to choose a life-cycle fund. But be careful. Because of poor employee investment education, workers tend to treat these funds as one more choice over which to spread their money. Make sure you don't mix a life-cycle fund with other funds, which would defeat the purpose.

My Company Offers a Brokerage Account under My 401(k). Should I Use It?

Emboldened by the easy money to be had in the late-'90s stock market boom, some employees pressed for even more choice, with the result being the Self-Directed Brokerage Account as a 401(k) plan option. This allows employees to pick investments almost as freely as they can outside their 401(k) plan. Typically, companies select a brokerage house to handle employee trades. To establish an account, workers transfer a lump sum out of their 401(k) account. They then allocate an amount to be transferred to their brokerage account from each 401(k) payroll contribution. Workers can buy stocks, bonds, or mutual funds with the transferred money. A recent Hewitt Associates survey found that 18 percent of plan sponsors currently offer self-directed brokerage accounts, and that another 5 percent will offer one within a year. Almost a third of sponsors say they are considering adding brokerage capabilities.

My own opinion is that these brokerage accounts are dangerous and should be avoided, unless you are a sophisticated investor. The IRS rightly prohibits trading exotic instruments, such as derivatives, or trading on margin (borrowing from a brokerage firm to trade) in these accounts. But that does not allay my fear that some investors will trade recklessly and lose their nest egg.

What Fees, Hidden or Otherwise, Am I Paying on My 401(k)?

For 401(k) plans, a key issue is fees. What might seem to be low fees, expressed in tenths of 1 percent, can easily cost an investor tens of thousands of dollars over a lifetime. Loss of assets to fees automatically reduces the amount invested, and thereby reduces returns. The compounding nature of returns can make fees a very expensive proposition.

Fees reflect two costs: plan administration and investment management. Those who closely follow 401(k) plans say it's difficult to compare fees among plans. Fees vary for obvious reasons, such as types of investments offered, the number of participants, and the size of each 401(k) account. But they also vary for less apparent reasons, such as whether a 401(k) plan provider expects to get additional business if workers roll 401(k) balances into Individual Retirement Accounts. A very rough rule of thumb might be that expenses ought not to exceed 1 percent of assets in a moderate-sized company.

You should carefully study differences in management fees among different investment options. You should also press your company for information on administrative costs, if not already provided. Administrative costs include sending out quarterly statements, paying auditors and lawyers, answering questions, and maintaining account balances.

At first, companies paid the bulk of plan administration expenses, but now they are increasingly passing those costs on to participants. For instance, in 1999, participants picked up 38 percent of record-keeping fees, up from 29 percent in 1995. Workers paid 41 percent of trustee fees, up from 33 percent, and 46 percent of miscellaneous fees, up from 18 percent.

Meanwhile, some companies are pressing the money managers and mutual fund providers handling their workers' 401(k) funds to grant rebates or revenue-sharing agreements. These considerations can offset a company's administrative costs. Or they can be provided in the form of additional services to workers, such as an investment education program.

But such practices raise ethical concerns. Workers' contributions fund the 401(k) system, and so workers should get their fair share of any rebates. But very few workers know of these arrangements, and employers are not required to disclose the details. This is not right. You should press your company to itemize any administrative fees and any rebates received from a fund company.

If I Need Cash, Should I Borrow from My 401(k)?   Many plans offer workers the ability to borrow against their account balances. The standard practice is to let you borrow up to 50 percent of your balance, up to $50,000. Knowing loans are available makes some workers more comfortable investing in 401(k) accounts.

Borrowing from yourself might sound attractive, but remember: There can be service fees, both one-time and annual; the money must be paid back; the interest rate is high—usually one or two percentage points above the prime rate. Here's the kicker: if you leave the company with a loan outstanding, you must pay it back immediately, and if you can't, the amount is considered a premature withdrawal subject to taxes. You'll owe a 10 percent penalty as well.

If you borrow from your 401(k), your money can't earn returns while you have borrowed it. True, you will be paying yourself back, with interest, but it may not be as much as what your money would have earned if left in the 401(k). In addition, if you stop making contributions to your 401(k) while you are repaying your loan, as many participants do, you are losing out on the earnings your own contributions would have made. You are also giving up any company match and earnings on the match, for the life of your loan.

Before you borrow from your 401(k), consider that a home equity loan may be a less expensive way to obtain funds, especially since the interest payments on most home equity loans can be deducted from your income taxes. The interest on a 401(k) loan is not tax-deductible. There may, however, be times when borrowing from your 401(k) makes sense, depending on the interest rate you'll pay and whether leaving your money alone would produce greater returns than borrowing from it. Luckily, there are several Web-based calculators to help you decide. One such tool can be found at the Web site of the mutual fund and 401(k) advisory company T. Rowe Price, at *www.troweprice.com*. Once at the site, click on "Retirement Investing."

My advice: borrowing from your 401(k) is a bad idea unless you are in severe financial difficulty.

Should I Take Advantage of My Company's Stock-Purchase Plan? As we saw with Enron, overreliance on company stock is an especially thorny problem with 401(k)s. Many plans make company stock available as an investment option. Some firms also make their matching contributions in the form of company stock, meaning that if you want the match, you're doubly yoked to the fortunes of one company through your salary and your retirement fund. On top of all that, many employees whose match is in company stock tend to put their own contributions into company stock. Although a company has a clear self-interest in making its match in the form of company stock—doing so reduces the amount of cash it must spend—employees view that as an endorsement of the stock, or a kind of implicit investment advice.

So much reliance on one company's stock violates the basic principle of diversification. "You would think if you'd already had a company match into company stock, the last thing in the world you'd do is put [your contributions] in company stock," says Jack L. VanDerhei, a research fellow at EBRI. "What we found is it's kind of like follow the leader: 'If it's good enough for the company match, it's good enough for us.' "

Overall, about 19 percent of 401(k) plan assets are invested in company stock, EBRI found. But among large plans, it's about one-third, and much higher still in some individual firms. Enron employees aren't the only ones feeling the sting from this overreliance. In July 2001 employees of ailing Lucent filed an unusual class-action lawsuit charging company officials with breach of fiduciary duty for giving employees the choice of investing in Lucent stock as part of their 401(k) plans. Lucent did not require employees to invest in company stock, and the company even occasionally told its workers about the need to diversify.

But the suit alleges that by offering its stock as an investment option, Lucent induced tens of thousands of employees to invest in, or maintain investments in, company shares, even though some executives knew of serious business problems that made the stock inappropriate for a retirement account. The company had been struggling financially and had shed tens of thousands of workers. Its stock price sank as low as $5.04 in mid-2001, down 94 percent from a high of $82 in December 1999. With more than 40 percent of Lucent's three 401(k) plans invested in company stock, many employees suffered devastating blows to their holdings, losing an estimated $7.6 billion. Lawsuits of this sort are difficult to win because they must show that the plan's trustees knew the company stock was a poor investment and offered it on the menu of choices anyway. The moral: be your own guardian of your 401(k), and keep the percentage of company stock below 10 percent. Any more than that and you don't have a well-diversified portfolio.

What Happens If I Leave My Company Before I Retire?   A 401(k) is portable; that is, you get to take it with you if you leave your employer. If you leave prior to reaching age fifty-nine and a half, you have four options:

- Leave your investments with the old employer's plan. Some employers allow workers to maintain 401(k) investments even after leaving the company. This would be a good idea if you are satisfied with how your funds are managed. Workers can check their Summary Plan document, or other basic documents, to see if this is allowed.
- Roll over the money in the old plan into a new employer's plan. If moving to a new job, check with that employer to see if such a rollover is allowed. Do this only after determining

that you are eligible for your new employer's 401(k) plan and that the plan is satisfactory.

- Roll over investments into a qualified Individual Retirement Account. Many financial institutions and investment companies allow workers to roll over 401(k) funds from their old employer into an IRA. This may be the best route if the new employer does not allow transfers from another plan, or if the IRA is superior to either the old or the new employer's plan.

- Cash out. If you are still working and haven't reached age fifty-nine and a half, this is the worst possible option. The funds are subject to federal income tax as well as state and local taxes. In addition, you will be charged a 10 percent penalty for early withdrawal.

Rolling over a 401(k) can be tricky, so be sure to ask plenty of questions before taking the plunge. There are special rules, for example, barring the mixing of funds in public and private retirement accounts. If you are leaving a private-sector job for a government position, IRS rules do not allow you to roll over your 401(k) into a 457, a type of retirement plan that is offered by state and local governments. Funds from a 401(k) also cannot be rolled over into a 403(b), a type of plan that schools, hospitals, and nonprofit groups offer.

Here is a short checklist to help you avoid problems:

- Check the rules of the old plan before withdrawal. Review the Summary Plan document for any restrictions on rolling over investments into another plan.

- Set up the next account before withdrawal. If a new account is not ready, funds will be idle and there's a risk of missing market upturns. Also, if a rollover takes more than sixty days, workers may be subject to the 10 percent penalty plus income tax.

- Make sure the rollover check is properly endorsed. It should not be made out to the worker, but to the company or entity that will manage the new plan. If the check is made out to you personally, the IRS could consider it an early withdrawal and levy taxes and penalties.

- Check for after-tax contributions. If the old employer allowed after-tax contributions to the 401(k) plan, those contributions—but not any gains based on them—can't be rolled over into another 401(k). Instead, that money will be distributed. If that happens, workers should consider putting the money into another tax-deferred option.

One disturbing aspect of today's retirement planning is "leakage" of funds from existing savings. According to a 1998 report prepared for the Department of Labor, only 20 percent of those getting lump-sum distributions rolled over the entire amount into another tax-qualified vehicle. "Leakage from retirement plans is a serious threat," the report warned.

I'm Only in My Twenties. Why Is It So Important That I Start Saving for Retirement Now? Today, about 25 percent of employees working for companies that offer 401(k)s don't use them. This is like turning down free money, and presents a worrisome public policy issue. Indeed, the number of workers who say they are saving for retirement dropped in 2001 after years of steady growth. The annual Retirement Confidence Survey, released in May 2001 by EBRI, the American Savings Education Council, and Mathew Greenwald & Associates, showed that the number of people saving for retirement declined from 75 percent in 2000 to 71 percent in 2001. Moreover, there is growing evidence that many Americans are willing to drain their already-inadequate retirement reserves. This is sheer folly, and reveals a lack of understanding of the power of saving regularly from an early age.

The beauty of a 401(k) comes down to two things: compound interest and dollar-cost averaging. These are easy concepts to understand. Compounding simply means that the returns you earn today get plowed back into your 401(k) so that you make returns on your returns.

Don't underestimate the power of compounding. An example from retirement planning Web site mPower (*www.mpower.com*) explains why. Suppose you start saving $2,000 a year at age twenty-five. Assuming a 10 percent annual return, you would have

$974,384 at age sixty-five. Only $80,000 of that would come from your $2,000-per-year contribution. The rest, $894,384, comes from the compounded return on your investment.

But for every year you delay saving, the amount of your nest egg drops precipitously. For example, if you don't begin saving $2,000 a year until you reach age thirty-five instead of age twenty-five, your nest egg will amount to just $363,887!

If you're putting off saving for another day, consider what's at stake: Assume a sixty-five-year-old retires today. She could live another twenty years, or at least should plan on that. Say she'd like to have $75,000 in annual income, and that Social Security will provide about $20,000 of that. Neglecting inflation for the moment, and assuming only modest investment returns of 5 percent annually, how much might she need in a 401(k) plan today? About $685,000—a sum clearly higher than most American workers have today or will in the future. Put another way, a thirty-five-year-old would need to save about $10,300 annually for thirty years to hit the $685,000 target.

The other great attraction of 401(k)s is that they force you to do what is known as dollar-cost averaging. This happens when you invest a fixed amount of money at regular intervals. By contributing, say, $100 a month every month, you will be buying more shares in a fund when the share price is low, and fewer shares when the price is high. Any drop in price lets you buy more shares with the same amount of money. When share prices go back up, you'll benefit again because you will have more shares. Most investment advisers agree that dollar-cost averaging is the best way to invest.

What Is Being Done to Boost Savings?   Ever-escalating household debt is one reason workers don't put more money into 401(k) plans. When Strong Capital Management Inc. surveyed more than one thousand participants, it found significant levels of nonmortgage consumer debt, and 11 percent of those responding said that made them unable to contribute to their retirement plans.

Concern about the low savings rate is spurring a search for new ways to boost 401(k) balances. The simplest is probably the most expensive: increase company matching contributions. In a recent survey, the ICI found that 80 percent of workers not participating in a 401(k) said they would be very likely or somewhat likely to enroll if their employers provided, or increased, the company match.

Short of that, one trend is toward automatic enrollment into plans. New or current employees become part of their companies' plans unless they exercise an option to get out. IRS rulings in 1998 and 2000 paved the way for automatic enrollment plans. Owing to employer fears of liability, the typical "default" option for those enrolled automatically is conservative: 3 percent of pay in contributions, placed into conservative investments such as money market funds.

Automatic enrollment clearly boosts 401(k) participation. The mutual fund giant Vanguard Group, for example, recently studied some of its clients, finding that among plans offering automatic enrollment to newly eligible employees, participation rose from 75 percent to 84 percent. For plans enrolling all eligible employees, not just the newly eligible, the jump was higher—from 73 percent to 90 percent.

But if you are automatically enrolled in a 401(k) plan, be careful. Studies show that many automatically enrolled participants stay with their company's default option. If that includes you, you are almost certainly contributing less than you will need for adequate retirement income. And your investment approach is almost certainly too conservative. Just because your company chose certain investments, such as a money market fund, as your default selection, that should not be viewed as an endorsement.

How Do I Know My Savings Will Be Safe?   In 1974 Congress passed a law called the Employee Retirement Income Security Act, or ERISA. The law sets standards for pension plans, including 401(k)s. Who is eligible for a plan, minimum performance standards, rules on vesting, how investments must be selected, and how plans are funded are all spelled out in ERISA. The law, administered by the Department of Labor, is there to protect your retirement income from abuse or misuse. For example, it says that your money must be deposited into a custodial account, which walls it off in case your employer goes bankrupt or is sold. The IRS also requires your employer to send you regular account statements (usually once a quarter) explaining how your investments performed, as well as educational materials about the investment choices available to you.

Still, you should be cautious and keep a watchful eye on your 401(k). The following is a list of ten warning signs that your funds may be in danger:

1.   Your 401(k) or individual account statement is consistently late or comes at irregular intervals.
2.   Your account balance does not appear to be accurate.
3.   Your employer fails to transmit your contribution to the plan on a timely basis.
4.   There is a significant drop in account balance that can't be explained by normal market ups and downs.
5.   You receive account statements that do not show contributions from your paycheck that were made.
6.   Investments listed on your statement are not what you authorized.
7.   Former employees are having trouble getting their benefits paid on time or in the correct amounts.
8.   Your account statement or a letter from your employer reports an unusual transaction, such as a loan to the employer, a corporate officer, or a plan trustee.
9.   There are frequent and unexplained changes in investment managers or consultants.
10.   Your employer has recently experienced severe financial difficulty.

However, there is no guarantee that your 401(k) balance will not fluctuate sharply, and even decline, as the stock and bond markets fluctuate.

Isn't There a Way to Guarantee My Pension?   Not if your pension is a 401(k) plan. Because there are no guarantees, labor unions and other worker-advocacy groups are trying to raise awareness of the dangers of moving en masse from defined-benefit to defined-contribution plans. In June 2001, for example, the United Food and Commercial Workers Union kicked off a nationwide "Worker Information Project" to warn employees that 401(k) plans are not real pensions, but tax-deferred savings plans. "Most companies switch to defined-contribution plans with some fanfare about giving individuals more choices," says Bill Patterson, director of the AFL-CIO's Office of Investment. "They can do it unilaterally, and we think the impulse to do it is very strong. We need to be more aggressive in defending defined-benefit."

Other groups are hoping to come up with a better mousetrap, and two of these may hold great promise for future retirees. The Public Policy Institute of AARP (formerly the American Association of Retired Persons) has proposed a guaranteed-return plan that changes the way employers make contributions. While the typical 401(k) bases employer matches on profitability or employee contributions, the AARP proposal calls for setting employer matches based on returns earned by 401(k) assets. A company would guarantee some minimum level of return, and if plan earnings fall short of the target, the firm would increase its contributions accordingly.

The AARP proposal represents a middle ground between defined-benefit and defined-contribution plans. Workers would get a guaranteed minimum, similar to that provided by a defined-benefit plan. Companies would get some of the cost advantage of a defined-contribution plan, but would still be responsible for ensuring some minimum level of retirement income.

Meanwhile, Ted Benna, the inventor of the 401(k), has designed a blueprint for future 401(k) plans that tackles two tough problems at once: relieving employer concerns about liability while boosting retirement savings. A key feature would be "structured portfolios" built according to standards that consider workers' risk tolerance and when they expect to begin drawing down their account. Employers and plan providers would then be freed from liability—provided a "safe harbor"—if:

- Worker-paid fees for each portfolio are kept at a prescribed minimum—0.75 percent of assets.
- Participants can select only one structured investment portfolio, thus avoiding the mixing problem noted above.
- Workers who stay in the same portfolio for at least twenty years receive a 7 percent guaranteed minimum average annual return.
- An Individual Retirement Account option is provided, to allow workers to keep the portfolio when they change jobs, in case their employer goes bankrupt or is sold.

Essentially, such a plan would allow a worker to pick a self-adjusting portfolio when young and stick with it forever. The minimum return after twenty years would encourage participants to keep their portfolios even when changing jobs. The portfolios would comply with yet-to-be-determined standards, such as independent review at least annually. The need for investment education would change dramatically, as participants in the structured portfolios wouldn't need to know many investment intricacies. "The only way, frankly, I see major change taking place in a relatively short period would be around the safe harbor idea," says Benna. The plan is attractive to workers who want a guaranteed pension from their 401(k), but plan providers, wary of the guaranteed return and fee-cap features, so far have not signed on.

What Sources of Advice Are Available on the Internet? Scores of Web sites offer financial and retirement information today. The following is a short list of what's available. Some require registration and/or fees, depending on the specific information you are seeking.

- More than one hundred financial planning calculators, including many for retirement, are available at *www.choosetosave. org*, a Web site developed by the American Savings Education Council and the Employee Benefit Research Institute. The education council also has the "Ballpark Estimate" retirement planning worksheet available at *www.asec.org*.

- The Department of Labor, the Small Business Administration, the Chamber of Commerce, and Merrill Lynch & Co. offer *www.selectaretirementplan.org*. This site is aimed at employers interested in offering retirement plans, but also has useful background information for workers.

- mPower, an Internet-based investment advisory service, offers its mPower Cafe 401(k) page at *www.mpower.com*.

- Financial Engines, a site cofounded by 1990 Nobel Prize–winning economist William F. Sharp, helps you set goals and track progress of retirement savings, at *www.financialengines .com*. Financial Engines is offering its advisory service on employer retirement plans, including 401(k) plans, free to Vanguard clients.

- The all-purpose financial site *www.quicken.com* includes a retirement section.

- Mutual fund company T. Rowe Price and Morningstar Associates, the mutual fund rating company, have teamed up to offer free online financial planning advice to 401(k) participants.

Now you should know more than enough to get started. Here's a quick checklist that summarizes what you've just read:

- First and foremost, participate in your company's 401(k) plan if one is offered.

- Sign up as soon as you can, even if it's your first job and you're still in your twenties. The younger you are, the more time your savings have to compound, and the less you'll have to contribute to reach your retirement goals.

- Contribute as much as you can, but at least enough to get your company's matching contribution.

- Diversify among investments, but don't be too conservative. To get the greatest returns and stay ahead of inflation, you need to have some exposure to stocks.

- If your company requires you to accept its matching contribution in the form of company stock, do not invest your own contributions in company stock. If your company matches in cash and you want to own the stock, keep no more than 10 percent of your 401(k) assets in company stock.

- Resist borrowing from your account. Although most plans allow you to take a loan from your 401(k), the money cannot grow if it's not in your plan. Fees and penalties can make the cost higher than it might seem.

- If you change jobs, don't cash out your 401(k) plan. If you do, you'll pay taxes and penalties, and have less money invested for your retirement. Instead, roll the money over into an Individual Retirement Account or into your new employer's 401(k) plan.

- If you choose a "lifestyle" or "life-cycle" fund, remember that it's not simply another fund option, and that selecting it along with other investment choices can defeat the original purpose.

- If you are automatically enrolled in a 401(k) plan, remember that the contribution levels and investment options must be adjusted, based on your personal savings needs and attitude toward risk.

- Remember to rebalance your portfolio occasionally so that the mix of investments you originally chose—the proportions of stocks and bonds in your asset allocation plan—is maintained.

- Don't overmanage your 401(k). Even if your employer provides you with Web access to your account and allows you to change your investment options as often as you wish, it's a bad idea to drop whatever went down yesterday in favor of whatever is going up today.

- Focus on the long term. Even if your 401(k) is not performing as well as you'd like today, remember that saving for retirement is a marathon, not a forty-yard dash.

Appendix I

POWER GAMES

In the spring of 2000, the Securities and Exchange Commission considered issuing rules to limit the amount of consulting work accounting firms could do for their audit clients. When the American Institute of Certified Public Accountants and the Big Five accounting firms got wind of this, they sought help from their Capitol Hill allies. This five-page letter, signed by the Republican chairman of the House committee that oversees the SEC and two of his subcommittee chairmen, is a classic example of how industry groups work the legislative process. The sixteen questions to which the authors demand answers within two weeks were meant as a shot across the SEC's bow and a warning that the agency could expect more of the same treatment if it went ahead with the new rules. Very often, accounting industry lobbyists wrote the questions Congress demanded we answer.

U.S. House of Representatives
Committee on Commerce
Room 2125, Rayburn House Office Building
Washington, DC 20515-6115

April 17, 2000

The Honorable Arthur Levitt
Chairman
Securities and Exchange Commission
450 5th Street NW
Washington, DC 20519

Dear Arthur:

In connection with its oversight of the securities markets, the Committee has a number of questions relating to accounting practice. Pursuant to Rules X and XI of the U.S. House of Representatives, please respond to the following questions:

1. What empirical evidence, studies or economic analysis does the SEC possess that demonstrates accounting firms having consulting relationships with audit clients are less independent than those firms that do not have such relationships? Are there any specific administrative findings that have concluded the provision of consulting services resulted in a specific audit failure by the same firm?

2. What empirical evidence, studies, or economic analysis does the SEC possess that demonstrates accounting firms providing tax advice to audit clients are less independent than those firms that do not provide such advice? Are there any specific administrative findings that have concluded the provision of tax advice resulted in a specific audit failure by the same firm?

3. What are the investment restrictions to which employees of the SEC are subject? How are they different from restrictions placed on accountants? What is the rationale for those differences? Is there evidence that share ownership by SEC personnel compromises their independence or ability to discharge their duties in accordance with the public interest? What are the similarities in access to material non-public information shared with auditors and with the SEC staff reviewing statements filed with the Commission? Estimate the number of violations that would exist if the stock restrictions applicable to the accounting profession were to be applied to the SEC and its staff on January 2, 2000.

4. You and members of the Commission staff have suggested a new regulatory oversight and disciplinary process for the accounting process be adopted. Is the SEC developing recommendations on this proposal? How would the SEC receive input on its recommendations? Under what specific grant of statutory authority would the SEC propose to implement these recommendations?

5. We understand the SEC has expressed its views on the question of independence primarily in interpretive guidance or no action letters issued by the staff. Have the policies in this interpretive guidance ever been subject to rulemaking subject to notice and

comment? Identify all guidance which was adopted by rulemaking and the date of consideration and adoption.

6. Members of the SEC staff have publically supported restricting the scope of services offered by accounting firms to audit clients beyond current restrictions such as the prohibition on audit firms acting in a management capacity for audit clients. Are such considerations currently under consideration by the SEC or the staff? How would the SEC receive input on and implement any such changes?

7. Under Section 3(f) of the Exchange Act and Section 2(b) [of] the Securities Act, the SEC is required to consider efficiency, competition, and capital formation when engaging in rulemaking under the public interest standard. The legislative history accompanying these provisions, as well as a plain reading of the statute, makes clear a thorough cost benefit analysis performed by the office of the Chief Economist must be undertaken prior to any such rulemaking. Has the SEC commenced cost benefit analysis of proposed changes to limitations on the scope of services offered by accounting firms to audit clients? If so, what are the findings of this cost benefit analysis?

8. Regulation S-X provides that the SEC "will not recognize any certified accountant or public accountant who is not in fact independent." Has the SEC defined the principles by which it determines that an accountant is not in fact independent?

9. Does the fact that audit firms are compensated for their services create an "appearance of conflict" problem? If direct compensation does not create an unacceptable appearance of conflict issue, how are more attenuated relationships between an auditor and its clients, such as the ownership of shares in an audit client by a spouse, child or son or daughter-in-law of an audit partner determined to be unacceptable violations of independence?

10. What is your view of the proper role of the SEC and its chief accountant regarding the Financial Accounting Standards Board's ("FASB") agenda? What is the proper role of the Commission and its Chief Accountant regarding FASB's deliberations on new GAAP rules? Please identify all non-public meetings between SEC person-

nel and members of the FASB or the FASB staff concerning recent proposals to change the accounting treatment of business combinations.

11. Identify all private sector committees, commissions, boards or other groups created at the request of the Commission or yourself during your tenure at the SEC. For each group, identify the method and criteria by which members of these boards were selected, including the role you played in selecting members. What is the legal status of each of these commissions or boards? What are the terms of existence of these boards and the terms of their constituent members?

12. In what ways did the SEC seek to influence the actions of the NASD and the NYSE as they considered the recommendations of the Blue Ribbon Committee on Improving the Effectiveness of Audit Committees? Did SEC officials meet with self-regulatory groups charged with reviewing the recommendations regarding listing qualifications?

13. What is the status of SEC consideration of rules issued by the Independence Standards Board (ISB) last December relating to investments in mutual funds and related entities? Given [that] consideration of these rules would be made under a public interest standard, what specific criteria would the SEC use to reject a proposed ISB standard?

14. The SEC Chief Accountant stated the SEC intends to move forward with proposals to modify independence rules. Is it the SEC's intention to make recommendations to the ISB for action, or to undertake action outside the ISB process?

15. In the area of rules and guidance on auditor independence please indicate whether each of the following situations would be a violation of auditor independence. For those that are a violation, justify why the situation should be grounds for an independence violation:

   • A partner's spouse participates in an employer sponsored benefit plan that invests in securities issued by an audit client with which the partner has no direct contact or responsibility. The benefit plan is the only option offered to the spouse by the employer.

- A partner's spouse participates in an investment club that owns 100 shares of stock of an audit client of the firm's Detroit office. The partner works out of the Seattle office and has no involvement with the client. The investment is not material to either spouse.

- The son-in-law of a tax partner is the beneficiary of a blind trust that has a de minimis investment in an audit client of the firm's Boston office. The tax partner works out of the Atlanta office and has no involvement with the client.

- A partner has a brokerage account with a securities firm that is not audited by the accounting firm. Cash in the brokerage account is automatically swept into a mutual fund that is audited by the firm's New York office. The partner works out of the Denver office, provides no services to the mutual fund, and is unaware the mutual fund is a client.

- The grandparents of a partner's children purchase a share of stock in an audit client and hold the share pursuant to the Uniform Gift to Minors Act. The partner has no control over the purchase or disposition of the stock and does no work for the client.

For the following situations also indicate what alternatives the couples would have to come into compliance with independence restrictions.

- A partner's spouse is an executive at company A, and through the only reasonable employer benefit plan has holdings in the company. The partner works for a firm which audits company B, though neither the partner's office nor the partner perform any work for company B. Companies A and B merge and the spouse retains both holdings and employment. The holdings are material to the couple. The firm audits the merged company.

- The spouse of a partner works in a non-management capacity for a non-public company that is an audit client. The spouse has holdings in the company which are material to the couple. Neither the partner's office nor the partner perform any work for the company. The company goes public.

- A manager's spouse is promoted to CFO of an audit client company. Neither the manager's office nor the manager perform any work for the company. The manager is promoted to partner.

- A partner's spouse works for a company as a non-management employee and participates in the stock option and 401(k) program. Neither the partner's office nor the partner perform work for the company. Due to fluctuations in stock price, the value of stock in the company represents 5.1% of the couple's net worth on particular days.

16. Accounting independence prohibitions were drafted at a time when few women worked outside of the home. Given the prevalence of women in the workforce, both as accounting partners and as workers, managers or executives in public companies, does the SEC agree current independence restrictions are outdated and in need of modernization? Do the restrictions as they stand discourage wives and daughters from participating in the workforce?

Please respond to these questions two weeks from the date of receipt of this letter. These responses will help to determine if hearings on the SEC's oversight of the accounting profession are warranted.

Sincerely,

Tom Bliley
Chairman

Michael G. Oxley
Chairman
Subcommittee on Finance and
Hazardous Materials

W.J. "Billy" Tauzin
Chairman
Subcommittee on
Telecommunications,
Trade, and Consumer Protection

cc: the Honorable John D. Dingell

*The accounting industry cited numerous reasons for its opposi-
tion to the SEC's auditor independence rules, and one of the
major reasons was the "New Economy" argument. In essence, it
said that accounting firms had to be able to perform consulting
work for audit clients because only then could the accountants
develop new ways to measure the value of technology, telecommunications, Internet, and other growth companies that make up
the New Economy. This argument is cited in the following letter
from three members of the Senate Banking Committee, which
also oversees the SEC (Bayh and Schumer are Democrats and
Bennett is a Republican). The trio request a hearing by the panel's
securities subcommittee chairman in an effort to slow down the
SEC rules until the New Economy issue could be vented.*

United States Senate
Washington, DC 20510

July 21, 2000

The Honorable Rod Grams
Chairman
Senate Subcommittee on Securities
United States Senate
Washington, DC 20510

Dear Mr. Chairman:

We commend you for taking the initiative to hold a hearing on financial reporting in the New Economy. The hearing began exploration of
the challenges that New Economy developments have placed on our
traditional accounting standards and securities laws. Indeed, it appears
that these standards and laws cannot fully represent the value of many

companies in the New Economy. Business reporting is a critical subject that continues to deserve Congressional attention.

In addition to this insightful hearing, we respectfully request that you hold a hearing on the Securities and Exchange Commission's (SEC) proposed rulemaking on auditor independence. Although the SEC's proposal was discussed briefly at Wednesday's hearing, the SEC, industry representatives, and others should be provided a full opportunity publicly to debate the appropriateness of the rulemaking. As you know, the SEC's proposal seeks to change its requirements for determining whether an auditor is independent in light of, among other criteria, the scope of services provided by audit firms to their audit clients. The proposal identifies broad categories of non-audit services that auditors would be prohibited from providing to their audit clients. The SEC issued the proposal with a 75-day comment period, due September 25, 2000.

Because of the relatively short comment period for this proposal, the SEC could finalize the rule when Congress is not in session and, therefore, is constrained from exercising its traditional oversight authority. This especially concerns us because it appears that the SEC has not demonstrated a substantive basis for imposing these far-reaching limitations this year. The SEC would be limiting auditing firms' expertise just when auditors appear to need it most in order to fully assess today's sophisticated New Economy companies. The broader issues of the New Economy require further study by Congress before the SEC implements this rule. Therefore, we believe that it is wholly appropriate for a hearing on the SEC's proposal, and other New Economy business reporting issues. Thank you for your consideration of this important request.

Sincerely,

Evan Bayh   Charles Schumer

Robert F. Bennett

*This letter from ten of the twenty members of the Senate Banking
Committee—eight are Republicans and two are Democrats—
also seeks to postpone the auditor independence rules. This time,
the banking panel members specifically request a delay until February 2001—after the November 2000 presidential election and,
possibly, after a new administration would take office—ostensi-
bly so Congress can better analyze the impact of the rules. I
viewed their request as nothing more than a device to wait me
out until the SEC had a new chairman.*

United States Senate
Washington, DC 20510

July 28, 2000

Arthur Levitt, Chairman
Securities and Exchange Commission
Washington D.C. 20549

Dear Chairman Levitt:

As you may know, the Securities Subcommittee of the Senate Committee on Banking, Housing and Urban Affairs held a hearing last week
entitled "Adapting a '30's Financial Model to the 21st Century." The
purpose of the hearing was to review the extent to which our current
financial reporting models capture what the markets perceive as value
on our current "New Economy." As you are fully aware, our current
financial models only partially capture value in an economy where so
much of corporate value is represented by patents, market access,
human talent and intellectual property.

We are writing today on a related topic. During the course of our
hearing, concern was expressed by committee members about the proposed SEC rules on Auditor Independence. Today Subcommittee
Chairman Grams received a request by three Senators for follow-up

hearings on that specific subject. The current intention is to hold this hearing in September following the August recess.

While we have heard many concerns expressed, our fundamental concern is the wide disparity between the impact of these proposed rules as described by SEC staff as opposed to the impact described by the accounting profession. At a time when our accounting standards will require significant modernization if they are to reflect value in today's economy, it is axiomatic that the accounting profession must retain the capacity to respond to these changes.

In light of the magnitude of your proposed changes, and the wide disparity in current opinion concerning their potential impact, we urge caution in arriving at final rules on this subject. Specifically, we request that you extend the comment period on the non-audit services portion of the Proposed rule until after February 1, 2001 in order to fully evaluate the impact of your proposal. This extension will allow for careful analysis of the proposed changes, and also address the concern about Congressional oversight authority expressed in the attached letter from Senators Bennett, Bayh and Schumer.

Sincerely,

Senator Rod Grams

Senator Robert F. Bennett

Senator Evan Bayh

Senator Wayne Allard

Senator Phil Gramm

Senator Jim Bunning

Senator Charles E. Schumer

Senator Chuck Hagel

Senator Mike Crapo

Senator Rick Santorum

Representative W.J. "Billy" Tauzin, a Louisiana Republican, is one of the lead Congressional investigators looking into the audit failures of Enron Corp. and WorldCom Inc., and the insider trading scandal of ImClone Systems Inc. But in 2000 he was one of Capitol Hill's leading voices against the SEC's auditor independence rules. Here he asks the SEC to include in the public comment file many of the letters he and his colleagues wrote to make sure the level of Congressional opposition was in full view. I wonder if he feels differently today?

Congress of the United States
House of Representatives
Washington, DC 20515-1803

September 11, 2000

Mr. Jonathan G. Katz, Secretary
Securities and Exchange Commission
450 Fifth Street, N.W.
Washington, D.C. 20549-0609

Re: SEC Public Comments File No. S7-13-00

Dear Mr. Katz:

Attached please find a number of letters from Members of Congress concerning the Commission's proposed rule on auditor independence. Please include all of the following letters in your public comments file: (1) from Representatives Tom Bliley, Michael G. Oxley and Billy Tauzin to Arthur Levitt, dated 4/17/00, (2) from Representatives Jennifer Dunn, Deborah Pryce, Tillie Fowler and Sue Myrick to Arthur Levitt, dated 5/2/00, (3) from Senators Charles Schumer, Robert F. Bennett and Evan Bayh to Arthur Levitt, dated 5/25/00, (4) from Representatives Jennifer Dunn, Deborah Pryce, Tillie Fowler and Sue Myrick to Arthur Levitt, dated 6/23/00, (5) from Representatives Ellen O. Tauscher, Jim Moran, Cal Dooley, Adam Smith, Peter Deutsch and Jim Maloney to Arthur Levitt, dated 7/18/00, (6) from Representatives Billy Tauzin, Roy Blunt, Paul E. Gilmor, Richard K. Armey, Nathan Deal, Bob Goodlatte, Barbara Cubin, John M. Shimkus, Brian Bilbray, Vito Fossella, Charles Pickering, Jr., James Greenwood, Jim McCrery, Richard H. Baker, Heather A. Wilson, Fred Upton, Richard M. Burr, Christopher Cox, Charles Norwood, Duncan Hunter and Cliff Stearns to Arthur Levitt, dated 7/20/00, (7) from Senator Robert G. Torricelli to Arthur Levitt, dated 7/21/00, (8) from Senators Richard C. Shelby and Phil Gramm, dated 7/27/00, (9) from Senators Rod Grams, Evan Bayh, Phil Gramm, Charles E. Schumer, Mike Crapo, Robert F. Bennett, Wayne Allard, Jim Bunning, Chuck Hagel and Rick Santorum to Arthur Levitt, dated 7/28/00, (10) from Representatives Tom Bliley, Mike Oxley and Ed Towns to Arthur Levitt, dated 8/2/00.

It is vital that this correspondence be promptly included in the public comment file, and be considered by the Commissioners. The correspondence reflects widespread and serious concerns about the proposed rule, particularly the impact of the proposal on the profession and the New Economy, and the obviously rushed and inadequate comment process that the Commission is pursuing with respect to the rule. I share those concerns, and the Commission should substantially extend the comment period, to permit greater participation by the public, by Congress and by the new Administration.

Sincerely,

W.J. "Billy" Tauzin

Enron Corp. Chairman and Chief Executive Kenneth L. Lay penned this letter to me a year before Enron collapsed. He cites the "success" of Enron's arrangement with its auditor, Arthur Andersen, which performed many of the internal audit tasks the SEC rules were seeking to curtail.

KENNETH L. LAY
Chairman and Chief Executive Officer
Enron Corporation
Houston, TX 77251

September 20, 2000

Arthur Levitt, Chairman
Securities & Exchange Commission
450 Fifth Street, N.W.
Room 6102
Washington, D.C. 20549

Dear Chairman Levitt:

I would like to take this opportunity to comment on the Securities & Exchange Commission's proposed rulemaking regarding auditor independence, on behalf of Enron Corp. Enron is a diversified global energy and broadband company that prides itself on a uniquely entrepreneurial business philosophy and on creating knowledge-based value in emerging markets.

For the past several years, Enron has successfully utilized its independent audit firm's expertise and professional skepticism to help improve the overall control environment within the company. In addition to their traditional financial statement related work, the independent auditor's procedures at Enron have been extended to include specific audits of and reporting on critical control processes. This arrangement has resulted in qualitative and comprehensive reporting to management and to Enron's audit committee, which has been found to be extremely valuable. Also, I believe independent audits of the internal control environment are valuable to the investing public, particularly given the risks and complexities of Enron's business and the extremely dynamic business environment in which Enron and others now operate.

While the arrangement Enron has with its independent auditors displaces a significant portion of the activities previously performed by internal resources, it is structured to ensure that Enron management maintains appropriate audit plan design, results assessment and overall monitoring and oversight responsibilities. Enron's management and audit committee are committed to assuring that key management personnel oversee and are responsible for the design and effectiveness of the internal control environment and for monitoring independence.

The proposed rule would preclude independent financial statement auditors from performing "certain internal audit services." The description of inappropriate activities included in your current proposal is so broad that it could restrict Enron from engaging its independent financial statement auditors to report on the company's control processes on a recurring basis as the company now has arranged. I find this troubling, not only because I believe the independence and expertise of the independent auditors enhances this process, but also because Enron has found its "integrated audit" arrangement to be more efficient and cost-effective than the more traditional roles of separate internal and external auditing functions. Frankly, I fail to understand how extending the scope of what is independently audited can be anything but positive.

The SEC has supported a number of measures to ensure that audit committees are informed of auditors' activities and feel the burden of determining auditor independence. Enron's audit committee takes those responsibilities very seriously. Given the wide-ranging impact of your proposed changes, I respectfully urge the Commission reassess the need for such broad regulatory intervention when the business environment is more dynamic than ever. I also respectfully suggest the SEC give the new measures regarding the enhanced role of audit committees in ensuring auditor independence a chance to work before regulations of this magnitude are considered.

Sincerely,

As the accounting war raged on, the industry opened a new propaganda front by convincing small businesses that the SEC's auditor independence rules would harm them. In particular, the AICPA and the Big Five said that the rules would result in accounting firms eliminating certain types of audit services and would force consolidation in the industry, thus driving up the cost of audit services for small companies. Our analysis showed that small businesses and CPA firms would not be affected that much at all. But they were frightened into seeking relief from their Washington representatives, twenty-three of whom promptly sent this letter to the SEC.

Congress of the United States
Washington, DC 20515

September 25, 2000

The Honorable Arthur Levitt
Chairman
U.S. Securities and Exchange Commission
450 Fifth Street, N.W.
Washington, D.C. 20549

Dear Chairman Levitt:

We are writing concerning the Commission's proposed rules to limit the range of services provided by accounting firms. While we share your belief that auditor independence is critical to meeting the economy's need for reliable financial data, we are not convinced that this level of regulatory intervention is appropriate at this time.

Our greatest concern about the proposed regulations is the likely negative impact they will have on small businesses. Specifically, we are concerned that the proposed rule will force some accounting firms to eliminate certain services, making it more difficult for smaller businesses to obtain the professional assistance they need at a reasonable cost. The rule may also reduce competition and encourage the consolidation of the accounting industry. This will have the negative impact of raising audit costs, which will severely disadvantage small businesses that already experience difficulty affording necessary auditing services in the current market.

Both of these changes in the auditing profession will place small businesses at a competitive disadvantage with respect to larger businesses and, as a result, have a detrimental impact on the American economy.

The rule may also have the effect of depriving accounting firms of the ability and/or incentive to continue the development of services geared toward the needs of businesses in the information age economy. It is important that American businesses—both large and small—are not deprived of this important service in our modern, technology and information driven economy.

Finally, we are concerned that the proposed rule may have a negative impact on the quality of service provided to businesses. By requiring auditors to be "walled off" from the expertise now provided to them by non-audit professionals, the firms may produce less effective audits simply because they will not have access to pertinent information.

Small businesses are the engines that drive America's economy. They are largely responsible for the economic growth we are now experiencing. To go forward with the implementation of such a broad rule without a thorough review of the rule's impact on the nation's small businesses would be irresponsible. We urge you to delay moving forward with this rulemaking until the impact its implementation will have on small businesses is thoroughly studied.

Overall, we question the need for such a comprehensive rule. We believe that regulatory intervention of the degree proposed should be undertaken when there is clear evidence that a problem exists. However, a recent study by the Panel on Audit Effectiveness, which was created with the endorsement of the SEC, concluded that the accounting profession is fundamentally sound. The Panel also reported that it found no evidence that audit quality was compromised by the provision of non-audit services to an audit client. In light of these findings, it is difficult to understand the necessity for such a comprehensive rule.

Furthermore, we have serious concerns about the proposed rule's assertion that the provision of non-audit services to audit clients represents a conflict of interest. The Commission's rule cites no empirical evidence or analytical studies that show a negative correlation between non-audit services and audit quality. In fact, a recent study conducted by a prominent panel of the Public Oversight Board concluded that they were "not aware of any instances of non-audit services having caused or contributed to an audit failure or the actual loss of auditor independence."

We are also concerned that the Commission plans to proceed with a regulatory ban on various non-audit services in light of the fact that new disclosure requirements have only recently been put in place. Last year the Independence Standards Board adopted a requirement that auditors annually disclose to audit committees all relationships between the auditing firm and the client which might bear on independence. Similarly, the SEC and the major stock exchanges recently adopted new rules expanding disclosures in proxy statements regarding auditor independence.

Government imposed restrictions on the services offered by any business are contrary to the free market system. Therefore, we would be more comfortable with an approach that would give the recent market-based reforms time to work before imposing outright prohibitions on the marketplace.

From a procedural standpoint, we believe the 75-day comment period established for this rule will not provide sufficient time for careful consideration of the proposed regulations. In addition, this short comment period does not provide for the affirmative outreach that is mandated by the Small Business Regulatory Enforcement Fairness Act. These proposals are very complex. Auditors have worked effectively for years without these proposed restrictions, and we believe the Commission should be in no rush to impose significant restrictions without adequate comment and review. A rulemaking that will have the major impact that this proposal will should only be considered through a thorough deliberative process that provides a meaningful opportunity for participation of the public. A 75-day comment period is not long enough to achieve that goal. Accordingly, we suggest the comment period be extended.

Mr. Chairman, for the reasons stated above, we urge you to reconsider the implementation of such a broad rule. At a minimum, we urge you to extend the comment period to December 31, 2001, and conduct a thorough analysis on how the rule will impact America's small businesses.

Sincerely,

Rep. Nydia M. Velázquez

Rep. Donald A. Manzullo

Rep. Juanita Millender-McDonald

Rep. Dan Burton

Rep. Danny K. Davis

Rep. Roscoe G. Bartlett

Rep. Carolyn McCarthy

Rep. Phil English

Rep. William Pascrell, Jr.

Rep. Tom Latham

Rep. Rubén Hinojosa

Rep. Thomas E. Petri

Rep. Donna Christian-Christensen

Rep. Robert A. Brady

Rep. Stephanie Tubbs-Jones

Rep. Dennis Moore

Rep. David D. Phelps

Rep. Charles A. Gonzalez

Rep. Brian Baird

Rep. Grace F. Napolitano

Rep. Mark Udall

Rep. Shelley Berkley

Rep. Jay Inslee

As the endgame approached for the auditor independence rules, members of Congress threatened to use the ultimate weapon: the power of the purse. If the SEC went ahead, Republican lawmakers said they would pass a law to prevent the agency from spending any money to implement the rule. With the SEC's independence at stake, I needed high-level Congressional and White House support. This letter, from Senator Tom Daschle, the South Dakota Democrat who is now the Senate Majority Leader, asks President Clinton to fight such efforts to tie the SEC's hands. The White House later issued a statement saying that it strongly opposed Congressional interference with the SEC's rule making.

United States Senate
Office of the Democratic Leader
Washington, DC 20510-7020

September 29, 2000

The President
The White House
Washington, D.C. 20502

Dear Mr. President:

The Securities and Exchange Commission is currently considering an important rulemaking regarding the independence of this country's accounting profession. I recently met with Chairman Arthur Levitt, who is concerned about efforts underway to persuade Members of Congress to restrict the authority of the Commission on this matter through an appropriations rider. Such legislation represents a real threat to America's investors and an inappropriate intrusion into the work of an independent regulatory agency.

Disagreement with the merits of a proposed SEC rule is not uncommon. Chairman Levitt has indicated his disappointment that the firms fighting the proposal have not taken the opportunity to engage the SEC but instead are focusing their resources on a legislative effort to limit the authority of the agency.

I will oppose any such legislation and respectfully request that the White House similarly oppose any efforts to thwart the work of the SEC in this crucial investor protection initiative.

With best wishes, I am

Sincerely,

Tom Daschle
United States Senate

CC: John Podesta
     Gene Sperling
     Jack Lew
     Bruce Lindsey

WHAT CHINESE WALL?

On April 28, 2003, ten Wall Street firms paid a total of $1.4 billion to settle charges that they routinely issued research that was biased in favor of corporations in hopes of winning lucrative investment banking fees. The Securities and Exchange Commission, the National Association of Securities Dealers, the stock exchanges (acting as self-regulatory organizations), and state securities officials all found that Wall Street's largest firms had used unscrupulous practices to enrich themselves at the expense of investors.

How so? Investment bankers at the ten firms pressured analysts to issue rosy reports on companies that they knew could not live up to the hype. The same firms also paid rival analysts to produce similarly puffy research to reinforce the illusion of success. The firms gave preferential access to hot initial public offerings to the executives of companies whose business they were hoping to obtain—or to reward those whose business they had already won. And they privately encouraged investment bankers and analysts to cross over the so-called Chinese Wall that they publicly claimed kept banking interests separate from stock research. Regulators went so far as to call research by three of the ten firms (Citigroup's Salomon Smith Barney unit, Merrill Lynch, and Credit Suisse First Boston) fraudulent.

The schemes worked throughout the go-go 1990s, when Wall Street firms raked in billions of dollars in fees for initial public offerings. But they severely damaged retail investors, whose paper wealth declined by some $6 trillion once the joyride ended in the spring of 2000.

While the ten firms neither admitted nor denied wrongdoing, they all agreed not to dispute the regulators' allegations or findings, which are explosive. Thousands of pages of e-mails and memos reveal the extent to which the ten firms deceived investors. The following pages contain just a small sampling of some of the most revealing, and damaging, documents.

1. CROSSING OVER THE WALL

Morgan Stanley analyst Mary Meeker, called "Queen of the Net" by the media because of her influence in determining which Internet companies' stock offerings would succeed, wrote a self-evaluation of her 1999 performance, shown in the first exhibit below. She states that her "highest and best use" is to help Morgan Stanley win IPO deals. And sure enough, Meeker was spectacularly helpful. In the second exhibit below, Meeker's boss states that she was instrumental in winning $525 million in investment-banking and other deal-making fees because of her ability to be "brought over the wall," a reference to the Chinese Wall that is supposed to prevent banking interests from influencing the conclusions of research analysts.

10/29/99
TO: MAYREE CLARK
FR: MARY MEEKER—F1999 Self Evaluation

Bottom line, <u>my highest and best use is to help MSDW win the best Internet IPO mandates</u> (and to ensure that we have the appropriate analysts and bankers to serve the companies well) and then to let them work their way through our powerful research and distribution system. Take priceline.com (the most successful Internet IPO of 1999) as an example—I read about the company in a trade journal, Andre called the company . . . Andre, Jim Liang and I met with the company . . . then five Morgan Stanley employees pitched the IPO (including Ruth Porat and Dick Fisher) . . . we won the mandate . . . now every MSDW employee knows the story . . . every institutional salesperson has met the management team . . . the market capitalization of the company is $10B and our New York PWM team manages a chunk of the wealth. This is how our business works.

2000 EVALUATION & DEVELOPMENT SUMMARY E.D.
EQUITY RESEARCH
ANALYST

Evaluatee: <u>Meeker, Mary G.</u>   Evaluation Director:
<u>Shea, Dennis F.</u>

    <u>Managing Director</u>   Co-Evaluation Director: __
Dept: <u>EQRES</u>

Review of 2000 Performance

C. Translation into Revenues for the Firm

(1) IBD Involvement (overall contribution to IBD franchise and involvement in specific transactions)

Highly involved. You continue to drive our Internet business on the primary side, are very involved in M&A assignments as they come up and as you can be brought over the wall on them, and are active in our private equity investment committee. A summary of revenues for the year is listed below.

- Total Booked IBD revenues for 2000: $379 million gross, $361 million weighted
- Realized Investment gains on Private Internet Equity Investments: $65 million
- Total Booked non-US IBD revenues for 2000: $81 million gross

2. BUILDING THE ILLUSION

Even regulators were surprised to discover that five of the ten firms (Morgan Stanley, UBS Warburg, J.P. Morgan Chase, Bear Stearns, and U.S. Bancorp Piper Jaffray) had paid rival analysts, or had received payments, to put out positive research and create the illusion that a banking client was on a roll. Morgan Stanley, for example, paid $2.7 million to 25 other securities firms to issue research on companies with whom Morgan Stanley had done deals. In the exhibit below, Morgan Stanley states that it is issuing to CSFB a check that includes $228,514.70 as a "research guaranty" on Agile Software Corp.

MORGAN STANLEY DEAN WITTER
1585 Broadway
New York, NY 10036
(212) 761-4000

March 15, 2000

Credit Suisse First Boston Corporation
11 Madison Avenue
New York, NY 10010
ATTN: Neal Keane

Dear Sirs,

We enclose a check to your order in payment of the credit balance, as set
forth below in settlement of your account as the same stands as of this
date, as an underwriter of Agile Software Corp. common stock, offered
12/13/99.

Research Guaranty $228,514.70

---

3. COMPENSATION DETERMINES BEHAVIOR

Wall Street firms held out their research departments as providers of
independent stock recommendations, based on the investment merits
of each stock. But in truth, the firms designed their compensation plans
to make sure that analysts played their part in landing investment
banking deals, thus compromising the integrity of their research. At
Lehman Brothers, one analyst's contract provided that he would earn
$200,000 in base salary and a minimum bonus of $4.8 million. The
bonus could increase in $1 million increments, up to another $4 million, if the investment banking division won $125 million in deal-
making fees from the companies he covered. In this January 22, 2001
e-mail, Lehman's director of U.S. stock research congratulates an analyst for generating ten potential banking deals:

> "Well done, we need senior bankers to see who [among the analysts] have the real relationships with the big companies. This is how we justify big comp. [compensation] packages."

4. CORPORATE CLIENTS CALL THE SHOTS

In announcing the settlement of the analysts' case, regulators promised to follow up with actions against individual analysts and their supervisors. One month later, the NASD filed charges against Phua Young, who for three years had been Merrill Lynch's senior research analyst covering Tyco International Ltd. The NASD alleged that Young published exaggerated reports on Tyco that he didn't personally believe, and that he broke NASD rules by maintaining a close relationship with company officials, including buying gifts for Tyco Chief Executive Officer Dennis Kozlowski, and flying on Tyco's corporate jet for business trips. Young's relationship with Tyco was so close that he remarked to a Tyco investor relations employee in an e-mail: "I am indirectly paid by Tyco."

The NASD complaint also alleged that Young often gave Tyco advance copies of his research, including proposed ratings, so that Tyco could make editorial changes. In one e-mail, Young submitted a draft report and rating to Tyco's chief financial officer, stating:

PLEASE REVIEW ASAP. I WILL NOT SEND OUT UNTIL I HEAR FROM YOU FIRST! LOYAL TYCO EMPLOYEE!

[Under NASD rules, Young is expected to request a hearing before an NASD panel to contest the charges. If the charges are upheld, the range of possible sanctions includes a fine, suspension, or expulsion from the NASD.]

5. EVERYBODY KNEW—EXCEPT INDIVIDUAL INVESTORS

In February 2001, the head of retail client investing at Citigroup's Salomon Smith Barney unit blew the whistle internally on shoddy research. He told a research manager that the firm's analysis was "basically worthless," and threatened to withhold his group's financial contribution to the research division. In turn, John Hoffman, the global chief of equity research, called for a meeting to discuss the problem. The exhibit below—Hoffman's request to get together—shows that top Citigroup managers knew that their analysts' work was viewed internally as shoddy.

TO: U.S. Research MD's.
FROM: John Hoffmann
RE: Stock Rating System
DATE: February 22, 2001

I would like to have a short meeting to discuss the current stock rating system in anticipation of a broader discussion on research integrity scheduled for the March Global Equity Research Directors meeting.

Second, a comment to me by Jay Mandelbaum (global head of SSB's Private Client Group) who stated that our research was basically worthless because of limited discrimination in stock ratings, wide inconsistencies in ratings and price targets and, as above, repeated occurrences of riding a stock down 50% or more and then, seemingly, capitulating at the very bottom. Most seriously, he threatened that the Private Client Group was considering whether they should contribute to the research budget (they currently pay about 25%, a substantial sum) anymore.

GLOSSARY

AICPA: American Institute of Certified Public Accountants, the trade association that represents 330,000 accountants who audit the financial statements of public companies.

Amex: American Stock Exchange.

amortization: Recording as an expense a portion of the cost of an intangible, or nonphysical, asset such as patents, trademarks, and copyrights.

analyst: A person who studies public companies, usually in a specific industry, and makes buy and sell recommendations. When they are employees of brokerage firms, they are called "sell-side" analysts; when employed by mutual fund companies, they are called "buy-side" analysts.

appreciation: Increase in value of an asset.

asset: Any property with monetary value, such as real estate, inventories, or accounts receivable. Listed on a company's balance sheet, they can be tangible (buildings, equipment, cash) or intangible (nonphysical assets such as copyrights, patents, or reputational value).

asset allocation: Process of deciding how much of an investor's money to put into stocks, bonds, real estate, cash, or other investments, based on age, goals, time frame, and comfort with risk.

balance sheet: Part of a company's financial statement that lists assets, liabilities, and shareholders' equity at a specific point in time.

benchmark: Group of stocks or bonds whose collective performance is a standard against which to measure the returns of a mutual fund or other investment. Some widely used benchmarks are the Standard & Poor's 500 stock index (large companies), the Dow Jones Industrial Average (30 blue-chip stocks trading on the New York Stock Exchange), the Russell 2000 (small companies) and the Wilshire 5000 (companies of all sizes).

bond: Debt security issued by a company or a unit of government. An investor lends money to a bond issuer, who pledges to pay back the loan on a preset date, and to pay interest at specific intervals. Most bonds carry a rating assigned by an independent rating agency, such as Standard & Poor's or Moody's Investor Services. When a corporate bond is below investment-grade, it is often called a junk bond. Bonds issued by the federal government are called Treasurys, while bonds issued by cities or a branch of local government are municipal bonds.

broker: Individual who advises investors on stocks, bonds, mutual funds, or other investments and acts as an agent by buying or selling on the investor's behalf. Most brokers charge a commission, or a percentage of each transaction's value; a minority of brokers charge a flat fee or a fee based on your account balance.

capital gain: Difference between an investment's original purchase price and the selling price.

capitalization: Sum of a company's stock, long-term debt, and retained earnings (or earnings that have not been distributed as dividends to shareholders).

cash flow: Measure of the funds flowing in and out of a company over a quarter or a year, as shown on a company's statement of cash flows. Calculated as earnings before depreciation, amortization, and other noncash charges.

churning: Excessive trading by a broker in a customer account in order to increase commissions.

closed-end fund: Publicly traded mutual fund with a fixed number of shares. Share prices fluctuate the same way a company's shares do, based on investor supply and demand.

commission: Fee paid by an investor to a broker for advice and help buying and selling stocks, bonds, mutual funds, or other investments.

common stock: Shares in a public company that provide ordinary voting rights (usually one share, one vote) and grant the owner the right to dividends, if any are distributed, out of earnings.

compounding: A mathematical function in which an investment's earnings also have earnings, leading to significant increases in value over time.

day trader: Individual who buys and sells stocks, usually through an online broker, by trying to anticipate minor changes in share prices. Day traders are not long-term investors, and usually close out their holdings at the end of each day.

debenture: Debt obligation that is unsecured, that is, backed by the borrower's general ability to repay credit.

debt-to-equity ratio: A company's long-term debt divided by stockholders' equity (assets minus liabilities). In general, the higher the number, the greater the risk.

defined-benefit pension: Company retirement plan whose payout depends on an employee's years of service and average salary. Employers contribute all the funds, determine how to invest them, and bear all the risks.

defined-contribution pension: Company retirement plan whose payout depends on the amount of money contributed by an employee (usually the employer matches employee contributions) and on the investment returns the account earns. Employees determine how to invest the funds in their plan, usually limited to a menu of choices offered by the employer, and bear all the risks.

depreciation: Recording as an expense a portion of the cost of a physical asset over a specified time period.

derivative: Financial instrument such as an options or futures contract whose price is derived from the value of another underlying security.

distribution fee: Fee assessed annually by mutual funds to support the fund's advertising and marketing activities; also called a 12b-1 fee after the SEC rule that allows such fees. For no-load funds, the fee cannot exceed 0.25 percent of the fund's assets.

diversification: Reducing risk by investing in different types of securities and different industries, or more simply, not putting all your eggs into one basket.

dividend: Distribution of a company's earnings to shareholders, usually on a quarterly basis.

dollar-cost averaging: Investing a fixed amount of money at regular intervals, regardless of whether the market is up or down. Financial advisers recommend this practice as a way of buying securities at lower prices.

earnings: Money left over after a company pays its bills, taxes, salaries, and other expenses. Companies usually report earnings at the end of each quarter and fiscal year. When called net income and reported to the SEC, this is the earnings number that is GAAP-compliant.

earnings per share: Earnings divided by the number of shares of common stock outstanding. Tells investors how much profit a company made for each share of stock it has issued. Diluted EPS takes into account all stock options that could be exercised.

EBITDA: Earnings before interest, taxes, depreciation, and amortization. This is a "pro forma" or "as if" earnings number that does not comply with GAAP. Companies with high debt loads prefer EBITDA, as it makes earnings seem better than they are.

ECN: Electronic communications network; an electronic marketplace that matches buy and sell orders, much like a stock exchange, but usually at lower cost and in fractions of a second.

EDGAR: Electronic Data Gathering, Analysis, and Retrieval. An SEC database that provides online access to company filings, such as quarterly and annual reports.

equity: Stock ownership in a public company. Also, the value of shareholders' ownership, as listed on the balance sheet.

ERISA: Employee Retirement Income Security Act of 1974, the main law that sets standards for private pension plans, including the investment practices allowed.

exchange-traded fund: Packages of shares traded on a stock exchange that combine the simplicity of index mutual funds with the flexibility of stocks. One popular ETF, the Nasdaq 100, comprises the 100 largest Nasdaq stocks, and goes by the ticker symbol QQQ, or Cubes. ETFs are managed by computer software, with little human intervention, and are designed to trade in lockstep with a benchmark. Unlike a mutual fund, ETFs can be bought and sold throughout the day.

expense ratio: A mutual fund's annual costs, expressed as a percent of the fund's assets. As disclosed in the fund prospectus, the annual cost to investors to own shares in that fund. Includes all recurring fees but not sales loads, which are charged only once.

FASB: Financial Accounting Standards Board, the private-sector body that determines and interprets Generally Accepted Accounting Principles (GAAP), which the SEC requires companies to follow when reporting financial results.

fiduciary: Individual entrusted with investment decisions on behalf of another. Is obligated to make decisions in the client's best interests.

financial planner: A professionally trained person who helps others determine how to invest, for a fee.

fixed-income securities: Another term for bonds; refers to the fact that the interest rate paid on a bond is fixed when the bond is sold.

floor broker: Professional who works on the floor of a stock exchange. A "house" floor broker is employed by a brokerage firm (such as Merrill Lynch) to execute the firms' and customers' trades. "Independent" floor brokers work for themselves, handling trades for mutual funds, smaller brokerage firms, or large firms during busy periods.

401(k) plan: Company-sponsored retirement plan in which employees make tax-deferred contributions from their salary; often the employer matches those contributions.

Form 10-K: SEC term for an annual report, containing a balance sheet, income statement, and cash-flow statement plus a description of the company's operations and results.

Form 10-Q: The SEC term for a quarterly report.

GAAP: Generally Accepted Accounting Principles; the standards that the SEC requires companies to follow when reporting their financial results.

goodwill: The premium a company pays over the fair market value of an acquired company's assets. It often represents the value of a company's brand name, market share, and customer relations.

growth stock: Stocks of companies that are growing faster than average. These stocks usually do not pay dividends. A growth fund is a mutual fund that invests in growth stocks.

guaranteed investment contract: Investment offered by insurance companies, often to a company pension or profit-sharing plan, that guarantees a rate of return over the contract's lifespan.

hedge fund: Private investment pool for wealthy investors that is not regulated by the SEC. Can use more speculative strategies, such as short-selling (borrowing shares in anticipation of the price falling) and investing with borrowed money. Doesn't have to disclose holdings or strategies, making it difficult to determine risk.

hedging: Strategy to reduce risk that involves locking in existing profits while giving up the chance for further gains.

ICI: Investment Company Institute; trade association that represents mutual fund companies.

income statement: Part of the financial statement that shows how a company performed over the past quarter or year. Also called the profit-and-loss statement or the statement of operations, its major components are revenues and expenses. The bottom line shows net income, or profit.

index fund: Mutual fund that invests in all or a representative sample of the stocks that make up a benchmark, such as the S&P 500. The fund tries to match the returns of the benchmark.

initial public offering (IPO): First public sale of stock by a company.

institutional investor: Pension fund or mutual fund.

investment adviser: Individual or organization hired by a pension or mutual fund to give advice on which securities to buy or sell and how to allocate assets. Also, another name for a financial planner.

investment bank: Type of bank that helps companies sell their equity or debt to the public, assists with mergers and acquisitions, and issues research reports on public companies. Many have a brokerage operation to trade stocks and bonds for their own accounts, institutional clients, and retail investors.

Investment Company Act of 1940: Main federal law, enforced by the SEC, that governs the mutual fund industry.

issuer: Company, government agency, or municipality that sells debt or equity securities to the public.

leverage: Use of debt to increase investing capacity.

liability: An outstanding debt.

limit order: When trading stocks, a type of buy or sell order that specifies a price.

liquidity: For an investor, the ability to get access to invested money quickly. In the stock market, the amount of trading interest in a particular stock.

loads: One-time fee charged to investors when they purchase mutual fund shares. Loads are usually assessed by brokers. A front-end load is paid up front and comes out of your initial investment; a back-end load, also called a deferred load, is paid when you take your money out of the fund.

margin account: Borrowing money from a brokerage firm to supplement your cash purchases, thus enabling you to buy more shares. The shares in your account act as collateral for the loan, and can be sold, sometimes without your permission, to cover the loan if the account's value drops.

market capitalization: Dollar value of a company's outstanding shares, calculated by multiplying the number of shares by the current share price. Also called market cap.

market-maker: Entity that acts as middleman in the Nasdaq Stock Market; trades for its own account by buying from sellers and selling to buyers. A market-maker, sometimes called a dealer, posts bid (to buy) and ask (to sell) prices for selected stocks, and must stand by those prices.

market order: When trading shares, type of order that does not specify a price, but instead directs a broker to buy (or sell) shares at the prevailing price.

market timing: Type of investment strategy that involves trying to predict the market's up or down movements. The aim is to get in before the market moves up, and to get out before it moves down, but rarely does market timing work on a regular basis.

mark-to-market: Computing the current value of an asset, based on the most up-to-date market price.

money market fund: Type of mutual fund that invests only in short-term instruments, not stocks or most types of bonds. Such instruments include commercial paper, bankers' acceptances, and repurchase agreements.

Moody's: Moody's Investor Services, a company that rates the debt of corporations and agencies.

mutual fund: Portfolio of securities in which investors can buy shares. The fund's stock, bond, or money market holdings are selected by a professional investment adviser to meet a specific goal.

Nasdaq: Stock market, also called the over-the-counter market, possibly soon to be spun off from the National Association of Securities Dealers. Trades are decentralized in that they are executed over a computer network, rather than on a floor, with Nasdaq dealers, or market-makers, acting as middlemen between buyers and sellers. Shares of a large number of technology companies trade on Nasdaq.

NASD Inc.: National Association of Securities Dealers, a trade group that acts as the self-regulatory organization for brokers and dealers by setting the rules governing their conduct. Currently NASD owns and oversees the Nasdaq Stock Market, but is in the process of spinning it off as a separate entity. National Association of Securities Dealers Regulation Inc. is the enforcement arm of the NASD.

net asset value: Market value of a mutual fund, minus its liabilities, expressed as a per-share figure. Mutual funds sell or redeem shares based on a daily NAV calculation.

net income: Number that appears on the income statement and conforms to GAAP. It is the bottom-line calculation of a company's profit for the quarter or the year.

no-load fund: Mutual fund that does not charge any sales commission or distribution (also called 12b-1) fee of more than 0.25 percent of the fund's assets.

NYSE: New York Stock Exchange, also called the Big Board. Unlike Nasdaq, the NYSE centralizes trades on a floor, with individuals known as specialists acting as middlemen to smooth out the buying and selling.

open-end fund: Type of mutual fund that stands ready to redeem investors' shares.

operating earnings: Net income excluding costs, such as restructuring expenses, that a company deems unusual. Does not conform to GAAP.

operating expense: Costs involved in running a business.

option: Type of investment that gives the owner the right, but not the obligation, to buy or sell stock at a given price by a certain date.

Investors can sell **put** or **call options** on the shares they own. A **put option** means the buyer believes the share price will fall; a **call option** means the buyer believes the price will rise.

penny stock: Usually speculative type of stock that typically sells for under $1 a share.

preferred stock: Shares without voting rights but that give the owner a claim superseding common-stock owners. Preferred stockholders usually get a regular dividend and priority in case of liquidation.

price/earnings ratio: Common measure to determine the relative price of a stock in relation to its earnings power. Calculated by dividing the current per-share market price by earnings-per-share.

pro forma: Also called operating earnings, a non-GAAP, hypothetical number calculated to show a company's earnings in a better light. Usually excludes costs, such as depreciation and amortization, that management deems not important to the health of the underlying business.

prospectus: Detailed document that describes a mutual fund's investment objectives, risks, and recent performance. Mutual funds must make a prospectus available to potential buyers of their shares. Similarly, when companies issue shares, they must make available to potential investors a prospectus, outlining the company's performance, business objectives, and risks.

proxy statement: Annual document mailed to shareholders outlining matters to be voted on at next annual meeting.

rating agency: Companies such as Standard & Poor's and Moody's Investor Services that rate the bonds, or debt issues, of a company or government unit.

reserves: Funds that are set aside when a company restructures, such as by closing down a factory and laying off employees, to cover the future expenses of the restructuring. Banks have reserves to cover anticipated loan losses. Reserves sometimes are based on exaggerated estimates and, if reversed, can artificially boost future earnings.

return on assets: Common measure of profitability, calculated by dividing net income by total assets.

return on equity: Common measure of how much a company earns in relation to amount invested in its common stock, calculated by dividing net income (before dividends are paid) by shareholders' equity.

revenue: Money promised or received when a product or service is sold to a customer.

SEC: Securities and Exchange Commission, the independent regulatory agency that oversees stock exchanges, mutual funds, brokers, and dealers, and the sale of stocks and bonds by companies.

secondary offering: Sale of new shares in a company that is already public but needs to raise more capital.

self-regulatory organization (SRO): Group that regulates its industry and the performance of individual members by adopting and enforcing rules of conduct. SRO rules are subject to SEC approval; the SEC then oversees the SRO's enforcement of those rules. The NASD and the NYSE are SROs.

shareholders' equity: Claim that shareholders have on a company's assets. On the balance sheet, it is calculated by subtracting liabilities from total assets.

SIA: Securities Industry Association, the trade group that represents brokerage firms, investment banks, and investment companies employing some 750,000 people.

specialist: Professional middleman who acts as an auctioneer by matching buy and sell orders in a specific stock on the New York Stock Exchange floor.

spread: Difference between the price that dealers pay to buy a stock or bond and the price at which they sell it.

stock options: Right to buy a defined number of shares in a company at a preset price, called the grant price, which is usually the market price on the day the option is awarded.

total return: Percentage change in value of an investment over a time period, usually at least one year, assuming dividends are reinvested.

trader: Professional often employed by a Wall Street firm who buys and sells securities not for long-term investment but to take advantage of small changes in market prices or to make a profit off the spread.

Treasurys: Bonds the federal government issues to finance its debt. Treasury bills mature, or come due, in one year or less; Treasury notes can mature in from one to ten years; and Treasury bonds have a maturity of ten years or more.

12b-1 fee: Fee that many mutual funds charge to cover the cost of distribution, such as advertising, marketing, and commissions; named after an SEC rule.

underwriter: Organization, usually an investment bank, that helps companies issue debt or equity securities to brokers and investors.

valuation: Estimated worth of an asset, such as a stock or an entire company. To figure valuation, analysts use a number of ratios, such as price/earnings and return-on-assets.

value stock: Stock that has fallen out of favor with investors, whose share price seems inexpensive compared to its peers. May offer outstanding returns.

variable annuity: Type of insurance contract sold as a retirement plan. Based on a portfolio whose overall value changes as the portfolio's assets change in value.

venture capital: Funds used to support start-up companies that are high risk but that offer potentially high rewards.

volatility: Amount of price fluctuation in the value of a stock, bond, mutual fund, or benchmark. In general, a widely traded security will have less volatility, or less of a gap between high and low prices.

Wall Street: Reference to the entire investment community or a specific geographic area of Lower Manhattan where the NYSE, American Stock Exchange, and many investment banks are located.

write-down: Declaring that an asset is worth less than the value at which it was previously carried on the balance sheet.

yield: Dividend paid to common stockholders, or the rate of interest paid to bondholders.

zero-coupon bond: Bond sold at a steep discount from its face value, which pays no interest.

INDEX